Frontispiece: Unnumbered and untitled 9th text plate by Gustave Doré illustrating *The Rime of the Ancient Mariner* by Samuel Taylor Coleridge

DEVIL ON THE DEEP BLUE SEA

The Notorious Career of
Captain Samuel Hill
of Boston

by
Mary Malloy

Mary Malloy

Bullbrier Press, Jersey Shore, Pennsylvania
2006

ISBN-10: 0-9722854-1-5
ISBN-13: 978-0-9722854-1-4

A portion of the material in Chapter One has appeared also in "Boston Men" on the Northwest Coast by Mary Malloy.

Printed on acid-free, permanent paper and bound in the United States of America by Cayuga Press, Ithaca, NY 14850. This book is available from Bullbrier Press, 873 Dutch Hollow Road, Jersey Shore, PA 17740. FAX 570 769 7345. Website: www.bullbrier.com.

Cover illustration:

Ship *Franklin* of Salem, Massachusetts, in Batavia, ca. 1790

Library of Congress Cataloging-in-Publication Data

Malloy, Mary, 1955-
  Devil on the deep blue sea : the notorious career of Captain Samuel Hill of Boston / by Mary Malloy.
    p. cm.
  Includes bibliographical references and index.
  ISBN-13: 978-0-9722854-1-4 (pbk. : alk. paper)
  ISBN-10: 0-9722854-1-5
  1. Hill, Samuel, 1777-1825. 2. Ship captains--Massachusetts--Boston--Biography. 3. Boston (Mass.)--Biography. I. Title.

VK140.H55M35 2006
387.092--dc22
[B]
                                                2006035756

*This book is dedicated to the memory of
Anthony J. Cave (1946-2005),
who loved seafaring and history.*

List of Illustrations and Maps

Table of Contents

Introduction

✺

Why Sam Hill?

During the course of his first command, Captain Samuel Hill received two astonishing letters. His vessel, the brig *Lydia* of Boston, was more than 20,000 miles from home by way of Cape Horn, cruising on the Northwest Coast of America when the letters were delivered to his ship.

"We are captives of the Indians" read the first. It was signed by John Jewitt and John Thompson, sailors from the American ship *Boston*. They were the only survivors of a massacre two years earlier at Nootka Sound; their Captain and twenty-five shipmates were dead.

The second letter was from Lewis and Clark. "We were sent out by the Government of the United States to explore the interior of the continent of North America, and did penetrate into the Pacific ocean," it announced.

The letter from Jewitt and Thompson was received in May 1805. Hill had already rescued the captives and had them on board when Lewis and Clark's letter was delivered aboard the *Lydia* a year later in July 1806. It was Hill's third visit to the Columbia River. The previous November, unknown to either party, the *Lydia* and her crew had lain at anchor less than a dozen miles from where the explorers were camped at Fort Clatsop.

Samuel Hill, at twenty-eight, had already made twelve voyages in fifteen years at sea. He had been on the coasts of Africa, Asia, North and South America; and to both the East and West Indies. In the course of his voyages he had, by his own account, twice risen to enormous challenges and saved ships in peril when no other man, including his more senior officers, could muster the right combination of daring, bravery, and skill. His current voyage would be his first of four circumnavigations of the globe.

He lived in Japan for three months in 1799, the first American ever to spend any significant time on Japanese soil. He spent a year as a prisoner of war in Halifax after his privateering vessel was captured by the British during the War of 1812. In subsequent voyages Captain Hill would rescue the victims of Malayan pirates and even become involved in events of the Chilean Revolution. He was attacked by Indians and tangled with the Russians on the coast of Alaska. He entertained Kamehameha, the great king of Hawaii, on board his ship, and witnessed the changes that came with the arrival of the first missionaries after Kamehameha's death.

Samuel Hill lived on the fringes of world-altering events and he documented his extraordinary chain of experiences in several published and unpublished articles and statements. He was an articulate and persuasive writer. If one judged him by his own word alone, Hill would be one of the great maritime heroes of the early nineteenth century

But Samuel Hill was not the only person to write about Samuel Hill. Men who served under his command described him as a villain of epic proportions. As captain of the *Lydia* he was a violent and unstable tyrant, subject to fits and seizures. He beat his men mercilessly, abused them with the foulest language, threatened them with abandonment, starvation, even shipwreck. He plotted against other captains, cheated his Indian trading partners, and kept a Hawaiian girl as his sex slave. A complex, sometimes tortured man, Hill underwent a religious conversion on his final voyage, but even then he could not admit the full extent of his evil doings.

In all his contradictions and complexities, Samuel Hill represented the fledgling United States during its first wave of expansion. In an age when Americans were first venturing into the Pacific and gaining knowledge of new regions and new people, Samuel Hill was in a position to affect, for good or ill, the subsequent relations between American citizens and native people around the globe, especially around the rim of the Pacific Ocean. He was not only an eyewitness to and participant in a number of the major events of his day, but he took active measures to shape the way posterity would view his role in those events by producing his own chronicle for the popular press. In these chronicles he also crafted images of native people that would continue to influence both savage and romantic stereotypes for the two centuries that followed.

It is one of the intriguing accidents of history that the first encounters of Americans abroad were never carefully planned diplomatic missions, but commercial voyages. The *de facto* ambassadors were men like Samuel Hill. The shipboard community, made up of young men isolated for months or years from the larger society of home and women, represented the United States. Sailors were the link through which the old world had encountered the new, and now Europeans and Americans entered the Pacific, transporting with them ideas, technology, and plants and animals that would transform the globe.

A half century before there was any notion of "Manifest Destiny" or organized westward expansion, before the Louisiana Purchase, Lewis and Clark, or the Oregon Trail, American ships swarmed into the Pacific Ocean, seeking profitable products for the China Trade. The first and finest commodities were sea otter pelts, acquired along the Northwest Coast, and the legacy of the voyages that procured them reached across the continent during the period when Americans were first beginning to look westward.

Captain Samuel Hill embodied the two faces of America on the eve of expansion. At home he appeared civilized and sensible, but as he sailed into the Pacific Ocean the mask slipped away to reveal the recklessness, ambition, and violence that largely propelled the United States from coast to coast and around the world.

Prologue

✍

The *Boston* of Boston

Events in which our hero plays no part,
but which will, nonetheless,
first bring him to public attention.

The sounds of a fight on the deck above him first brought John Jewitt up from the hold of the ship. An axe blow to the head sent him plummeting back down. As he lay unconscious and bleeding, the Yuquot Indians of Nootka Sound slaughtered his shipmates.

It was March 22, 1803, and the ship *Boston* lay at anchor on the west coast of Vancouver Island. The Yankee ship was acquiring sea otter pelts to sell in Canton, and negotiations between Captain Jonathan Salter and Chief Maquinna had gone horribly wrong. Salter had been insensitive and Maquinna had been incensed—heaping on the *Boston's* crew the frustrations of two decades of insults and abuse by the captains and crews of British and American vessels.

When Jewitt finally regained consciousness and was dragged up on the deck, Maquinna recognized him. In the ten days before the attack, Maquinna had often been on board the *Boston* and he knew that Jewitt was a blacksmith. It was a skill the Yuquot lacked and Maquinna wanted. He decided to spare Jewitt's life in order to get his knowledge and expertise. "Will you be my slave?" he asked him. "Will you fight for me, repair my muskets, make my daggers?" Jewitt answered that he would and Maquinna ordered him to kiss his hands and feet in submission.

During the time that this bargain was being struck, Jewitt shivered from cold and terror. His head throbbed with pain and he was dizzy from loss of blood. Maquinna went to the cabin of the ship and returned with the captain's coat, which he wrapped around the young man's shoulders. He put a flask of rum to his lips and made Jewitt drink. These small acts of kindness were followed by the most horrible moment of Jewitt's life. Maquinna took him by the hand and led him to the quarterdeck of the ship, where he beheld an unimaginably horrific sight. Rolling gently on the blood-soaked deck was a line of severed heads. It was all that was left of twenty-five men who had been Jewitt's shipmates and friends. For six months they had lived together in the isolation of the ship. Now they were gone, their bodies cast overboard during the massacre.

One by one, Maquinna grabbed each head by the hair and held it up to Jewitt's face, asking him to identify the man by name. Though one of his eyes was swollen shut from his injury, the horrified nineteen-year-old murmured their names as he recognized each man. Some of the heads were so mangled that they could not be identified. Among those he did recognize, and whose names he spoke, were the captain, John Salter, and the mates, John DeLouisa and William Ingraham. These three men had been Jewitt's close friends; Salter had been his mentor, the potential key to his future success.

The ship was from Boston, Massachusetts, but Jewitt was from Boston, England. He joined the crew at the nearby port of Hull, where the ship had come to take on an English cargo before heading south around Cape Horn. The voyage was to take him up through the Pacific to the Northwest Coast, across to Canton, and on to the ship's home port in Massachusetts. Jewitt had not meant to be a sailor; he signed aboard the *Boston* because he liked Captain Salter and especially his mate, William Ingraham

In conversations with young John and his father, Captain Salter had offered his help in setting the young man up in America, a step which both father and son thought would lead to his advancement in life. The voyage was to be the means by which he would move from Old England to New England. The bonus of seeing the world along the way, in the company of friendly and like-minded men, made it the perfect adventure.

Before they left England, Captain Salter and his mates often had dinner at the Jewitt home. The old salt told stories of his voyages to the East Indies and around the world. The young mates took Jewitt to the theater. By Jewitt's account Salter was a good captain, the mates popular and the ship a happy one. Ingraham sketched and painted, Jewitt indulged in his love of singing—he was only one of several musicians on board—, and Captain Salter was an enthusiastic audience. Though there was an arduous passage around Cape Horn, beating against unfavorable winds for over a month, the long stretch through the South Pacific was glorious. The wind was steady, the weather temperate, the company pleasant, the captain kindly. Only one other ship, a British whaler bound home around the Horn, was seen during the whole cruise.

For six months, the *Boston* comprised the whole of John Jewitt's world; his shipmates were his sole companions. He had a blacksmith's forge on deck and a workbench below in the mid-ship area called the steerage, where he spent time with young John Dorthy of Scituate, Massachusetts. Dorthy had been the original blacksmith, but Captain Salter didn't trust him to keep up with the heavy production schedule that they would face on the Northwest Coast, and Jewitt had come aboard as Dorthy's senior, the "armourer." As the ship progressed northward in the Pacific Ocean, Jewitt and Dorthy prepared muskets and blades for sale to the Indians.

The other men on board were a mixed bunch. Six of them, including the captain and the first mate, were from Boston, Massachusetts, the ship's home port. There were five other Americans, including second mate William Ingraham from New York, and John Wilson a black man from Virginia, who was the ship's cook. Another black man, Jupiter Senegal, was probably a runaway slave; it was not uncommon to find them on ships from New England. Seven other Englishmen were on board besides Jewitt, most of them hailing, as he did, from the north of England. Also aboard were two Scots, an Irishman, a Norwegian, a native of the Isle of Man, and a Portuguese speaker who may have come from Cape Verde or the Azores.

These men ranged in age from early teens to middle age. Mostly common seamen, several had specific roles on board as carpenter, tailor, or gunner. They were called John and Johnny, Bill or Willy, Robbie, Sam, Ben, Philip, Tom, Adam, Andy, Joe, and seem to have been a well-matched crew, more contented than one often found on shipboard. They had high expectations for success with their mixed cargo of blankets, bolts of cloth, mirrors, beads, knives, razors, and guns. They did not expect to die that March day in 1803.

The attack came without warning. Several of the men were away from the ship. Abe Waters of Philadelphia, the steward, was ashore washing clothes. Ten men, including first mate John DeLouisa, were fishing when they were suddenly attacked with guns and clubs. The men who were still aboard the *Boston* were mostly killed with their own jack knives, their throats cut, their heads severed. Though John Jewitt survived, the course of his life was so deeply altered by those moments that he would never recover from the experience.

At Maquinna's order, and under Jewitt's direction, the Yuquot ran the *Boston* up onto the beach at Friendly Cove and began to move the cargo ashore. The savage violence of the massacre contrasted with the treatment that Jewitt began to receive immediately upon his arrival in the village. Maquinna's young son, Sat-sat-soks-sis, instantly took a liking to him and became his constant companion. Maquinna himself bound Jewitt's scarf around his head to stop the flow of blood, pressing a tobacco leaf on the wound at Jewitt's request. The women in his house treated the stranger with kindness. Though there was a vocal element among the Yuquot who thought that Jewitt's death was necessary to protect them from retaliation by other American ships, Maquinna would not hear of it.

Within a few days the *Boston* was in flames and the evidence of the incident was destroyed. Before the ship's arsenal exploded, though, it was discovered that there was another survivor on board. When Jewitt heard the news, he wracked his feverish brain, trying to determine who it might be. He forced himself to remember the heads he had seen held up one after the other by Maquinna. Who was missing? He became convinced that it must be John Thompson, the sailmaker, a man who, like himself, had been working below when the attack came.

Thompson was almost forty and had what Jewitt called "an old look." Jewitt assumed, and was soon after assured by Maquinna, that Thompson would be executed in the morning, and he concocted a plan to save him. At dawn the next day, Jewitt accompanied Maquinna back to the ship. "Father!" he declared upon seeing Thompson. The difference in age between the two men made the relationship believable and Jewitt banked on the affectionate nature of Sat-sat-soks-sis, and the great love that Maquinna obviously felt for his son to argue for Thompson's life.

The ruse worked. Maquinna had already taken a liking to Jewitt, appreciated the relationship that the young Englishman had with his son, and had an idea that sailmaking, like blacksmithing, might prove a useful skill at Nootka Sound. The Indians had not traditionally used sails on their canoes, but Maquinna was eager to experiment, and John Thompson could make him a sail. Jewitt and Thompson consequently found themselves residents of the village of Yuquot. Their position within the elaborate social structure was clear. They were the slaves of the highest-ranking person in the village, Maquinna, and would, thereafter, live in his house.

Despite the horrors of the situation that brought him there, Jewitt adapted quickly to the rhythm of life at Nootka Sound. He set about learning the language, developing relationships with the people around him, and putting his skills to work for Maquinna. He was, by all accounts, a remarkably affable young man, social and gregarious by nature, and seemingly adapted to this new life as he had to that on shipboard.

John Thompson, on the other hand, was not so affable or adaptable. He had spent most of his life as a sailor and turned forty while at Nootka Sound. A native of Philadelphia, Thompson ran away to sea at the tender age of eight, as cabin boy on a ship bound for London. Arriving alone and friendless in the English capital, he worked his way from ship to ship, was pressed into service on a man-of-war, and served almost thirty years in the Royal Navy. Unlike most Americans of the period, he could neither read nor write. According to Jewitt, he was "a very strong and powerful man, an expert boxer, and perfectly fearless."

Thompson did not accept his captivity. He hated the Indians, refused to learn their language, often entered into stupid scrapes or violent bouts, and did not engender any of the fondness that came so naturally to Jewitt. At one point Maquinna said to Jewitt, "You must have had a very good tempered woman indeed for your mother, as your father is so very ill-natured a man."

Three things kept Thompson from being killed during the time he was at Nootka Sound: the constant intervention of Jewitt with Maquinna, his skill with a needle, and a growing reputation for violence that earned him a measure of respect among the Yuquot. Years later, Jewitt would recount a number of instances where Thompson lashed out in a temper and struck someone, usually someone who was taunting him as a "white slave." One time he struck Sat-sat-soks-sis and it took all of Jewitt's efforts to pacify Maquinna. Yet Thompson was also able to gain some favor with Maquinna on his own account. He made him a sail for his canoe and a garment out of fabric salvaged from the *Boston*. The latter item, sewed in a style patterned after a common article of native garb, was described by Jewitt as "a most superb dress."

> This was a Kootsuk or mantle, a fathom square, made entirely of european vest patterns of the gayest colours. These were sewed together, in a manner to make the best show, and bound with a deep trimming of the finest otter skin, with which the armholes were also bordered; while the bottom was farther embellished with five or six rows of gilt buttons, placed as near as possible to each other. Nothing could exceed the pride of Maquina when he first put on this royal robe, decorated like the coat of Joseph, with all the colours of the rainbow, and glittering with the buttons, which as he strutted about made a tinkling, while he repeatedly exclaimed in a transport of exultation.

On more than one occasion, Thompson killed native men, but as Maquinna identified all of them as his enemies, this enhanced rather than damaged his position with the chief. Though never as comfortable or accepting as Jewitt in his role as captive, Thompson nonetheless became a fixture in the village. He was feared while Jewitt was liked.

For over two years, Jewitt and Thompson lived among the Yuquot. Their lot was sometimes very hard as they were expected to fend for themselves and they were not very good at it. They never mastered the native techniques of fishing, nor did they ever develop a taste for the local cuisine of dried clams, berries, fish, and sea mammal meat, all dipped in fish oil or whale oil. Their skills as blacksmith and sailmaker or tailor had value though, as did their labor hauling firewood, and they were able to trade work for food, especially salmon, which was their favorite dish.

The two men were often cold and hungry. They were regularly harassed when Maquinna was out of earshot. But they began to understand the cycles of native life. They moved with the Yuquot from their summer village at Friendly Cove to their fishing camp at Tahsis and later to their winter quarters at Cooptee and back, through the cycle of three summers and two winters. Both came to know Maquinna and his people well. Through the long winters they joined them in the big cedar long house for ceremonial feasts, dancing, speeches, and songs.

The Yuquot were whalehunters and Jewitt observed their preparations and even made an iron harpoon for Maquinna to replace the Chief's traditional mussel-shell blade. Jewitt had been a blacksmith in the English whaling port of Hull and was consequently knowledgeable about the harpoons used by the British Arctic fleet. The harpoon he made at Nootka Sound was a rousing success.

When Maquinna went to war, Jewitt and Thompson went with him; Jewitt prepared enough armament for the Yuquot to massacre their neighboring rivals, and Thompson gaining a legendary status for killing seven men with his cutlass. Jewitt would later say that Thompson's thirst for revenge was vented that day in a murderous frenzy.

In the fall of 1804, when the two men from the *Boston* had lived at Nootka Sound for a year and a half, Maquinna announced that it was time for Jewitt to marry. Jewitt was not inclined to agree, even though he acknowledged that his life would be easier with a wife. Maquinna insisted, threatening the lives of both Jewitt and Thompson if Jewitt did not take a wife. "Reduced to this sad extremity," Jewitt would later write, "with death on the one side, and matrimony on the other, I thought proper to choose what appeared to me the least of the two evils, and consent to be married." Jewitt's seventeen-year-old bride, Eu-stoch-ee-exqua, beautiful, charming, and well connected, became pregnant immediately and bore a son the following summer.

Though Jewitt seemed settled in his new life, he dreamed constantly of rescue. Sixteen times he placed a letter in the hands of one of Maquinna's rivals, in the hopes that it would reach an American ship. On at least two occasions he saw ships in the distance, but they didn't come into Nootka Sound. The attack on the *Boston* successfully discouraged them and other vessels from visiting the area in the months and years that followed. Thompson never gave up his hopes for a return to his former life, as hard as that life had been. He preferred the dried and salted fare of the ship to the salmon, berries, and whale oil of the Yuquot. He would not wear Indian clothing, though his own deteriorating shirt and trousers hung on him in rags.

As their relationship developed, Jewitt had a chance to ask Maquinna about the circumstances that led to the attack on his ship. The incident that precipitated the massacre of the *Boston* crew was minor enough on the face of it. Captain Salter gave Maquinna a gun and Maquinna broke it. When he brought the gun back to the American captain, insisting that it was "peshak—bad!" Salter grabbed it angrily and threw it to Jewitt to repair. Salter made disparaging comments about the chief which Maquinna, having a fair command of English, understood better than Salter ever could have imagined.

The American's actions and comments were embarrassing and insulting to a man of rank, who was accompanied on this occasion by several of his subordinates.

Salter had lost patience with Maquinna, who could be petty and irritating, but it was obvious in the days that followed that Salter didn't realize the extent of Maquinna's anger. On its own, the insult would not have warranted the killing of a shipload of men, but for Maquinna it was the straw that broke the camel's back.

There had been a number of incidents over the years, ranging from insensitive remarks to accidents, mishaps, and murder. The Spanish had kept a garrison at Nootka Sound for several years, during which time the commander, Esteban José Martinez, summarily executed a high ranking and popular chief. A British captain, James Hannah, had turned his cannon onto a party of Yuquot canoes, killing twenty people, including children. Most outrageous of all, the American Captain Robert Gray, commanding the ship *Columbia,* ordered the complete destruction of the nearby village of Opitsat in 1792. The chief there was Wickaninish, a man well known to American captains and the brother-in-law of Maquinna. John Boit, a member of the *Columbia* crew, regretted having to take part in the event. He was, he wrote in his journal, "grieved to think Capt. Gray shou'd let his passions go so far. ... This fine Village, the Work of Ages, was in a short time totally destroy'd."

Jewitt was sympathetic to Maquinna's anger at these hostile and unwarranted acts of violence, and would ultimately speak in defense of his captor. "Maquina's conduct in taking our ship," he wrote, "arose from an insult that he thought he had received from captain Salter, and from the unjustifiable conduct of some masters of vessels, who had robbed him, and without provocation, killed a number of his people."

Maquinna clearly regretted that Americans had abandoned their trade with his people in the wake of the *Boston's* destruction. News traveled quickly on the Northwest Coast. The Indians were extremely mobile, traveling between villages in their dugout canoes, and American captains depended on native informants for news of trade. Other Americans on the coast knew the attack on the Boston, and the fact that there were two survivors, within days of the event.

Jewitt and Maquinna conversed frequently. It seems obvious that a real bond formed between the two men during the time that they lived in close quarters in Maquinna's long house. The Yuquot chief knew that Jewitt was writing in a journal, but not that he had, through the whole of his captivity, been slipping secret notes into the hands of visiting chiefs.

In May 1805 one of Jewitt's messages was finally delivered to an American ship. Chief Utiller of Classet, a village on the southern bank of the Straits of Juan de Fuca, saw the brig *Lydia* in the distance and paddled several miles to meet it. The letter gave him an opportunity to ingratiate himself with an American trader and damage Maquinna in the process, and though he couldn't read it, he had a very good idea of its contents.

The *Lydia* eventually changed course and sailed into Nootka Sound. It had been more than two years since the Yuquot had seen a ship this close to their village. The *Lydia* fired three cannon shots, the customary signal on the Northwest Coast of a desire to initiate trade. Maquinna went instantly to Jewitt, who with some effort maintained a calm and disinterested demeanor. How, Maquinna asked him, should he approach this unknown captain? If Jewitt would write a letter, he suggested, saying that all was well in the village, that he and Thompson had been kindly treated...

It was almost too much for Jewitt. As Maquinna continued explaining how he would bring the letter, along with some prime pelts, to the ship, Jewitt's mind raced. Maquinna was interested in bringing the prosperity of American trade back to Nootka Sound; Jewitt knew that the moment of his rescue was near. Slowly and cautiously he agreed to write the letter. He knew that Maquinna would be easily convinced that he did not want to leave. His month-old son, his kind and beautiful wife, his position as Maquinna's friend, all were inducements to stay.

Most importantly, he knew that Maquinna could not read. He wrote a letter and Maquinna carried it on board the *Lydia* where it was read by the Captain, Samuel Hill.

To Captain ———
    of the Brig ———
    Nootka, July 19, 1805.

Sir,

    THE bearer of this letter is the Indian king by the name of Maquina. He was the instigator of the capture of the ship Boston, of Boston in North America, John Salter captain, and of the murder of twenty-five men of her crew, the two only survivors being now on shore—Wherefore I hope you will take care to confine him... keeping so good a watch over him, that he cannot escape from you. By so doing we shall be able to obtain our release in the course of a few hours.

        JOHN R. JEWITT, Armourer
           of the Boston, for himself and
        JOHN THOMPSON, Sail-maker of said ship.

    Jewitt's prediction was true. Within a few hours, he and Thompson were standing on the deck of the *Lydia.* For two years and four months they had dreamed constantly of rescue, they had thought of home, where English was spoken and the food and customs were familiar. They knew that their families and friends thought they were dead. Now their captivity was over. They were free men—or so it seemed.

    In 1807, Jewitt published the journal he had kept in captivity. Eight years later he expanded it into a narrative of his "Adventures and Sufferings" as the captive of Maquinna. His story ends when the *Lydia* sails away from Nootka Sound.

    What did not become part of the story was that at that moment Jewitt and Thompson entered into a new captivity, of greater confinement, equivalent violence, and almost equal length. They traded one master, Maquinna, for another, Captain Samuel Hill.

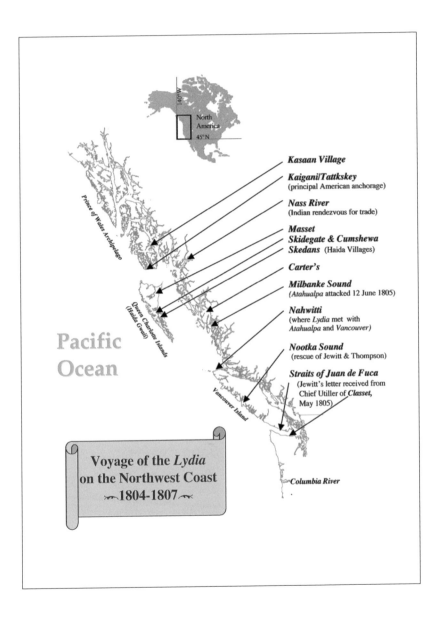

Kasaan Village

Kaigani/Tattkskey
(principal American anchorage)

Nass River
(Indian rendezvous for trade)

Masset
Skidegate & Cumshewa
Skedans (Haida Villages)

Carter's

Milbanke Sound
(Atahualpa attacked 12 June 1805)

Nahwitti
(where Lydia met with
Atahualpa and Vancouver)

Nootka Sound
(rescue of Jewitt & Thompson)

Straits of Juan de Fuca
(Jewitt's letter received from
Chief Utiller of Classet,
May 1805)

Columbia River

Pacific
Ocean

Prince of Wales Archipelago

Queen Charlotte Islands
(Haida Gwaii)

Vancouver Island

Voyage of the Lydia
on the Northwest Coast
1804-1807

Dramatis Personae of Chapter One

Captives of Maquinna:

> John Jewitt
> John Thompson

Aboard the American ship *Lydia*:

> Samuel Hill, *Captain*
> Isaac Hurd, *Supercargo*
> William Walker, *Clerk*
> *MATES:* Mr. Low
> James Bennett
> Mr. Hewes
> Sailors, carpenter, boatswain, steward
> Girl of Atooi, *Captive of Sam Hill*

Other American Ships, and their Captains:

> *Vancouver,*   Thomas Brown
> *Pearl,*   John Ebbets
> *Atahualpa,*   Oliver Porter (later David
>   Adams)
> *Hamilton,*   Lemuel Porter
> *Juno,*   John DeWolfe

Indian Chiefs:

> Maquinna, *Chief at Nootka Sound*
> Utiller, *Chief of the Classets*

Offstage:

> Lewis and Clark, Explorers
> George & Theodore Lyman, Owners of the *Lydia,*
>   *Atahualpa, Vancouver*
> Thomas & Francis Amory, Owners of the *Boston*

Chapter I

✧

Lydia, 1804-1807:
Devil on the Deep Blue Sea

*In which Samuel Hill proves disappointing as a hero,
although he rescues Jewitt and almost meets
Lewis and Clark.*

When the first raptures of being rescued had faded,
John Jewitt and John Thompson found out soon enough
that they were on what sailors referred to as a "hell ship."
The *Lydia* had a dysfunctional chain of command. The men
were always poised and ready to mutiny. The original first
mate and supercargo had already been dismissed and put
off the ship for challenging the authority of the captain.
Three different men served as chief mate in the course of
the voyage, each more brutal than his predecessor. A
young Hawaiian woman lived in the captain's cabin as his
sexual hostage, and the captain himself behaved like a
madman. This was the situation into which the *Boston*
survivors escaped.

The *Lydia's* voyage seemed ordinary enough when it
began, and the purpose for the trip was the same as it had
been for the *Boston:* to go from Massachusetts to the
Northwest Coast and there to trade with the Indians for sea

otter pelts, which would then be brought to Canton and exchanged for Chinese tea, silk, and porcelain. The owners, brothers George and Theodore Lyman, were experienced managers of Pacific voyages and the vessel was well outfitted for the purpose. On August 31, 1804, the *Lydia* sailed out past Boston Light into the North Atlantic. Their route took them east by south to Cape Verde for supplies and from there into the great swirl of winds and currents that would carry them through the South Atlantic and around Cape Horn. Christmas found them rounding the Horn at the height of the southern hemisphere summer and heading north again into the Pacific Ocean.

Living aft, in private cabins surrounding a central ward room, were Captain Hill, two mates (referred to as "Mr. Low" and "Mr. Bennett" by all on board), and the supercargo, Isaac Hurd. There was a steward who served the men in the aft cabins, and a cook who prepared food for the entire crew. In the central or "steerage" section of the ship were the accommodations for the men who practiced the specialized trades of carpentry, blacksmithing, and sail-making, as well as the boatswain, who was responsible for the upkeep of the ship. The common sailors lived forward in the forecastle.

The brig *Lydia* was not a large vessel. At 180 tons she was not even eighty feet long—tight quarters for a crew of twenty or so men. She had two masts, both square rigged, which means that in order to set or strike sails, the men had to climb aloft and out along the yards. There they hovered, their feet balanced on a single rope, as the ship rolled through an arc that suspended them alternately over the deck and the sea. Sail handling was required most when weather conditions were at their worst, and being aloft could be a miserable and dangerous business for the sailors.

This was a world constantly in motion and run on a rhythm established by the schedule of watches: four hours on duty, four hours off, through the whole of the twenty-four hour day. In the evening, two two-hour "dog" watches broke up the schedule and reversed the order of watch standing for the next day. The men were always at least a little sleep-deprived. The fresh provisions were long gone by Christmas, and the menu was a monotonous repetition of reconstituted dried stores: beans, rice, peas, beans, rice, peas. What meat there was had been preserved long before in salt or brine. The sailors' bread, called hardtack, was either months old if baked ashore and packed in the hold (in which case it was likely bug-infested) or was mixed by the cook from flour and seawater. There were occasional boiled or steamed sweets made with raisins or molasses. There was no privacy and few secrets.

Unlike the *Boston,* which Jewitt described as a happy ship, a power struggle had begun on the *Lydia* immediately after she set sail from Boston. A mercantile venture to the Northwest Coast and Canton had two business components, the business of the ship and the business of trade. The captain was always completely responsible for the business of the ship. With him lay both the responsibility and the authority for the safety of the vessel and its crew, and for its movement from one place to another. He needed to know navigation, ship handling, meteorology, and personnel management, as well as a smattering of medicine, law, international relations, and finance.

The business of trade was the purview of the supercargo. His job was to decide when and what to trade, what price to fix on goods, when to hold back in the expectation of getting a better price, and when to surrender to conditions and take a loss. He needed to know numbers and be able to keep a record of transactions. It helped enormously if he knew other languages, though it was impossible for any mariner in the early nineteenth century to have more than a rudimentary knowledge of even a small number of the languages that would be encountered in the course of a circumnavigation.

A good supercargo had a feel for human psychology, and an ability to read people and their intentions despite a difference of language and culture. Often he would have to make quick decisions and accommodate completely different situations than had been anticipated when the voyage was planned. If one cargo was not going to work, he had to be prepared to come up with another. Twenty thousand or more sea miles from home, the success of a voyage often depended on the supercargo's ability to draw a rabbit from his hat.

In the course of American trade on the Northwest Coast, clever supercargos had been known to strip captains' cabins of their furnishings and sailors of their clothes to acquire sea otter pelts. (Just a few years before the *Lydia* voyage, Ralph Haskins, supercargo of the ship *Atahualpa*, bartered his violin, his pocket watch, and the ship's cat to get pelts!) The blacksmith and carpenter were often called into service to make items for trade; the sailmaker could expect to act as a tailor-on-demand for custom clothing made from trade cloth, signal flags, Polynesian tapa, and spare sails.

The best captains functioned as their own super-cargoes. They managed both the ship and its business and there was, consequently, no conflict between the two. In any case, the success of a voyage depended upon the ability of the two offices to work together, a situation that was never achieved on the *Lydia*. Isaac Hurd, the supercargo, was clearly a favorite of the Lyman brothers, who owned and managed the vessel. The twenty-one-year-old Hurd was seven years younger than Hill, better educated, and well connected in Boston social circles; his father was a minister in nearby Concord. Most importantly, Hurd had already made a voyage to the Northwest Coast on another Lyman ship, the *Vancouver*, serving as clerk under Captain Thomas Brown. Hurd and his former captain had developed a warm friendship and a smooth working relationship as Hurd learned the business under Brown's tutelage.

Prior to becoming captain, Samuel Hill had commanded just one other vessel, the *Mary*, on a voyage that ran along the Atlantic coast from Boston to Virginia, from Virginia across the Atlantic to the Spanish port of Cadiz, and then back to Boston. A transatlantic voyage was much less com-plex than one that rounded either Cape Horn or the Cape of Good Hope, and on Hill's subsequent voyage (the one that immediately preceded that of the *Lydia*) he had been unable to secure a captain's position and was obliged to accept the lower rank of mate on the Batavia-bound *Indus*.

Hill was twenty-seven years old. He had been at sea for fourteen years, and following the usual progression was promoted from boy to steward to seaman to mate to master in ten voyages. He had crossed the Atlantic eight times, been twice each to the East and West Indies, and even to

Japan on the Salem ship *Franklin,* one of the first American vessels to visit there. His education was rudimentary but sound, he read extensively, wrote beautifully, and was obviously intelligent. There is nothing surprising about his having achieved command of the *Lydia.* But he had not been around Cape Horn to the Pacific, and he had not been to the Northwest Coast, Hawaii, or Canton.

The Lymans had originally hired Hill to be both captain and supercargo, but just before the ship left Boston, they had second thoughts about Hill's abilities to handle both jobs. Isaac Hurd was added at the last minute to be responsible for the business part of the venture, and it was a blow to Hill from which he did not recover. The mantle of command did not yet rest easily on his shoulders, and having a self-assured, experienced, and somewhat arrogant supercargo didn't help. Hurd never gave the captain the respect that his position required. Hill and Hurd should have been collaborators but instead they were competitors, and it was a bad way to begin.

Relations between the two men went awry very early in the cruise. As Hill was subject to violent outbursts on the slightest provocation, and as Hurd was the more experienced man, it is not too surprising that Mr. Low, the first mate, began to look to the supercargo rather than the captain for direction. The situation was disturbing enough to Hill that he fired Low and ordered him off the ship when the *Lydia* reached Hawaii in early March 1805.

The *Lydia* spent a few weeks in Hawaii, making repairs to the vessel, stocking up on fresh provisions, and bringing aboard wood and water. The men took liberty ashore and brought native girls back to the ship for sex. Even though the language there was entirely unknown to them, sailors looked forward to a sojourn in the "Sandwich Islands" and it was an important break in the routine before a ship headed to the Northwest Coast. Few American ships left there without hiring Hawaiian men for crew and the *Lydia* was no exception, bringing four new sailors into the already crowded forecastle.

There was also an addition to the party living in the aft cabin when the ship left the islands. She was a young Hawaiian woman, brought on board by Samuel Hill to be his sexual partner. James Bennett, who advanced into

Low's position as mate, speculated that she was about fifteen years old, and Hurd called her a "poor innocent Sandwich Island girl." She certainly spoke little or no English, and in his extensive writing Hill makes no mention of ever having learned any Hawaiian beyond basic greetings and place names. What her expectations were when she came on board the ship isn't known, or even if she came willingly. She could not have realized when she first went into Sam Hill's cabin that he would sail away and keep her there for more than a year and a half.

Though she is mentioned often in the two shipboard journals that survive for this voyage, she is never referred to by name. Isaac Hurd calls her "the Captain's Lady." William Walker, who came aboard later, refers to her repeatedly as "the Skipper's whore" or his "wife," in snide and disgusted terms aimed more at Hill than at her. To distinguish her from a Chinook Indian woman brought aboard more than a year later, Walker once identified her by her home island as Hill's "Atooi lady," but she is otherwise a nameless shadow on the *Lydia.*

From the time Hill brought her on board, what little civility there had been on the ship ceased. The captain paid little attention to the working of the ship unless a crisis was imminent. The new first mate, James Bennett, was consistently undermined by Hill, and could be a vengeful brute to the men. Before they left the islands, Isaac Hurd persuaded John Young, an Englishman who was living in the islands and working for the Hawaiian King, to use his influence to place Mr. Low on another American ship at the earliest opportunity.

The *Lydia* proceeded to the Northwest Coast and arrived at the Columbia River on April 6th. Hurd wrote in his journal that he and the captain went ashore to find the first signs of spring in evidence. The flowering shrubs and smell of land made Hurd somewhat hopeful for the success of the venture, but it was short-lived. The next day Captain Hill began what would become a pattern of behavior, leaving the ship for an extended period of time with his Hawaiian companion. Often he would require several hands to row him ashore in the ship's boat, while the supercargo waited impatiently on the anchored brig.

The Chinook Indians, who lived along the bank of the Columbia River, recognized Hurd from his previous voyage on the *Vancouver* with Captain Thomas Brown, and remembered the prices given at that time for the tanned moose hides called *clemmels* that American mariners regularly purchased here to exchange farther north on the coast. Hurd had hoped for a better deal, quickly became frustrated, and was anxious to proceed north. As he continued to carry out the business of the ship, the captain absented himself with the Hawaiian girl, usually for a day or more, sometimes several days. Once, after an absence of five days, Hurd in his frustration ordered the mate to ready the ship for an immediate departure upon Captain Hill's return. After another two days, Hurd confided to his journal that he began to be "very concerned for them." More than once the Chinook told Hurd that they believed Hill's party was lost, but there was no evidence.

Finally, more than a week after leaving the ship, Hill returned, having gone further up the Columbia River than any foreign party had yet ventured, but being disinclined to report about it to Hurd. To Hurd, Hill's boat crew looked "rather thin as though they had had poor keeping." He told the captain that he was ready to depart, but Hill dallied for almost another week with little trade, and then the two men could not agree on where to go next.

From the Columbia River north to the Straits of Juan de Fuca there were few opportunities to trade unless one was willing to go into Gray's Harbor, one of two large shallow bays along the coast of what is now Washington State. Hurd was for proceeding on, trading with the Chehalis Indians along the way only if they came out of Gray's Harbor in their canoes. He specifically "instructed" Hill *not* to go into the harbor itself, because of the shallow sandbar at its mouth. That was enough for Captain Hill. In they went, striking the bottom several times in the process. Hurd could not restrain himself from scolding Hill.

It was a foolish and dangerous move; Hurd was clearly overstepping the bounds of his position and Hill rightly resented it. But Hurd also felt his responsibility to the owners, and his concerns for the financial success of the voyage were not unwarranted. Hill was a weak and obsesssive man, unable to control his emotions, and subject to petty grudges. He did not have the cool, level-headed sense of command that Hurd had seen in his former captain.

In the absence of a working relationship with the captain, Hurd consistently turned to the chief mate, first in the person of Mr. Low, and subsequently James Bennett. On a successful ship, the mate speaks with the voice of the captain, and any visible conflict between the two is felt by the crew and undermines their confidence. The mate is *not* the employee of the supercargo, and Hurd's attempt to bypass Hill led to a further breakdown of the chain of command.

The whole of this drama was played out on a stage less than 80 feet long and 20 feet wide. Samuel Hill and Isaac Hurd worked, ate, and slept within a few feet of each other day after day as their battle raged on. It was impossible to keep it from infecting the whole ship. Hurd gossiped about the captain with his mates; Hill, unable to control his temper, exploded in tantrums of foul language and threats.

The fact that Hill had a female companion can only have added to the frustration of all the other men on board. William Walker, quartered in the forecastle at the other end of the ship, was able to report on the Captain's sexual activity, so Isaac Hurd, living in the adjacent cabin, must have been a hostage audience to the sounds of Hill's behavior next door.

From the fiasco at Gray's Harbor, the *Lydia* proceeded north to the Straits of Juan de Fuca, the passage between the Olympic Peninsula and Vancouver Island. They were not planning to make a stop on the south coast of the Straits, but they saw a canoe paddling furiously toward them, with a man in the bow waving a piece of paper. He was Utiller, the chief of the Classet Indians, and in his hand was one of the letters that John Jewitt had written and distributed among the various tribes in the vicinity. It was dated September 2, 1804, eight months earlier. Hurd quickly wrote a letter to Jewitt and Thompson, whose names were signed to the note, and gave Utiller a small present to deliver it if the opportunity arose.

American traders had already established a regular sort of route by the time the *Lydia* arrived on the coast, though the success of a voyage depended on the captain or supercargo being canny enough to get to remote villages before other ships either reduced the stock of furs or drove the price up too high for commercial success. The Columbia River was the southernmost point of the "North-west Coast" for Americans engaged in the trade. The northernmost destination was the Russian fort at Sitka. Trade farther to the north and west, where the coast of Alaska swings out toward the Aleutian Islands, was controlled by the Russians.

South from Sitka lay the "Inside Passage," along what is now the coast of southeast Alaska and British Columbia. Here the waters were protected from the full force of the Pacific Ocean, but the tradeoff was difficult navigation through narrow channels and along poorly charted coasts with submerged rocks and ledges. Sandbars made the entrances to bays and rivers dangerously shallow and they shifted and changed constantly. Hurd was always sugges-ting prudence, but Hill was not necessarily putting the ship in more danger than any other captain sailing along that coast when he attempted various narrow or shallow passages.

There was a rendezvous point for American ships near the Haida Indian village of Kaigani, which sailors called "Tattiskey" or "Tatter's Key." It was a place where Yankee mariners could obtain news of home from newly arrived ships, and information on trade in the region from those who had been working the coast. The Native population was sparse here, and there was abundant wood, fresh water, and several protected anchorages. In the first decade of the nineteenth century as many as a dozen Yankee vessels are known to have anchored at Tattiskey at the same time.

The *Lydia* bypassed Vancouver Island and the Queen Charlotte Islands and headed directly north from Gray's Harbor to Tattiskey. A number of small rocky islets mark the passage into the anchorage, growing larger, higher, and greener until a stretch of protected beach opens behind one of them to reveal Kaigani. Beyond it lies a series of passages into deep narrow coves, surrounded on all sides by thickly forested mountains that rise steeply up from the sea floor.

When the *Lydia* arrived there in May 1805, the *Pearl* was riding at anchor and tethered to the shore by lines attached to nearby trees. The *Pearl* had followed the *Lydia* into the Hawaiian Islands two months earlier and Isaac Hurd, anxious to hear what had happened to his friend Mr. Low, went aboard to meet with the Captain, John Ebbets. Ebbets had been easily persuaded to take Low on board at the Hawaiian Islands, and when the *Pearl* arrived on the Northwest Coast just a few weeks earlier, Captain Brown had offered him a position as mate on the *Vancouver,* so Low was even now in the area, serving under Hurd's former captain and good friend.

Having received enough information to develop a plan for trade, Hurd told Hill to head south to the Native village of Skidegate in the Queen Charlotte Islands. As they approached their anchorage, the mate, James Bennett, called out to the captain that he thought the rocky bottom might foul their anchor cables. Captain Hill exploded in a torrent of abusive language. Hurd was shocked. "This young man is the only one I place any dependence on when in danger," he wrote in his journal, "and he receives the harshest treatment from Capt. Hill of any one on board—he has often told me were it in his power he [would] work his passage home before the mast."

Trade did not appear to be very favorable at Skidegate, and Hurd would certainly have requested that Hill move on to the next village, but the captain almost immediately left the ship. Hurd poured his frustration at this behavior into his journal.

> Friday, 24 May, 1805: Trading with the Natives. Capt. Hill & Wife with 4 hands & a Cocksw'n gone in the Boat as usual, surveying the N.W. Coast. A Stranger w'd suppose that Mr. Lyman had fitted the Brig out on a Voyage of discovery - If I save my life and get to Boston safe, it is more than I at this time expect. The Indians I fear not so long as every Man, under pay on board the Brig is attending to their respective duties on board - At Columbia River, at three different times, Capt. Hill with 5 & 6 hands was near being lost.

The *Lydia* carried three boats that could be launched from the deck. These were the vehicles that carried men ashore and brought supplies and provisions back to the ship. Two of them were whaleboats, 25-foot double-enders that could be rowed, paddled, or sailed; the third was a longboat that was then being used only with oars. Hill regularly commandeered these small boats for his exploring expeditions. When he returned on board after his foray ashore on May 24, Hurd scribbled angrily that Hill had almost lost his life, the crew, and the boat in trying to land. Almost as if to spite him, Hurd sold the two whaleboats to the Indians three days later.

Several days were spent cruising in the Queen Charlotte Islands, with little trade, growing anxiety, and rising tempers. They returned to Tattiskey and learned from the Kaigani Haida that Captain Brown of the *Vancouver* was in the region and that he was bound for a place on the mainland coast that the British and Americans called "Carters." "Thither I intend going," Hurd wrote in his log. His former mentor and friend could guide him through the morass that was the *Lydia's* voyage.

Before they could depart, however, Hill was off again on a private cruise in the longboat. "I had forgot when I sold the Whale [boats] that the Long Boat could have Sails," Hurd wrote, "but no sooner was they gone, then a new sail was rigged... this morning Capt. Hill with his wife set out upon a cruise." His plot to keep the captain on the ship by trading away the two boats had failed.

Hill can not have wanted to meet with Captain Brown, who was certain to be an ally to Hurd. Besides, his former chief mate, Low, was on board the *Vancouver* and he had, no doubt, already given Brown an earful about life on the *Lydia*. Hill dallied at Tattiskey until June 5, when a sail was seen in the distance. The cannon was fired as a signal and within a few hours the Boston ship *Atahualpa* was alongside. This was good luck for Hill. Captain Oliver Porter of the *Atahualpa* was a man he claimed as a friend and, like the *Lydia* and Captain Brown's *Vancouver,* the *Atahualpa* was owned by the Lymans. In the battle for reputations that was inevitably going to transpire back in Boston, Porter could be an ally of Hill's if the captain played his cards right.

The *Atahualpa* had been built for the Lymans specifically for the Northwest Trade, and was currently on her second of four voyages to the region. The ship was well known to the Indians. Captain Oliver Porter was from an active seafaring family in Boston. His brother, Lemuel, was even then bound to the Northwest Coast as master of the *Hamilton*. The *Atahualpa* was having a more successful cruise than the *Lydia*. Captain Porter reported to Hurd that they had taken 4300 skins and 3000 sea otter tails. The officers of the two vessels passed an afternoon together, and Hurd made a note later that day about the *Atahualpa*: "all well on board."

Porter had already seen Hurd's friend Captain Brown and echoed the information, received from the Indians, that he was then at Carter's. Two days later, Hurd finally saw the *Vancouver* in the offing and had a chance to meet with his old friend when he came on board the *Lydia*. The next day Hurd returned the visit and had a chance to see Mr. Low. "I am happy to find," he wrote later, "that Capt. Brown thinks Mr. Low is capable of the Duty he shipped to do." Hurd was sorry to return to the *Lydia* from his expedition to the *Vancouver*, where he had been able to vent his frustrations about Captain Hill to a willing and sympathetic audience.

In the constant bickering between captain and supercargo over where to go next, they missed the biggest Indian rendezvous of the summer, an extravaganza of fishing and trade at the Nass River. The *Lydia* arrived there too early, left prematurely, and then passed the Indians in a fog enroute back when the ship returned to the Queen Charlotte Islands. Consequently, they missed out on the trade at both ends of the Indians' annual pilgrimage. To make matters worse, when Hill and Hurd finally agreed to proceed next to Skidegate, they found that another American ship, the *Juno*, had beaten them to their destination.

At Skidegate, Captain John DeWolfe of the *Juno*, and his mate, Mr. Morefield, came aboard the *Lydia* to report on their trading success. It was bad news for Hurd. Wherever the two ships might meet thereafter, DeWolfe would dominate the trade. Hurd had been complaining to Hill that trade was off all over the coast. None of the *Lydia's* cargo was selling; neither bolts of cloth nor provisions could command the price he hoped for. Now here was DeWolfe, giving three fathoms of cloth, a woolen coat, rice, molasses, and "several small articles" for each prime pelt. It was a price Hurd could not afford to pay.

The *Juno* was owned by the DeWolfe family of Bristol, Rhode Island, and the captain, John DeWolfe, was Herman Melville's uncle. As captain, supercargo, and owner, DeWolfe had enormous latitude in controlling the trade, and he had a secret motive as well. It was his intention to get rid of all of his cargo enroute to Sitka and then sell his ship there to the Russians. There was no way that the *Lydia* could compete. There was nothing Hill and Hurd could do but leave the *Juno* behind and start to cruise from village to village. With any luck they would find one or two where they had not been preceded by another American ship.

Early on the morning of June 24, the *Lydia* weighed anchor and began to tack out of Skidegate harbor. In the distance the crew could see the sails of two ships, and before long they heard the sound of a signal cannon. It was the *Atahualpa* and the *Vancouver,* and Captain Brown came aboard immediately.

He had devastating news. Captain Oliver Porter and eight of his men were dead, murdered by the Indians at Milbanke Sound. Many more of the *Atahualpa* crew were wounded, some mortally. It had been just three weeks since the men of the *Lydia* had seen the *Atahualpa* and reported "all well" with their comrades aboard. Captain Porter had sailed directly from that rendezvous toward Milbanke Sound.

As the *Lydia, Atahualpa,* and *Vancouver* were all owned by the same company, Captain Brown thought that the three ships should be brought into some safe anchorage so that the officers could decide how to proceed next. Hurd went aboard the *Atahualpa* to take charge of the business papers, and the three vessels sailed into Nahwitti harbor at the northern tip of Vancouver Island. The *Juno* followed soon after.

The men of the *Atahualpa* reported that the attack had come without warning and without provocation. Several of them were terribly wounded, "some had Six or seven Stabs with large Daggers," Hurd wrote in his journal. Most were expected to make a good recovery, except for one Hawaiian crewman who "had the chords & arteries of his wrist cut off, three stabs on his body, & 3 on his head."

Gradually, the survivors were able to tell their story. The attack had taken place on the morning of June 12. It was a sunny summer day and the men of the ship were relaxed as they went about their shipboard duty. Sails were spread out on the deck to be mended. A number of local Indians milled about on the deck. At around ten, the local chief called out to Captain Porter from his canoe. He had, he said, several fine pelts. Porter had just come up from the cabin below and strolled to the side of the ship to look at the sea otter skins, spread open in the canoe below him. As he leaned over the railing, one of the Indians on board stabbed him in the back and threw him overboard.

According to Joel Richardson, one of the survivors, it was the signal for "a general Massacre." The first mate was shot in the chest but despite being mortally wounded, managed to make his way to the cabin and get a musket. He struggled back up the companionway to the deck, "shot the Chief, delivered the Musket to the Boatswain and died."

Richardson then provided Hurd with a list of the casualties as he had noted them in his own shipboard journal: Mr. Goodwin, the second mate, was "shot dead." The clerk was "stab'd stagered below & died immediately." Lyman Plummer, a young kinsman of the owners who had been sent to sea to learn the business (and was probably the supercargo), was "Dagger'd in six places" and lived for four hours. Before he died, he "desired the few alive to take the Ship to Kaigani, in search for some other Vessel."

Among the dead were Peter Spooner, the cooper; Samuel and Luther Lapham, two brothers from Boston; Isaac Sammers, a seaman, "all Kill'd." The cook, John Williams, "defended himself in the Galley untill he had expended all his hot water, was mortally wounded and died the next morning." Among the injured were seamen Ebenezer Baker and Henry Thompson, who were described as "dangerously wounded." Seaman Ebenezer Williams and tailor Ebenezer Clinton were "slightly wounded." The unfortunate Clinton had been on the *Atahualpa* for less than a month. Captain Porter had borrowed him from Captain Brown to make clothes to order for his Indian customers. He was set to return shortly to the *Vancouver* when the *Atahualpa* was attacked.

Some of the men were below deck during the attack and were able to get to the ship's arm chest. They fired up through the hatches, and then charged the Indians on deck with their jack knives and muskets. When the muskets were empty, they used them as clubs. The ship was retaken by the surviving crew, only four of whom were left uninjured at the end of the battle. With three of the wounded men, they "cleared the Decks of the dead bodies, loosed the Top Sails & waited for the Ship to swing the right way, cut the Cable, & were just able to clear the Village rock, afterwards made all Sail & beat out of Milbank Sound." They were not out of danger until they had cleared all of the various rocky obstacles that lay in their way.

On June 17, five days after the attack, they committed the bodies of their dead shipmates to the deep. Eventually they made their way to Tattiskey, where they could be almost certain to find a Boston ship. A number of the Kaigani Haida visited the ship over the next few days until the crew of the *Atahualpa* began to fear that the short number of hands on board made them an easy target for another attack. It was not until June 23, eleven days after the attack, that they saw a sail, "which proved to be the *Vancouver* (Capt Brown) the most welcome of any ship on the Coast, not only [did] the Ship belong to the same Owner, but having a Man of good understanding & a friend to the unfortunate for her Commander, made them all rejoice at the sight of Capt. Brown on their Decks."

The *Atahualpa* had lost her captain, two mates, clerk, and supercargo, leaving the boatswain as the highest ranking man on board. When he saw Captain Brown, the relieved teenager immediately turned the vessel over to him. Brown sent his chief mate, David Adams, to take command of the *Atahualpa;* Mr. Low, who had left Boston as first mate of the *Lydia,* now took up that post on the *Atahualpa.* The ships then set sail for Nahwitti.

Word of the attack moved quickly along the coast. By June 27, six ships were at Nahwitti, the three Lyman vessels: *Atahualpa, Vancouver,* and *Lydia;* the ships *Pearl* and *Mary* of Boston; and DeWolfe's *Juno.* (On a previous voyage more than two years earlier, the *Mary* and *Juno* had been seen by Jewitt approaching Nootka Sound in the week after the *Boston* was taken; they had unsuccessfully attempted a rescue.) Between the various New Englanders, a plan was devised to make up the lost crew of the *Atahualpa* with men from the other ships, and to establish a new hierarchy of command.

Isaac Hurd was happy to volunteer to move to the *Atahualpa* as supercargo. He was sick and tired of Samuel Hill and his shenanigans. It was agreed that the *Atahualpa*, with David Adams as captain, would proceed immediately to Canton. Her guns and cargo were consequently moved to the *Vancouver,* and the ship was hauled ashore and made ready for the long trans-Pacific passage.

Hurd wrote that Captains Ebbets of the *Pearl* and DeWolfe of the *Juno* "had their Carpenters & several hands assisting to get the ship ready—even the Capts. themselves while the Ship was on Shore (which was two days) attended themselves to be ready to give any assistance." Of the captains who responded, only Samuel Hill did not volunteer to help, choosing instead to "tarry on board the brig" with his Hawaiian girl.

On July 3, the *Atahualpa* was ready to go to sea. Brown and Hurd decided that the *Atahualpa's* sea otter pelts would bring a good price in Canton, but felt that the remaining goods on the *Vancouver* and *Lydia*, which had been brought from Boston to trade with the Indians, were not going to be profitable in the competitive market then current on the coast. They thought that the cargos of the two ships should be consolidated, and one of the vessels should accompany the *Atahualpa.* As the *Vancouver* was bigger and could easily take the *Lydia's* goods, while the smaller brig could not accommodate all of the consolidated cargo from the larger vessel, prudence dictated that the *Lydia* should now leave the coast. Captain DeWolfe of the *Juno* had already agreed to take the less valuable items, including the excess provisions (mostly rice, molasses, and bread). This arrangement, Brown and Hurd felt, would best serve the interest of the Lymans.

Having pretty much settled the business, Hurd went back to the *Lydia* and informed Captain Hill of their plans. Hill exploded in a rage of obscenities. He accused Hurd of trying to ruin him. As captain, his income was tied, in part, to the margin of profit made by the owners at the end of the voyage. Hurd offered to let Hill have his own commission to make up the loss, but Hill angrily declined. Hurd told Hill that the *Lydia's* trade goods must go onboard the *Vancouver* within the next few days. Hill refused. The two men, who had never liked or respected one another, screamed at each other in the cabin of the ship. Eventually, Hill had to give in. Hurd told him that if he did not give up the cargo he would report it to the owners, and he stormed back to the *Vancouver.*

The next day Hill was sullen. Hurd returned on board. As he expected that the *Lydia* would soon be leaving the coast, Hurd asked Hill to let the *Atahualpa* have one of the anchor cables, and whatever "provisions & hands he could spare." Hill assented. July fourth was the day that would liberate Isaac Hurd from Captain Samuel Hill forever. The men met on board the *Vancouver,* where Hill announced that he had decided not to give up any of his cargo after all. He would, he said, remain on the coast and continue the voyage as originally planned.

Brown and Hurd tried to reason with him, suggesting a number of alternatives to the plan that they had already agreed upon. Eventually Hill was persuaded to comply, and said that he would deliver the cargo whenever they wanted it. Hurd asked him to be ready the next morning. Hill said "the sooner the better."

Again Hurd offered Hill his commission, but Hill again refused. Hurd told him that the *Lydia* need not accompany the *Atahualpa* to Canton but could proceed immediately home to Boston if that was preferable to Hill. "I likewise offered him his choice whether to go to Boston round Cape Horn or by Canton & Europe, he chose to leave it to my discretion."

On the fifth, Hurd rowed over to the *Lydia* ready to supervise the transfer of the cargo to the *Vancouver.* Hill greeted him from the deck, charged him with having "deserted the Brig and Cargo" and refused either to deliver the cargo or let Hurd come aboard.

"I certainly shall!" Hurd declared, attempting to board.

"I forbid it!" Hill screamed.

They finally agreed that Hurd could come aboard only to take his personal clothing and that he must be accompanied by a witness at all times. He had already put his personal journal onboard the *Atahualpa;* it was his

evidence against Captain Hill. Hurd rowed back to the
Vancouver and described what had happened to Captain
Brown and the officers. The *Atahualpa* was lying nearby
and David Adams and Mr. Low, standing on the quarterdeck, heard the whole exchange.

When Hurd finally went on board the *Lydia* to get his
personal effects, Hill hovered over him with a club. At that
point Captain Brown threw up his hands and declared that
he would never again have anything to do with Hill. Hurd
obviously felt the same way, but had one more encounter,
when the *Lydia,* under sail, approached the departing
Atahualpa.

"Where's my cook?" Hill bellowed through his
speaking trumpet.

Captain Adams insisted that he was not on board
the *Atahualpa.*

"I'm coming aboard!" Hill demanded, lowering the
brig's boat as he said it. He declared his intention to search
the *Atahualpa.* David Adams was adamant that he would
not allow such a breach of protocol. As the *Atahualpa*
picked up the breeze and sailed beyond Hill's reach, the
runaway cook came up on deck and waved good-bye. Hurd
and Low, both earlier victims of Hill's wrath, both escapees
to the *Atahualpa,* had protected him.

"I fear that I shall never see that Brig again," Hurd
wrote. "Hill appears very strangely... the crew are all
resolutely bent against him." As he closed his own chapter
on his strange cruise with Captain Hill aboard the *Lydia,*
Hurd wrote, "I believe, had he not a poor innocent Sandwich
Island Girl on board, he would behave with more reason. I
hope he will do well with the Cargo, and return the Vessel
with a rich Cargo to her owner, & himself to his wife &
family if he has any."

Before the *Atahualpa* left the coast, Hurd went
aboard the *Vancouver* one last time to say goodbye to his
mentor and friend, Captain Thomas Brown. "When wishing
him a prosperous Voyage and a safe return to Boston & the
same compliment from him," he wrote, "I left one of my best
friends the World can produce. Capt. Brown, whilst I was
clerk to him, treated me like a Brother & has done the same
whenever we have met since I have left him." The contrast
between the two testimonials Hurd gave to the captains

with whom he had served on the Northwest Coast could not have been more pronounced.

As the *Atahualpa* beat out to sea, bound for Hawaii and Canton, the crew unfurled the main topsail and hoisted the yard into place. It was one of the sails that had been lying on the deck at the time of the massacre. Hurd looked up to see it catch the wind and saw that it was covered in blood. Hill must have seen it too.

***

As the *Atahualpa* sailed away with her blood-splashed sails, and the *Vancouver* headed off to the north toward the Queen Charlotte Islands, what must Samuel Hill have thought? His reputation and future sailed with them. In fact, he *was* married; he had left a pregnant wife back in Boston. For almost a year he and Isaac Hurd had shared close quarters in the aft cabin area of the *Lydia* and Hill had never mentioned his family. Hill had apparently thought little enough of his family anyway, as he romped across the Pacific with his Hawaiian lover.

Hill knew that Isaac Hurd would reach Boston before he did, and the report that his former supercargo would give, especially when witnessed by his former mate and the venerable Captain Brown, could pretty well be predicted at that moment. It would sink him. He would certainly never work for the Lymans again. What about the other firms? Would they hire a captain so tainted? He was still a young man—to be master of a ship had been his goal since he first went to sea as a teenager. What would he do if he couldn't be a captain? Though it was not uncommon for a captain to sign on to a subsequent voyage at a lower rank, this would be an especially awkward and difficult situation for Samuel Hill. It had taken him long enough to get a command, and it was the position best suited to his aberrant personality.

On the Northwest Coast he was the equal of the highest ranking individuals ashore. He was the chief, the king, the dictator of his little world on the ship. In Boston he was a sailor, and sailors were no better than bums unless they became merchants. The only way he would become a merchant was through connections with men like George and Theodore Lyman. As the *Atahualpa* sailed away, so did Sam Hill's future.

The action that could not only save his reputation, but enhance it, must have occurred to him in a flash, because he proceeded immediately from the *Atahualpa* fiasco for Nootka Sound. He would rescue the survivors of the *Boston.* If the massacre of one ship's crew precipitated his professional damnation, perhaps that of another could be his salvation.

Before he left Boston, Hill had heard a report that Thomas and Francis Amory, the owners of the *Boston,* were offering a reward for the rescue of the survivors at Nootka Sound. If the Lyman brothers didn't want him upon his return to Boston, perhaps he could insure that the Amory brothers would. And it was not only the reward that motivated him. He was in danger right now of being known only as a savage brute. Among other charges, he knew that Hurd had recorded in his log that he had threatened the life of seaman John Nicholson, and that his crew was in a mutinous state. To rescue men who had been abandoned by every other captain on the coast, however, was an operation that could salvage his reputation. It might even make him appear heroic.

Two months earlier he had received Jewitt's letter via Utiller, the chief at Classet. Now, on July 16, 1805, the *Lydia* sailed into Nootka Sound. Onshore, the Yuquot people saw the ship come in with mixed feelings. It was a long time since they had had direct access to American goods. Maquinna paced. He knew that *they* knew (whoever *they* were) that he had taken the *Boston* and that there were survivors. The word had been all over the coast for more than two years. He went to Jewitt. "Write me a letter," he instructed, "to bring out to that ship. Tell them I have treated you well."

Within a few hours, Maquinna was in irons on the *Lydia,* John Jewitt was negotiating the Chief's release from Captain Hill in the cabin of the brig, and John Thompson was drunk in the forecastle. The men from the *Boston* had been "rescued." Samuel Hill was their unlikely hero and their new home was the powder keg known as the brig *Lydia.*

Jewitt and Thompson now entered into their second captivity. Within days they had even settled into their accustomed roles. Jewitt was the accommodating chap who never offended and tried to get along with everyone, even in the worst of situations, while the strong-willed Thompson was constantly challenging the authority imposed upon him by a tyrannical master.

In the wake of all the excitement of the past two weeks, there were some changes on the brig. Hurd was gone and Captain Hill could now serve as his own supercargo. He still needed a man to keep the books for him, however. William Walker, who had come aboard in the recent swap of hands among the several Boston ships, was appointed clerk.

Jewitt gave one of the blank ledger books he had salvaged from the *Boston* to Walker to use as his personal journal. The title page was inscribed "John Thompson. His Book, 1803" and there were several columns of sums labeled "Addision" and "Subtraction." There had obviously been a time when Thompson had intended to learn rudimentary arithmetic, but it had long been abandoned. In the back someone had written Thompson's name for him in a beautiful script and he had copied it out several times in his own uncertain hand. The ledger also had some miscellaneous accounts kept by Thomas Amory back in Boston, but most of the book was blank, and so Walker had almost the whole of it to use as his own.

Walker's journal starts out promising enough. He tried to keep a businesslike tone in describing events, but the *Lydia* was not like other vessels, as he quickly learned. They sailed from Nootka Sound back to the Queen Charlotte Islands, coming to anchor in the harbor of Skedans, where they "had a little falling out" with the natives and had to make a run for it up to the safety of Kaigani and Tattiskey.

The *Lydia* made her approach to Kaigani on the night of August 7. The moon was bright, the weather was clear, and there was a slight breeze. The second mate stood at the bow watching for obstacles. When he called back to the captain that the land was on their weather bow and the breakers were close at hand, Hill obstinately refused to acknowledge him. With increasing urgency the mate called back to the captain from the bow of the brig. All eyes were on Hill who made no motion to respond. The vessel struck hard, tearing the rudder off its mounting. "By the blessing of God," wrote Walker, "she got off again." The *Lydia* tossed about for a few days, unable to steer, and finally came to anchor near Skidegate.

Walker was perplexed by Hill's behavior. "He came very near losing us all several times," he wrote. If one of the mates made a report to him with a suggestion of altering course or sail, Hill ignored him. The sails were blown out in a high wind, the ship struck several times on sandbars and even once on a rocky ledge. Finally, at Skidegate, the *Lydia* met up with another vessel. It was the British ship *Myrtle,* and Hill immediately went on board to complain about his crew. Another swap of hands was arranged. The *Lydia's* third mate was fired and sent to the other vessel, Walker was demoted from the position he had held for only a few short weeks, and three new men came on board. The unfortunate Walker was doomed in the job. He did not, like Isaac Hurd, have the backing of the owners behind him; he had no mentoring friends among the other captains. Within a month he moved into the forecastle.

At the village of Kasaan, Hill ordered the majority of the men left from his original crew to go on shore, but they believed he meant to abandon them there and refused to go. Trade continued sporadically, but the crew was angry and the captain uncommunicative, except in sudden bursts of rage. The Indians who came alongside found themselves the hapless victims of the violence bubbling up inside the ship. There was very little discipline, despite Hill's threats of violence. A number of Indian women were living in the forecastle with members of the crew.

Hill had a regular pattern of cruising, and he had now reached the northern end of it. By late November he made his way back to the Columbia River and came to anchor at the same place where he had started his assault on the coast seven months earlier. It was his plan to spend some time repairing the damage that the ship had suffered in the hard weather and haphazard navigation of the northern cruise.

When the Indians paddled out to meet the ship, they brought interesting news. Another party of Americans had just been there and they had not come by sea. It was the Lewis and Clark expedition.

As proof of their encounter with the overland Americans, the Chinook showed medals bearing a portrait of Thomas Jefferson, which they had received from the explorers. It had been the President's intention to have the expeditionary party return by sea, or at least to send their journals home on one of the American vessels that frequented the Columbia River. The *Vancouver,* under Hill's nemesis Captain Brown, had actually been instructed to proceed there to rendezvous with the explorers. Now Hill knew that Brown had failed in his mission and he must have welcomed the news.

According to the Indians, Lewis and Clark had been at this very spot some two weeks before. They didn't bother to say that they were still nearby, making a winter camp not ten miles away. Hill didn't ask any questions. It was enough for him that Brown had failed.

The Indians had goods to offer and a great willingness to trade. It was not to their advantage to have the Lewis and Clark party leave on the *Lydia* rather than stay for the winter. But the explorers would certainly have been relieved to make a connection with an American ship. They were facing the prospect of a winter on the damp and chilly coast and they knew exactly what stood between them and the end of their journey: a rugged continent, the Rocky Mountains, the Great Plains. They were short on supplies. As much as it would have made the expedition easier if they had been able to return by sea, given the conditions on the *Lydia* it was probably just as well they missed the ride.

***

Lewis and Clark found around them ample evidence that they had been preceded there by their seafaring countrymen. The Chinook Indians not only had plenty of articles of New England and European origin, but wore "sailor jackets, overalls, shirts and hats independent of their usual dress" and had a "considerable quantity of sailor's cloaths, as hats coats, trousers and shirts."

On several occasions near the end of their stay at their winter fort, Lewis and Clark asked the Indians what traders were expected and when. On November 6, 1805, William Clark wrote in his journal that "we over took two Canoes of Indians going down to trade one of the Indians Spoke a few words of english and Said that the principal man who traded with them was Mr. Haley, and that he had a woman in his Canoe who Mr. Haley was fond of & c. he Showed us a Bow of Iron and Several other things which he Said Mr. Haley gave him."

Though the name "Hill" became altered to "Haley" as it went from Sam Hill's lips to Chinook ears, and subsequently back from them to be written down by William Clark, there can be no doubt that the man described was Samuel Hill. The "woman in his canoe" was the Hawaiian girl who had traveled extensively around the Columbia River in one of the *Lydia's* small boats seven months earlier.

The following January the explorers made a "List of the names of Sundery persons, who visit this part of the coast for the purpose of trade." "Mr. Haley," they noted, "Visits them in a Ship & they expect him back to trade with them in 3 moons to trade— he is the favourite of the Indians (from the number of Presents he gives) and has the trade principally with all the tribes." In his honor, Lewis and Clark named a bay near the mouth of the Columbia River "Haley's Bay." (It had been named Baker's Bay in 1792 by the cartographers of the Vancouver expedition, after James Baker, a British captain who was in the bay when they arrived. As it appeared by that name on Vancouver's chart of the river, it was never referred to as Hill's or Haley's Bay except by members of the Lewis and Clark expedition themselves.)

Before they turned east again, the expedition members collected a number of artifacts from the Chinook Indians, including two distinctive whaler's hats from Nootka Sound, which must have been brought to the Columbia on the *Lydia.* No other vessel had been at both locations since the capture of the *Boston* almost three years earlier, and these hats, used only by persons of rank, were likely obtained from Maquinna by either John Jewitt or Samuel Hill.

Figures 2 – 5:

During their sojourn in the Columbia River, Lewis and Clark collected a number of ethnographic artifacts, including several woven basketry hats that had been manufactured on the northern coast and traded to the Chinook by American mariners. Upon their return to St. Louis in 1806, one of the hats was sent to Thomas Jefferson in Washington, D.C. and by 1810 a number of them were in the collection of the Peale Museum in Philadelphia. Today, the surviving collections can be found at the Peabody Museum of Archaeology and Ethnology at Harvard University. Among them are two similar hats from Nootka Sound. The distinctive knob-topped shape was drawn into the journals of both explorers, and each described the whaling scene woven into the body of the hats. Tomas de Suria, a Spanish artist who visited Nootka Sound in 1791, drew a sketch of a young Maquinna wearing a similar hat, more than a dozen years before John Jewitt and Samuel Hill met him.

These hats were almost certainly conveyed into the hands of the Chinook by Samuel Hill. His was the first vessel to travel from Nootka Sound to the Columbia River since the attack on the *Boston* had stopped all trade with Maquinna and his people in 1802, and no other ship arrived there before the departure of the exploring expedition.

Figures 3 and 4 are details from larger images.

Figure 2, Hat collected by Lewis and Clark

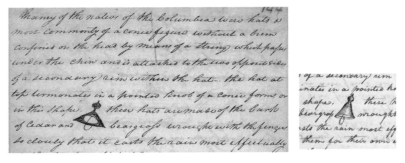

Left, **Figure 3,** Entry in William Clark's journal showing hat (detail).

*Right***, Figure 4,** Entry in Meriwether Lewis's journal showing hat (detail).

Figure 5, Portrait of Maquinna by Tomas de Suria, 1791

***

When the *Lydia* left the Columbia River, it retraced the route of the previous spring, heading north again toward the Queen Charlotte Islands. This time, however, Hill did not avoid Nootka Sound. They made a brief stop at the Yuquot village to trade and to let John Jewitt meet with his former captor. Between Jewitt and Maquinna there was an affectionate reunion, while Thompson remained steadfastly on the ship.

As the year came to a close, the weather was wet and cold, conditions felt more keenly on a wooden ship than on shore. The men living in the forecastle had no source of heat and no means of drying out damp clothes. With fog and adverse winds preventing them from cruising, they anchored again near the Alaskan village of Kasaan. Tempers rose steadily. On December 14, 1805, the cook went aft to the captain to receive the crew's daily allowance of rum and was informed that rum would no longer be served to the men. The men rushed aft when they heard the news and stood near the companionway into the cabin.

William Walker tried to negotiate a peaceful settlement of the explosive situation. He went to Hill and told him it was "the request of the ships company" that he come on deck and speak to them. Hill refused. The men's allowance of rum, he said, was stopped because of the Indian women living in the forecastle. At that point the men refused all further work.

The mate, James Bennett tried to convince them to resume their duty. Even the captain's steward, John Paul, was sent forward to attempt to persuade them. Eventually Hill went down into the forecastle in a rage. He carried a club.

"I will see if you will come up or not," he shouted. "I am ready for you." He turned to seaman Joseph Crane. "Go on deck you damned rascal!"

As Crane cowered before him, begging him not to strike, and putting his arms up to protect himself, Hill began to beat the man with his club.

John Thompson, the fearless tar who had seen so much hardship in his forty years, had now had enough. He put himself between the captain and his victim. His strong physical presence brought an end to the beating.

"I will blow your brains out," Hill threatened Thompson as he backed away. He turned to his mate, James Bennett. "Go on deck," he told him. "Fire a gun and hoist the flag to half mast." It was the signal to nearby ships that there was a mutiny on board.

He turned back suddenly to Thompson and struck him a blow with his fist. "You are the cause of all this disturbance," he roared. He asked the crew if he had ever shortchanged them on essential provisions. Had he ever stopped their allowance of beef, pork, or bread? They acknowledged that they had always had plenty to eat.

"Will you return to work?" he asked them. Not without their rum allowance they answered.

He turned to Thompson again. "You would like to see another ship taken! You damned old scoundrel! You mutinous villain!"

Thompson had his temper well under control. "I should be very sorry to see any such thing," he said softly. "I have seen too much trouble already."

Hill was still in a rage. "I will seize you up in the Rigging and flog you!" he shouted, again calling him a mutinous villain.

"You do not know what a mutiny is if you call this a mutiny," Thompson replied.

"It is no matter whether it is a mutiny or no," Hill sneered, "as long as I think so, that is enough." He continued to rant for several minutes, at one point lashing out with his fist and striking a seaman named Richard King. Hill informed Thompson that his wages were stopped and he was banished from the quarterdeck. If he saw him there he would certainly blow his brains out.

"Let me go ashore," Thompson requested.

"If Captain Ebbets will take you then you can go," Hill answered.

"I don't suppose he will take me," Thompson said. "You will give me such an infamous character."

"I shall give you the character you deserve," Hill said, "that is an old scoundrel."

"I am not an old scoundrel. I have that to show in my past that I am a man and always in a man's station."

"You ought to be hung," Hill concluded, "I will get you hung or something as bad." He cursed at Thompson and the other men for several minutes as he returned to his cabin.

The entire exchange was dutifully recorded by Walker. Since he no longer had any official position on the brig and was not required to keep the ship's business, he dedicated his journal to an obsessive documentation of the captain's behavior, including regularly noting the abusive language he directed at the crew.

It was a dangerous situation, and not just from Hill's violence. With none of the crew on deck, the *Lydia* was in danger of dragging her anchor toward the rocky shore. There was also a growing feeling among the crew that they were now constantly in danger of an Indian attack. They had seen firsthand the deck of the *Atahualpa* soaked in the blood of men they had known, full of life, just a short time before. And Jewitt and Thompson must have given them a full report of the attack on the *Boston* and their two years in captivity.

Jewitt was the first to break ranks and go to stand his watch on deck. The captain saw him and ordered him to go away.

"It's my watch, sir," Jewitt answered.

"Leave the deck," Hill commanded, "when I want you I will call you."

After threats to stop their wages, cease all rations, and eventually a demand that they either go ashore or return to duty, all of the crew except for Thompson went back to work. Thompson launched the long boat and began to go ashore.

Though he had been in an uncontrollable rage moments before, Hill had a sudden change of heart. His plan to regain his reputation by rescuing the *Boston* survivors would hardly work if he didn't return home with both of them alive and well. "I don't turn you on shore," he called out to Thompson. "You may return again if you like."

Thompson came back.

Hill then gave the man a lecture in front of the whole crew. "You were the means of the Ship *Boston* being taken," he said. "Captain Salter thrashed you on the passage from England to the Pacific."

It was a blatant falsehood and Thompson very emphatically said so. Salter had been a good master. Through all of this exchange, Jewitt remained silent. Though he had several times saved Thompson from Maquinna's rage, he never spoke in the man's defense aboard the *Lydia*. The older man never accepted captivity, either in the Yuquot village or under Captain Hill, and his behavior embarrassed Jewitt. In his later publications, Jewitt is entirely silent about Hill's abuse of Thompson after their rescue. Hill was, in Jewitt's eyes, always more important as his rescuer than he was to blame as Thompson's abuser.

The morning after Thompson's confrontation with the captain, the *Pearl* came in to anchor beside them in Kasaan harbor. Captain Hill sent his boat over and requested that the *Pearl's* tailor come over to the *Lydia*. "To make some cloaths for the Skipper & his whore," reported Walker. Hill's behavior was becoming ever more erratic and he began to display symptoms of some physical ailment as well. Over the next several weeks, Walker reported on a number of occasions that the captain "had a fit & was verry ill." His navigational judgment was definitely impaired. "Every time lately he has come out of a harbour," Walker wrote, "we have been... in the most imminent danger." Asked if there was a problem he answered, "I cant help it my boys."

There was trade on and off through January 1806, though Hill was often unfit to conduct it, hampered either by bad temper or bad health. The abuse that he had heaped so soundly on his officers and crew now began to extend regularly beyond the bulwarks of he ship to encompass the Indians on shore. In the middle of January, Walker reported that "the Skipper treats the Natives so bad they hate to come on board he tells them he dont care whether they trade with him or not he says he dont want their skins." The next day the Indians came again with pelts to trade, but Hill told them to "Go to Hell!"

Toward the end of the month, the *Vancouver* approached as the *Lydia* lay at Skidegate in the Queen Charlotte Islands. First mate James Bennett invited

Captain Brown aboard the brig to see Captain Hill, who was apparently too sick to leave his cabin. Hill probably took this opportunity to let Captain Brown know that he had missed the hoped-for rendezvous with Lewis and Clark, and that the expedition had turned east again. If so, he kept Brown from proceeding to the Columbia River, where the explorers were still camped, and where they would remain for another two months. There was still time for Brown to have proceeded south to meet them, and Samuel Hill may well be the reason the attempt was never made.

For over a week Hill was unable to leave his bed. After the *Vancouver* departed, he threatened to flog the steward who served him his meals in his cabin, but wasn't strong enough to carry it out. At week's end he crawled on deck, but was unable to stand. When he finally did return to the quarterdeck, he was testy and impatient. If Walker is to be believed, he hardly spoke except to curse.

There was trade to be had, but Hill was often too obstreperous to make the deal, refusing to give in one village the same price he had given in the last, or on a previous visit. Every small incident on shipboard was blown out of proportion by the captain. Several men on board, evidently including the mate, began to doubt Hill's ability to complete the voyage. On February 11, he "crawled on deck" only to tell the mate to go to hell.

"You think I am going to die," Hill said to Bennett, "but I am not! God damn you." Walker reflected with some irony that though Hill had "one foot in the Grave & the other not half way out," he couldn't speak to a person without damning him!

A few days later Walker complained again about the effect Hill's relationship with the Hawaiian girl had on the running of the ship.

He dont allow his officers Nothing but spruce tea to drink Night & Morning but he has Coffee for himself & his girl dont like Coffee so she has Green tea made for her at dinner. He always culls all the best of the victuals for her before any one is allowed to help themselves. His lady Belongs to the Sandwitch Islands. When he gets Jealous of any of his officers haveing anything to do with her [he] turns to flogging her to make her tell him if they have, then he will begin with him & threaten to blow his brains out. Several Times I have heard him threaten his Chief officers life"

In March 1806, the *Lydia* encountered the *Hamilton,* under the command of Lemuel Porter. This vessel had recently arrived on the first of four voyages to the Northwest Coast. Captain Porter's brother Oliver had been master of the *Atahualpa,* and was murdered in the incident at Milbanke Sound. Though Porter certainly learned of his brother's death on his Hawaiian stopover, and probably obtained additional details from the Indian grapevine when he arrived on the coast, Hill was the first person he met with who had been on the ship in the aftermath and had spoken with the survivors. Consequently, Hill was in a position to give Lemuel Porter real information about what had happened to his brother, and to provide some support as Porter worked through the grief and anger that followed his brother's violent death. But Hill had neither a compassionate ear nor a shoulder to cry on.

When he met Porter for the first time, Hill launched immediately into his litany of complaints. He had, he said, "the damdest set of Rascals for men that ever a man had god damn them."

For chief mate James Bennett it was the final straw. He had been repeatedly abused in front of the crew, his life threatened, his immortal soul damned to hell. Now he was the subject of the captain's malicious gossip. He resigned or was sacked and left the ship to take a position on one of the other Boston vessels. David Nye from the *Pearl* came on board at Tattiskey on March 22 to take his place as first mate.

It was three years to the day since the *Boston* had been taken at Nootka Sound. Though no one on the *Lydia* would even have imagined it, far to the south, the members of the Lewis and Clark expedition were finally giving up all hope for a rendezvous with an American ship. The next day they would break camp, turn east, and begin the long trek home.

***

On the anniversary of the massacre of the crew of the *Boston,* Samuel Hill began a series of actions that seemed to invite a similar tragic event. He abused the native people at every port he visited. Before leaving Kaigani, Hill cheated the Indians by filling the bottom of gun powder kegs with rope fragments, an action which the Haida immediately detected and angrily resented. Later he would find that he could mix molasses with sea water, and that practice was also detected by the Indians.

As they cruised south, Hill began blatantly to steal furs. In May at Masset he took six hostages, forcing the people of the village to pay a ransom in pelts. As they sailed from the harbor, shots were fired toward the ship, but fell short. Hill tacked and fired a broadside into the village. Upon returning to its course the ship went aground and lay for several hours in a very precarious position until the flood tide came in and floated it again. His men were clearly very afraid that their captain was ripe to reap the seeds of violence and abuse he had just sewn.

Enroute to the next village a canoe approached with furs to trade. Hill greeted them with his gun and demanded the furs. He then gave them five buckets of watered down molasses as payment.

At Skedans he invited two chiefs into his cabin to share a meal and then told them they were his prisoners. A hundred skins would buy their release, he told them, a huge number for any village. Individual pelts dribbled in over the next few days, but it was clear that the Haida at Skedans simply didn't have that many furs. They went to other villages in desperation. Eventually they told Hill that they could not get a hundred skins. They offered their boats in exchange; he told them they should take the boats to their neighbors at Cumshewa and trade them there for skins and bring them back to him.

Hill attempted to justify his actions by telling the Haida that they were being punished for having made an attack on an American ship. The attack he spoke of had occurred more than a dozen years earlier, and he was not the first captain to use it as a justification for making demands on Haida people.

Hill's behavior was a recipe for disaster, if not for himself and the *Lydia's* crew, then for the captain and crew of the next vessel that followed them, unsuspecting, into one of the communities he had plundered. One of the negotiators at Skedans told Hill that because of him, they would attempt to "to kill the first Ships Company" that followed them into the village. Hill's response was to make him a prisoner "for his Sauce" and demand additional skins for his ransom. He could not, or would not, see that his actions were of exactly the sort that had led to the deaths of Captains Salter and Porter and their crews. The Indians knew better than any one on board what other ships were in the region, and Walker heard one grumbled threat to attack the *Hamilton* in retaliation for Hill's abuse.

Walker thought that Hill was "acting very unwisely in staying to plunder the Coast. [We] might have been of[f] the Coast the first of April if he had been a mind to; he had 22 Hundred Skins on board at the time but he seems as if he wants to lose the Brigg & all our lives by his Carrying on."

The *Hamilton,* meanwhile, was sailing nearby, unaware of the behavior of Samuel Hill and others. At Tattiskey a shore party was attacked, one of the men "badly wounded with arrows." The crew, in response, "flew in a great rage to the arms chest, and with muskets opened a brisk fire on the numerous innocent creatures about the ship, and killed a great many."

All of the men began to wish for a departure from the coast. If Walker's count was correct, then the Lydia had some 2200 pelts in the hold by April 1806. On such a small vessel, this could certainly constitute a full cargo, but Hill seemed unwilling to leave the coast. "He dont seem to Care whether he loses the Brig & all hands or not," wrote a frustrated Walker, "he has got his compliment of Skins."

Around this time Walker began to notice that Hill was instructing his clerk to record fewer pelts in his ledger than were actually acquired in trade. Though Walker said he could not understand why, it seems clear that Hill was positioning himself to conduct some trade on his own behalf when the *Lydia* reached Canton. He may, at last, have begun to contemplate a departure from the coast. He would make one more run up to the northern reaches of his cruising ground in June, and then head south to the Columbia River in July to prepare for the Pacific Ocean crossing.

The northern leg of the trip was filled with his usual woes. They struck a rock at Cocklanes, were threatened by the Indians at Kasaan. Eventually it became difficult to get any of the Indians to come aboard the ship in the region of the Queen Charlotte Islands. Walker lamented that his captain had done more damage to the trade than any captain in the business, and had endangered the lives of all visiting Americans in the process. There was, he said, a time when he could "goe on shore amongst any of the Tribes of the Northwest & not be afraid but Now it is dangerous to goe in to a harbour with the Vessel when she lays within Musket shot of them."

They turned south again and Hill's health finally began to improve. On June 5, Walker reported with disgust that "Skipper Hill & his whore Slept together for the first time this two months" and everyone on the ship knew it. Thereafter, Hill's sex life ran the ship.

On one occasion, Mr. Hewes, the mate in charge of the watch, went down to the cabin to inform Captain Hill that a gale was on the horizon. Hill was in bed with the Hawaiian girl and shouted to Hewes that he thought he must be mis-taken, the weather would hold. As the storm came down on them, Walker wrote caustically that the captain thought he knew "better when he is laying embracing his Indian how the weather is than his officer does that is on deck."

On the first anniversary of the rescue of Jewitt and Thompson, Hill gave the Hawaiian girl the pocket watch that had belonged to Captain Salter of the *Boston*. This was an item that Jewitt had gone to some pains to recover during the frenzied pillaging of the ship that took place after the attack. Hill took it apart to show it to its new owner and could not reassemble it.

Now that he was sleeping with her again, Hill became obsessively jealous of how other men on the ship behaved toward his Hawaiian partner, and she toward them. He began to beat her when he became suspicious that she might have conversed with any of the other men on board. Little more than his slave, this unfortunate woman was once again regularly dragged ashore when the *Lydia* reached the Columbia River again in July 1806.

During one of the captain's absences from the ship, a Chinook canoe approached and the Indians delivered a letter from Captain William Clark of the exploring expedition. The Chinook had been holding it, at Clark's request, for the next ship into the river. It announced Lewis and Clark's departure in March and commended the local people who had treated them very hospitably.

Hill paid little attention to this letter at the time. He was involved in personal problems of his own. He discarded his Hawaiian companion to the mercies of the crew and took up with a Chinook Indian woman, who lived with him in the aft cabin for the duration of his time in the Columbia River. He set John Jewitt to work making brass rings and bracelets for her. By the end of the month, she had replaced her Hawaiian predecessor on Hill's jaunts ashore. On July 25, Walker reported that Hill and "his Chenook Lady has returned from her Journey he went on Shore & tarried till half past Eleven. After a night with her he has done with his Atooi lady entirely." Over the course of the next few weeks, as the men went about preparing the ship and its cargo for the long stretch across the Pacific, Hill's attention was all on his new girlfriend. He made her presents from the cargo, including cloth, beads, candles, brass and copper wire, and various trinkets.

Through the first week of August 1806, Hill and his new partner were inseparable. She was constantly on the ship, staying overnight, sometimes with her parents. While the carpenter was ashore preparing new spars, and Thompson was hard at work making sails and hatch covers, Jewitt was mostly employed in making jewelry for her, although the ship was scheduled to leave imminently and she was not going to be on it.

Finally, on August 10, the *Lydia* weighed anchor for the last time on the Northwest Coast. Years later, John Jewitt would write about that day when, "having completed our trade, we sailed for China, to the great joy of all our crew, and particularly so to me." It is unlikely that he was the most relieved. William Walker wrote simply "Thank god for getting Safe off the Coast."

The *Lydia* proceeded to Hawaii, arriving at Oahu on the 6th of September. Three weeks had apparently been too long for Samuel Hill to spend alone in the cabin. The

Hawaiian girl was back in his clutches in those last few weeks before he finally let her off the ship.

The brig stayed three weeks at the Islands, during which time Hill purchased fresh provisions, sold the guns from the *Boston* to a British captain and the Hawaiian King, had sex with Native girls, and discharged the four Hawaiian men who had come aboard a year and a half earlier. Walker made a record of what one of them was paid for his service of eighteen months: two muskets and powder, a pair of shoes and stockings, needles and thread, a jack knife and tobacco.

No mention was made of the girl who, having been taken on board a year and half earlier, was summarily dumped ashore at home.

***

As the *Lydia* began the passage from Hawaii to Canton, Captain Hill must have taken stock of the disastrous wake he left behind him on the coast. He had viciously abused his crew. He had cheated and threatened the Indians and, in the process, endangered the lives of other ships and crews. He had proved a poor navigator in the complex inland waters of the coast, having run aground on numerous occasions. He had embezzled from the *Lydia's* owners. He had had sexual relationships with at least two Native women that had obviously and negatively impacted the business of the voyage.

What evidence was there against him? Certainly Isaac Hurd, Thomas Brown, James Bennett, and Mr. Low had all observed him at his worst, and John Ebbets, the captain of the *Pearl,* must have heard plenty of complaints against him from Hurd, Bennett, and Low. These were all very credible witnesses, as was David Adams, now the captain of the *Atahualpa.*

His abuse of sailors and Indians could be explained to those who hadn't seen the viciousness of it as a necessary part of the job—certainly he had plenty of successful predecessors to point to. Common sailors like William Walker and John Thompson were not much of a threat to Hill. Their testimony could always be dismissed as whining. Besides, what some might have seen as a second "captivity" for Jewitt and Thompson was the job they had agreed to do. They were sailors, and the consequent loss of rights and privileges, the subjugation by brute force and threats of violence, the inability to make personal decisions that altered one's schedule or routine, all were considered within the realm of their profession. "Just sailors," like "just Indians," didn't get much sympathy or interest from Bostonians in 1806.

Hill probably had little fear that his embezzlement would get back to the owners, and the *Lydia* wasn't the only ship to run aground in those treacherous uncharted waters. The vessel was sound enough to make the run to Canton and home, so he might be able to persuade some new employer that those experiences were even valuable.

It was extremely unlikely that he would be hired again by the Lymans, but he did have three things going for him: a valuable cargo of pelts in his hold, a letter from Lewis and Clark in the strongbox in his cabin, and a story to tell about how he had rescued the slaves of Maquinna. It almost doesn't matter that Hill didn't actually meet up with Lewis and Clark. At least Brown hadn't either, and Hill had the letter! As he headed to Canton, he began to lay the foundation for the plan that would let him emerge as the hero rather than the villain of this voyage.

He knew that the *Atahualpa,* with Isaac Hurd aboard, was probably already back in Boston. The *Pearl* had arrived at the Hawaiian Islands during the *Lydia's* recent sojourn there, so there was a chance that James Bennett would also precede him home. Thomas Brown was still on the coast when he left, so Hill would at least get back to tell his story before the return of the *Vancouver.*

Hill made two strategic decisions. He would send the Lewis and Clark letter back to the United States by the first convenient vessel he could identify when he got to Canton, and he would write an article for the Boston newspaper about how he had rescued Jewitt and Thompson, to be published immediately upon his arrival home.

On November 1, the *Lydia* arrived at Canton and Captain Hill went ashore. It took him a week to find the perfect vessel for the Lewis and Clark letter. It was the *Rousseau* of Philadelphia. The fact that it had no connection to Boston was clearly an advantage. Hill was unknown in Philadelphia, and his reputation would consequently be built entirely on the fact that he had received and delivered the important letter. It also meant that the letter could be conveniently in the hands of the President well before the explorers were able to return. Thomas Brown would be entirely out of the picture. All that remained for Hill was to describe the rescue of the *Boston* survivors in a way that put himself in the best possible light and to get the story published quickly. The *Lydia* arrived home on May 12, 1807. Hill's article appeared in the *Independent Chronicle* on the 14th and in the *Columbian Centinel* a week later.

The article is a masterpiece of storytelling. After describing the receipt of Jewitt's letter, Hill wrote that while his business had to come first, his humanity eventually got the better of him, despite the fact that none of the other captain on the coast was willing to take such a step.

> As my business was of a commercial nature, I could not, consistent with my duty, pursue any measures whereby the success of my voyage might be endangered; yet common humanity demanded that an attempt should be made to relieve these unfortunate men. The contents of the above mentioned letter was made known to several commanders on the coast; but the idea of an attempt to recover the men, was generally deemed rash and imprudent. Whether from want of judgment or that my humanity got the better of discretion, I do not pretend to say; but it appeared to me, it could not be thought rash or imprudent to go to *Nootka,* and take a view of the harbour, and discover whether the natives were disposed to be friendly or not.

Hill then gave a brief description of sailing into Nootka Sound and stated: "In the course of twenty four hours after my arrival, I recovered the two above mentioned captives, and the guns, anchors a few muskets and some other articles of less consideration; these were all they had left in their possession, belonging to the BOSTON."

The natives were, of course, "very unwilling to deliver up the two men," he explained.

But they were given to understand that if they did not immediately bring the men on board, alive and unhurt, I would most assuredly punish their chiefs and destroy the village. This had the desired effect; and I was happy in recovering the men together with the guns and ammunition, without entering into a quarrel, which would have occasioned the loss of the lives of many young Indians who were entirely innocent.

Hill made it all seem remarkably simple. He gave no credit to Jewitt for having planned out the details of the escape. When Jewitt wrote about the same situation several years later, the complexities of the situation were born out: how he dealt with the villagers upon getting word that Maquinna was a hostage on the *Lydia;* how he sent Thompson aboard the ship first, while he stayed ashore, making the arrangements to get the *Boston's* guns, papers, and other surviving effects; and how when he finally got on board the *Lydia,* he had to convince Captain Hill not to kill Maquinna. In a comparison of the stories told by Hill and Jewitt, one has to give the benefit of the doubt to Jewitt. He knew the language; he knew Maquinna; he knew what gear of the *Boston* survived in the Yuquot village. Jewitt, not Hill, orchestrated the escape.

The rest of Hill's article is a description of how the *Boston* came to be captured, and how the *Juno* and *Mary,* having an opportunity to rescue Jewitt and Thompson within days of the attack, failed miserably in the attempt. As his knowledge of the events of the capture could only have come from Jewitt, it is not surprising that his account is very similar in most respects to what Jewitt himself would write later. In those places where the two accounts differ, it is in Hill's denigration of Captain John Salter. Hill made the captain of the *Boston* more violent and more culpable for the attack. According to Hill, Salter struck Maquinna on the head with the butt of a rifle, an incident that never occurred in Jewitt's telling.

When it came to describing the actual attack, Hill says that Captain Salter was seized by Maquinna and thrown overboard where "the old women in the canoes along side, killed him with their paddles, and he expired, crying out 'WHACOSH, MAQUINNAH,' while MAQUINNAH, looking over the ship's side laughed at the farce of the old women beating SALTER'S brains out with their paddles!"

This is completely inconsistent with Jewitt's later account. Salter was thrown overboard and died in the water, but Jewitt didn't actually see what happened. Thompson was in hiding in the hold, and there were no other witnesses except the Indians themselves.

Captains Gibbs and Bowles of the ships *Juno* and *Mary* are also roundly criticized by Hill in the article. Learning of the attack almost immediately after it occurred, they pro-ceeded to Nootka Sound "for the express purpose of taking the ship *Boston* from the Indians, by force," Hill wrote.

> Let us see how they conducted this business:—Both ships stretched up close to the entrance of *Friendly Cove,* where they each let go an anchor in very deep water, but neither ship brought up by her anchor; in much haste and confusion they fired three broad sides and one of the ships swinging on the rocks, without the Point they both cut their cables and stood out to sea again: Thus ended the expedition. It appears by the best accounts that the guns were fired from that side of each ship which was next the village; but whether the guns were directed towards the village, or to the tops of some trees standing on a hill behind the village, is not certainly known as some double headed shot have been found on the aforementioned hill since that memorable expedition. It is very certain that none of their shot struck near the village; yet these ships were in smooth water, and about 230 yards from the village of *Nootka.*

Hill's snide tone implies that he was the only competent captain on the coast, Salter and the captains of the *Juno* and *Mary* falling far short by comparison. He clearly was diminishing the reputations of his brother captains in order to enhance his own. Salter had been stupid and brutal. Hill turned his death at the hands of screeching old women into a humiliating farce. He described Gibbs and Bowles as fools. They handled their ships and shot their guns badly. If only, he implied, they had been more competent, Jewitt and Thompson would have been rescued years earlier. What Hill had accomplished with such straightforward, commanding ease, they had blundered, despite the fact that they acted in concert and had two well-armed ships at their disposal.

To adopt such a tone back in Boston, where there were people who knew him, was the height of audacity. But Hill's ploy worked. Jewitt's version of events would not be published for another eight years and it didn't include an account of life aboard the *Lydia*.

Hill had a chance to revisit the story many years later. A dozen years after the conclusion of the *Lydia* voyage, he had an evangelical conversion experience and wrote an account of what his life had been up to that point. Though he laments "an almost infinite number of Crimes & Offences against the established Laws of the Almighty," his memory of what happened aboard the *Lydia* is remarkably free of guilt. He was the victim of the machinations of Hurd and every other captain, the only honorable man in a world of schemers.

He wrote that upon first receiving Jewitt's letter, he "proposed to proceed Immediately to Nootka & attempt their Rescue, but Mr. Hurd strongly opposed me in this determination, & represented the undertaking as impracticable & as the extreme of Rashness & folly."

This opinion of Mr Hurd's produced some effect on the minds of the Officers & Seamen, & from Various Considerations but principally from a desire to preserve a spirit of harmony I relinquished the attempt for the present though much against my inclination. — When we arrived on the Northern part of the Coast I met with five other American Ships to all of whom I made proposals to go in Company & attempt the Rescue of these unfortunate men, but they all from Motives of Interest or Fear absolutely refused & represented the attempt as rash & imprudent.

On the 17th July 1805 I entered Nootka Sound alone & on the 18th Succeeded in Rescuing the two Captives & sailed again from thence on the same day. ... I also Succeeded in recovering all the Cannon, & Muskets, which they had left of the Ships arms they had Captured. ... Thus it pleased the Almighty will that I should succeed in effecting what so many of my countrymen

Laughed me to Scorn for wishing to attempt & they who had branded my Character as a fool or Madman, were now ashamed of themselves. But many of them became my Enemies, from what motives is I believe hard to explain, except it was a bad one, but I Judge them not. Their Conduct on Various Occasions while I remained on that Coast, Caused me much Uneasiness, & many Months of painful Sensations which produced So deep an effect upon my Spirits that my Health was impaired, & I did not again recover from its effect untill two Years afterwards.

In reality, his recovery was prolonged more by political exigencies than personal plots. After a two-year suspension of foreign trade by a Congressional embargo, Samuel Hill was signed to command another voyage to the Northwest Coast. Thomas C. Amory, one of the owners of the *Boston,* hired him to take the brig *Otter* on a voyage similar to that made by the *Lydia.* Thus it was that on April Fools Day, 1809, Captain Samuel Hill was signed to command another voyage to the Northwest Coast, and the cycle began again.

Nicholas King drew the map shown on the next page from notes and sketches compiled by Lewis and Clark, of which this is a detail. The mouth of the Columbia River is visible just north of the line indicating 46° North latitude. The bay behind Cape Disappointment was named "Haley's Bay" by the explorers, after Captain Samuel Hill.

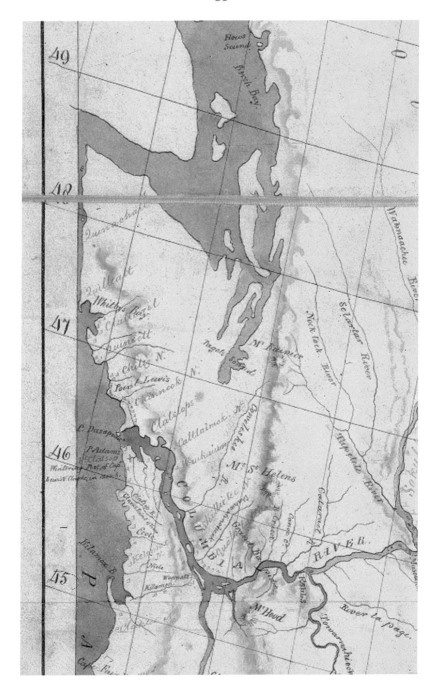

Figure 6 Map of Lewis and Clark route (detail)

A note on the Lewis and Clark letter received on board the *Lydia*, July 15, 1806.

On March 18, 1806, just prior to his departure from Fort Clatsop, the expedition's winter encampment on the Columbia River, William Clark wrote the following in his journal:

We were now ready to leave fort Clatsop, but the rain prevented us for several days from caulking the canoes, and we were forced to wait for calm weather, before we could attempt to pass point William. In the meantime we were visited by many of our neighbours, for the purpose of taking leave of us. The Clatsop Commowool has been the most kind and hospitable of all the Indians of this quarter; we therefore gave him a certificate of the kindness and attention which we had received from him, and added a more substantial proof of our gratitude, the gift of all our houses and furniture. To the Chinnook chief Delashelwilt, we gave a certificate of the same kind: we also circulated among the natives several papers, one of which we also posted up in the fort, to the following effect:

"The object of this last, is, that through the medium of some civilized person, who may see the same, it may be made known to the world, that the party consisting of the persons whose names are hereunto annexed, and who were sent out by the government of the United States to explore the interior of the continent of North America, did penetrate the same by the way of the Missouri and columbia rivers, to the discharge of the latter into the Pacific ocean, where they arrived on the 14th day of November 1805, and departed the 23d day of March, 1806, on their return to the United States, by the same route by which they had come out."

On the back of some of these papers we sketched the connexion of the upper branches of the Missouri and Columbia rivers, with our route, and the track which we intended to follow on our return. This memorandum was all that we deemed it necessary to make; for there seemed but little chance that any detailed report to our government, which we might leave in the hands of the savages, to be delivered to foreign traders, would ever reach the United States. To leave any of our men here, in hopes of their procuring a passage home in some transient vessel, would too much weaken our party, which we must necessarily divide during our route; besides that, we will most probably be there ourselves sooner than any trader, who, after spending the next summer here, might go on some circuitous voyage.

The *Lydia* returned to the Columbia River on July 15, 1806, and William Walker reported in his shipboard journal that the Indians delivered "a paper on board that Capt. Clark Had Left with them declaring them Citizens of America," and saying that "the Natives here treated him very Civil on his travels."

Though Hill wrote extensively about this voyage, both immediately after it was concluded and years later in retrospect, he never specifically mentions the letter. The letter did return to the United States, however. Nicholas Biddle, the Philadelphia lawyer who was invited by William Clark to prepare the journals for publication, included the following note in *The Journals of Lewis and Clark:*

By a singular casualty, this note fell into the possession of captain Hill, who, while on the coast of the Pacific, procured it from the natives. This note accompanied him on his voyage to Canton, from whence it arrived in the United States. The following is an extract of a letter, from a gentleman at Canton to his friend in Philadelphia:

Extract of a letter from ----- to ----- in Philadelphia.

CANTON, January 1807

I wrote you last by the *Governor Strong,* Cleveland, for Boston; the present is by the brig *Lydia,* Hill, of the same place.

Captain Hill, while on the coast, met some Indian natives near the mouth of the Columbia river, who delivered to him a paper, of which I enclose you a copy. It had been committed to their charge by captains Clarke and Lewis, who had penetrated to the Pacific ocean. The original is a rough draft with a pen of their outward route, and that which they intended returning by. Just below the junction of Madison's river, they found an immense fall of *three hundred and sixty-two* feet perpendicular. This, I believe, exceeds in magnitude any other known. From the natives captain Hill learned that they were all in good health and spirits; had met many difficulties on their progress, form various tribes of Indians, but had found them about the sources of the Missouri very friendly, as were those on Columbia river and the coast.

Biddle, unfortunately, left out both the addressee and recipient of the letter, and the original has not been located. The publication of the letter in *The Journals of Lewis and Clark* in 1814, however, solidified Hill's place in the Lewis and Clark story, as did his appearance in several places in the journal as "Captain Haley."

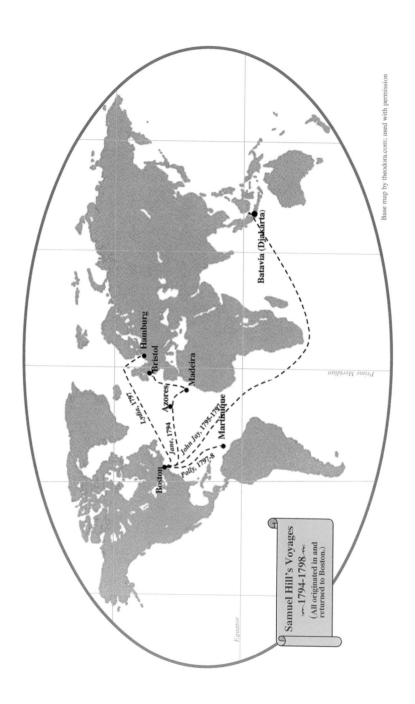

Samuel Hill's Voyages
1794-1798
(All originated in and
returned to Boston.)

Chapter II

❧

Jane, John Jay, Lydia, Polly, 1777-1798:

Roots of Violence and Routes of Voyages

*What's in a name? Or, would Sam Hill
by some other name be as rotten?*

It certainly wasn't Sam Hill's fault that his parents gave him a name that was, or would become, a common euphemism for Hell, but he grew into it.

Samuel Hill was born in February 1777 in the New England coastal village of Machias. Now part of Maine, but then part of Massachusetts, Machias is almost as far "Down East" as a ship can sail before it slips into Canadian waters. Isolated by a rugged and roadless interior, it was dependent on sea transportation, and almost everyone in the village had a link to the maritime trades. Maine lumber was exported from Machias during the Colonial period and on those logs the prosperity of the town was built. Before they was shipped, many of the logs were milled and fashioned into boards and shingles, oars and spars for the maritime trades, and barrels that were broken down into their component staves and bundled together as "shooks."

The principal destination was the West Indies, where the soft wood of northern evergreens was used to build the houses in which the slaves of the cane fields lived, and the boxes and barrels in which sugar products were packed. Dried salted codfish and potatoes rounded out the southbound cargo. Sugar and molasses came north again in the same ships, bound for Newport or Boston where the molasses was made into rum. Logs were also shipped from Machias to Boston, where all the trees within easy reach had been felled before 1700. Bostonians depended on Maine lumber for building materials and even firewood, and it was easier and cheaper to ship it down the Maine rivers and load it at Machias than it was to drag it by ox power from the distant woods into Boston.

During the American Revolution, the British thought that Machias lumber might still be available to them. The port was a long way from Boston and much closer to the Loyalist communities of the Canadian Maritime Provinces. In 1775 two vessels were, consequently, sent into Machias for a cargo of lumber that would be used to build British barracks and fortifications around Boston. The *Margaretta,* an armed schooner of the Royal Navy, accompanied them. To the surprise of the British, Machias rose against them and merchant sailors from the port took the *Margaretta* in a surprisingly successful encounter—the first naval battle of the American Revolution. In retaliation, Machias was intermittently bombarded by the British throughout the rest of the war.

In this small port, pummeled by British guns, Samuel Hill was born on February 20, 1777. Though Machias was a seaport, Hill's father was a prosperous farmer, the son of one of the original settlers of the town. Among his other crops, he planted the seeds of violence in his young son.

Sam Hill would forever justify, rationalize, romanticize, and fictionalize his own actions, until he could not, near the end of his life at the age of forty-nine, distinguish fact from fantasy. In a heart-rending shipboard confessional, a forty-two-year-old Hill, having converted to Christianity and seen the errors of his life, still could not acknowledge the truth of it.

He described his father as "much respected & ever Honored... an Honest Man," who died when the son was eight years old. He described himself as having "arrived at the age of sixteen Years or thereabouts" when he left home and "embarked on the Ocean." His grandson, F. Stanhope Hill, told a different story, one in which a thirteen-year-old Sam Hill received a savage beating from his father, a "good old-fashioned flogging," after which the boy was locked in the barn for a day.

Samuel took the punishment—in both kinds—quietly, but that night he packed up a bundle of clothes, and telling his younger brother that he would never give his father an opportunity to whip him again, he stole out of the house to which he never returned again, and making his way on foot to the nearest seaport, he shipped as a boy on a brig bound to the West Indies, and commenced his life career as a sailor.

Sam left school when he left home and though his education was interrupted early, it had laid the groundwork for the very literate and persuasive writing that he would produce all his life. He read the Bible, along with works of literature, geography and history. He specifically remembered reading about the voyages of Captain James Cook to the Pacific Ocean, and was "excessively fond of reading Poetry & possessed a most retentive memory."

He wrote about his experiences in shipboard logbooks, newspaper articles, and in an "autobiography" which purports to be a confessional statement written at the moment he was born again as a Christian. This last document is particularly puzzling, because at a time when it seems most likely that Hill would honestly admit to and reflect upon his actions, he instead obfuscates his early history and much of his subsequent behavior. His articles about the rescue of John Jewitt, which appeared in the Boston newspapers, are clearly filled with manipulated facts, half truths, and bold-faced lies, but different tactics are expected in a confessional statement, written at what was seemingly a genuine moment of piety and faith. One can only conclude that over the course of his life Hill revised and reorganized his memories until he believed his own version of events. Nonetheless, it is impossible to reconcile even the dates he gave for his early voyages with the shipping records that survive in other sources.

"I think it was in November 1794 I entered as Steward of the Ship *Jane* of Machias, Capt M. Inglee," he wrote, neglecting an earlier voyage, which he likely made from Machias to the West Indies. There were plenty of opportunities in a place like Machias to run away to sea and be many miles beyond the reach of family before being missed. It may have been in the West Indies that Hill encountered Captain Moses Inglee, who hailed from his hometown. Inglee signed the boy to serve as steward aboard the ship *Jane* of Machias. His role was, essentially, to act as a servant in the main cabin, principally to the captain, who was an experienced Machias mariner and must have known the lad and his family. The *Jane* made a trans-Atlantic voyage to fetch Madeira wine for the Boston market, with a landfall at the Azores and a side trip from Madeira to Bristol, England, carrying passengers described by Hill as "Ladies & Gentlemen of Respectable English Families." The ship remained several months in Bristol and returned to Madeira with the ladies.

On these early voyages the young Sam Hill was, for the first time, away from the influence of his family. He would not return to Machias until he was twenty-one years old and then would not return for long. By that time, the pattern of his life was inextricably woven into a lanyard that tied him to the sea

Those visits to the West Indies, Bristol, Madeira, and the Azores, were his first introductions to the sights, sounds, and smells of foreign lands after weeks or months at sea. He had begun to feel the motion of the ship in his bones, to taste the tang of salt in the air, to recognize the patterns of wind and wave, and to note what was familiar and what was unfamiliar and to file both away in his active brain. The *Jane* did not bring him home to Machias, but to Boston, where he took lodgings in a boarding house as a transient sailor.

When he was eighteen, he sailed from Boston to Indonesia and back on the *John Jay* with Captain Robert Haswell. The voyage, which lasted almost a year and a half, is described in a single enigmatic paragraph in his autobiography.

In the Autumn of 1795 I entered as an Ordinary Seaman on board the Ship *John Jay* of Boston under the Command of Robert Haswell Esquire, we proceeded to Battavia in the Island of Java, where we loaded a Cargo & returned to Boston in Jany 1797. While in Battavia it pleased Capt Haswell to permit me to live on shore with him at the Company's Hotel, & where he allowed me to use his Coach, to Ride in the Country or elsewhere, whenever I pleased provided I returned before Eight O'Clock in the morning or more properly from day light until Eight in the morning and as Capt. H. required but a few hours of my time each day I had much leisure, by which means I acquired some knowledge of the Malayan Language, as spoken at Battavia, & also a very considerable addition to the Stock I already possessed of a knowledge in the ways of Iniquity.

There can be no doubt but that the iniquitous ways that young Sam Hill came to know so well were principally sexual in nature, and Robert Haswell is was an interesting potential co-conspirator in the degradation of the younger sailor's morals. Ironically, the captain's sister, Susanna Haswell Rowson, was then the best selling author in America. Her book, *Charlotte Temple: A Tale of Truth,* described in vivid and horrifying detail what happened to a nice young woman if she had sex without being married.

The gulf between the desires and expectations of a young sailor, and the rigid and rigorously patrolled acceptable behavior of a young woman of his own background, was more difficult to navigate than the widest part of the Pacific Ocean. In the age of sail, many boys and young men went to sea just at that point in their emotional and social development when they would ordinarily begin to seek out female companionship and explore romantic and sexual relationships. Had they stayed home, their own society would have provided them with a framework for meeting suitable young women. Within the context of family, church, and community, potential partners could be brought together for flirting, courtship, and marriage.

On shipboard there were no options for meeting marriageable young women, and sailors like Sam Hill were robbed by circumstance of normal socializing experiences for the whole period of their pubescent and adolescent development. The picture they got of girls from books like Rowson's (which must certainly have been in the possession of her brother, and consequently available on the *John Jay)* did not allow for any kind of relationship to be considered that did not start with the expectation of a direct and rapid road to the altar.

Though marriage was clearly the only acceptable road to sexual relations, it also served social functions that could make it seem less than desirable, for both women and men. The father of the heroine in Rowson's story considered his sisters to have been "legally prostituted to old, decrepit men," by marriages that were arranged principally to provide them with social position. Young love might have made for a more perfect union, but if love did not lead directly to marriage, the girl was in a far worse position, because in passion she might forfeit, as Charlotte Temple did, "the only gem that could render [her] respectable in the eye of the world." Rowson ranted quite vigorously about this.

> Gracious heaven! when I think on the miseries that must rend the heart of a doating parent, when he sees the darling of his age at first seduced from his protection, and afterwards abandoned, by the very wretch whose promises of love decoyed her from the paternal roof... her bosom torn between remorse for her crime and love for her vile betrayer ... my bosom glows with honest indignation, and I wish for power to extirpate those monsters of seduction from the earth.

> Oh my dear girls—for to such only am I writing— listen not to the voice of love, unless sanctioned by paternal approbation: be assured, it is now past the days of romance.

Rowson believed that there was a "natural sense of propriety inherent in the female bosom." Men did not share it. Even a good man might be unable to resist his nature, and the results could then be disastrous. Once a girl had "surrendered" herself to a man—even a good man, and even under pressures which might as easily be interpreted as rape as "seduction"—she could no longer expect his respect. She had, in effect, made herself unmarriageable. Rowson documented this in the scene where her heroine, Charlotte Temple, is abducted from her English school to be taken on shipboard and thence to America.

"I cannot go," said she: "cease, dear Montraville, to persuade. I must not: religion, duty, forbid."

"Cruel Charlotte," said he, "if you disappoint my ardent hopes, by all that is sacred, this hand shall put a period to my existence. I cannot—will not live without you."

"Alas! my torn heart!" said Charlotte, "how shall I act?"

"Let me direct you," said Montraville, lifting her into the chaise.

"Oh! my dear forsaken parents!" cried Charlotte.

The chaise drove off. She shrieked, and fainted into the arms of her betrayer.

Though Montraville has clearly kidnapped Charlotte, and will subsequently "seduce" her on shipboard, he ultimately rejects her as unworthy because she submitted. The premarital sexual encounter became "misfortune worse than death." Charlotte knew this would happen, of course. "Never did any human being wish for death with greater fervency or with juster cause" than she, unmarried, pregnant, and abandoned in New York City.

Other books that Samuel Hill was reading at this point in his life had a very different message. "I had accidentally fallen in with some immoral Books previous to my going to Sea," he wrote, "& those parts which most easily caught my attention were Profane & Lascivious Allusions, & quaint expressions of Ridicule." Among the books that he "perused with much delight" were the novels of Laurence Sterne.

Unlike the fevered Charlotte Temple, the heroes of Sterne's novels *Tristram Shandy* and *A Sentimental Journey through France and Italy* were casually, even hilariously sexual. Handsome matrons and lovely chambermaids fell against them by accident, hands strayed, and before they knew it, Sterne's heroes were "winding the clocks" of females thrown unexpectedly into their paths. There were never any consequences from these liaisons, no expectations of marriage, no fear of pregnancy; the men simply moved on to the next encounter.

Voltaire's *Philosophical Dictionary,* purchased by Hill while "strolling into a Book Store one Evening ... in a foreign Port," also provided his eager imagination with new ideas about love, sex, and religion. For the first time, Hill began to consider different belief systems among the Native people whom he encountered around the globe, and to ponder "natural" impulses in contrast to cultural and religious mores. Love came directly from a man's "constitution," wrote Voltaire. It was "natural, and embroidered by imagination."

Shall I give you an idea of Love? View the sparrows in thy garden; view thy pigeons; behold the bull led to thy heifer; look on that spirited horse, which two of thy servants are bringing to thy mare, who quietly waits his coming, and turns aside her tail to admit him; how his eyes glare! how he neighs! observe how he prances; his erect ears, his convulsed mouth, his snorting, his turgid nostrils, his fiery breath issuing from them; the fluttering of his mane; the impetuosity with which he rushes on the object that Nature has appointed for him:

But, Voltaire told his readers, "forebear all jealousy" of the stallion, for men have certain advantages as well.

Most creatures in copulation receive pleasure only from one sense, and that appetite satisfied, sink into insensibility. Thou alone, of all animals, art acquainted with the warm endearments of embraces; thy whole body glows with ecstatic sensations; thy lips, especially, enjoy a most sweet delight, without satiety or weariness, and this delight is peculiar to thy species. Lastly, thou canst at all times give thyself to love; whereas other creatures have only a stated season.

This was powerful stuff for Hill. "It was the Specious arguments, the witty Sarcasms, & Oblique allusions of Voltaire," he wrote, "which produced more effect than all the other books I had met with. Yet I must attribute to my own evil propensities the Chief if not the whole Blame of my Ill spent life, for I certainly knew I was doing wrong, & cannot plead even Ignorance in excuse." When he considered Voltaire and Sterne more than twenty years later, he wrote that he was "now of Opinion that, to a mind susceptible of the finer feelings their effect will be rather productive of Evil than Good, although they do unquestionably include many Sublime & Beautiful Sentiments." The close attention which he had paid to these authors he now saw as "pernicious," but still "owing to the depravity of my heart," and to "gratify a foolish & wicked ambition of Knowledge."

Beyond the simplistic notion that women could be identified as either chaste or loose, some very mixed messages appeared in the books that Hill and his shipmates were reading, which presented very real conflicts for young men becoming sexually active and having to make decisions about how they would behave with women. Few foremast hands in Sam Hill's day actually had normal relationships with women in the communities from which they came, and such fevered and melodramatic descriptions as they encountered in books like *Charlotte Temple* did not make the possibility of such a relationship seem very likely. For girls, this book—which had a wide readership among both females and males—was a lesson in how not to behave. For boys, the message was much more confusing. Clearly men had desires that had to be fulfilled, whether they were in a position to marry or not.

For most sailors, a wife was simply out of the question. The structure of pay did not allow anyone but captains and those mates who were clearly advancing to a captaincy, to support a wife during their absence on a voyage. The ship was consequently divided into two worlds, one in the aft cabin where the captain and possibly the chief mate were married, and everything forward of that where the single, young (often very young) men lived. Within the forecastle there was also a clear dichotomy of expectations. On the one hand, many or most of these young men were sentimental. They were homesick, missed their mothers and families, and were still hoping that a sweet young wife was in their future. But the macho swagger of the shipboard boys' club also demanded that they trumpet their sexual conquests. The only female sexual partners available in the course of the voyage were either prostitutes in the more developed seaports, or native girls and women in less-developed ports of call. Both the girls at home and the girls abroad were subjected to a rich and exotic development in the fantasy culture of young sailors.

In ballad texts scribbled into shipboard diaries are dozens of songs about beautiful and constant lovers, virginal shepherdesses, and women desired by rich and powerful men who resolutely save themselves for their absent sailors. An alternative view was strongly articulated in the chanties sung on American and English ships in the nineteenth century. These songs, which drove the work and were sung together, more often degraded women, describing a sailor's easy conquests from port to port or even from body part to body part. In the chantey, a woman could be compared to a ship with hilarity. Even the prostitute with syphilis, the "fire ship" who set poor Jack's bowsprit ablaze, was grist for the shipboard song mill.

The sailors' view of women and of relationships with them was formed in a womanless vacuum that was very much influenced by rumor, humor, fantasy, and exaggeration. The macho posturing on shipboard was not unlike the competition among a pack of dogs each seeking to be the alpha male, except that no female dogs were available.

The only sexual partners actually available in the isolation of the ship were other sailors, and sexual encounters with his shipmates may have played a role in Hill's "iniquity." Communities of young men and boys, isolated from female contact in boarding schools, ships, or prisons will, not infrequently, turn to one another to find sexual partners. For the vast majority of sailors, homo-erotic behavior did not define their sexual identity in the sense that we understand that concept today; it was simply a physical act in which they engaged while on shipboard.

Voltaire wrote openly about "Socratic Love" in the *Philosophical Dictionary,* which Hill acknowledged reading.

> How could it be that a vice which, if general, would extinguish the human species, an infamous crime against nature, should become so natural? It ... is usually found in those who have not had time to be corrupted. It makes its way into novice hearts, who are strangers to ambition, fraud, and a thirst after wealth; it is blind youth, which, at the end of childhood, by an unaccountable instinct plunges itself into this enormity. ...
>
> The young males of our species brought up together, coming to feel that play which Nature begins to unfold to

them, in the want of the natural object of their instinct, betake themselves to a resemblance of such objects. It is nothing uncommon for a boy, by the beauty of his complexion, and the mild sparkle of his eyes, for two or three years to have the look of a pretty girl.

Voltaire ended this passage with a quotation from Ovid's *Metamorphoses,* noting that Orpheus "offered the example to the people of Thrace by giving his love to tender boys, and enjoying the springtime and first flower of their youth."

Few contemporaneous sources from Samuel Hill's day speak openly of homosexual activity on sailing vessels. In both the American and British Navies, sodomy or "buggery" was a capitol offense through the middle of the nineteenth century. Most of what we can glean from eighteenth- and nineteenth-century sources comes from Admiralty records that describe the courts martial of naval men. Though the Royal Navy, especially, was ferocious in punishing men convicted of the crime of sodomy, bringing formal charges forward required a great deal of care. There was never only one man on a ship who participated.

In 1816 on the man-of-war *Africaine,* for instance, the captain found that once he began to collect evidence of "buggery" on the ship, twenty-three men were implicated, including one officer. Eventually four men would be hanged; two others were flogged for the lesser charge of "uncleanliness," for which one received 200 and the other 300 lashes. Others were dishonorably discharged. The captain himself was eventually held morally culpable for having failed to perform religious services on Sundays, and for failing regularly to read the "Articles of War"—one of which prohibited sodomy.

Later in the nineteenth century men would speak more openly about sexual behavior that they witnessed or participated in while at sea. The poet John Masefield, in a letter to a female friend, confessed what he never acknowledged in his romantic odes to seafaring. In describing life aboard the merchant sail-training vessel *Conway,* on which he served for two-and-a-half years in the 1890's, Masefield wrote:

The tone of the ship was infamous. Theft, bullying, barratry, sodomy, and even viler vice were rampant. ... I'd not been on board more than three days when a great hulking brute tried to make me submit to him, and when I refused, he led me such a hell of a life that I nearly drowned myself. I've seen boys committing sodomy on the ship's deck quite openly. I've seen worse things still.

Masefield wrote about homoerotic sexual activity as commonplace, and while his experiences were removed from Sam Hill's by several decades, the culture on shipboard in the Anglo-American world remained remarkably unchanged from Hill's time. The technology and hierarchy of the ship, the schedule of watch standing, the food, the lingo, the isolation, the separation from home, and the exposure to foreign places, were factors that did not see significant changes until steam power was introduced.

It is important to acknowledge that many kinds of relationships between men do not include sexual activity. In recent decades a number of scholars have explored the loving, even romantic nature of men's friendships in the eighteenth and nineteenth centuries which still remained non-sexual, and a number of such relationships in literature were read for a century and more without raising eyebrows. But in societies like those on shipboard, where there were *only* men, the line was clearly crossed more regularly. One historian of the early nineteenth century, in a chronicle of naval courts martial, wrote that there was a class of legal actions about which he would not speak other than to say, "To ignore the fact that it is there would be dishonest. To dwell on it would be an outrage." Even Winston Churchill, while First Lord of the Admiralty, referred to the three traditions of the British Navy as "rum, sodomy, and the lash."

In the specific case of Samuel Hill, he raised the flag himself when he wrote in his autobiography of "an almost infinite number of Crimes & Offences against the established Laws of the Almighty, in defiance to, & against the light of that knowledge & Reason which he has given me." His behavior aboard the *Lydia*, where he abducted a Hawaiian girl to be his sex partner on a long voyage, was well known. Even his wife, left pregnant on shore when he departed, and holding their young son when he returned, must have known about it, as James Bennett described it in court testimony during legal proceedings that Hill took against the owners of the ship. Consequently, that incident is likely not the sin that cannot be described.

Hill wrote of conquering his "natural timid & feminine disposition," which, he says, was "altogether unsuitable for the profession I had adopted, & the Society in which I had placed myself."

'Twas this had induced & Stimulated me to Superiour & practical knowledge of all the modes of vice & profaneness known among Seamen, except Drunken-ness, which, Blessed be God, I was not addicted to, & which perhaps prevented me from becoming one of the most abandoned of Mortals. — nay more, I was not satisfied with the approbation of the oldest Sailors in this respect, but aiming at Superiority among them. To the Grosser Sensualities & vices practised among Seamen, I added improvements in Vice which I had observed amongst Other classes of Society. ... I was prompt in devising plausible modes of defence or excuse in case of detection. By these & other foolish practices, & a prompt attention to the discharge of Ship duty whenever called on, I generally enjoyed the esteem & approbation of the Seamen, & also of the Officers, more particularly the Commanders, from Several of whom I received attentions which I was not deserving of, & which of course was owing to the Success of the deceptions which I practised on their understandings in concealing my real character.

It is hard to imagine what actions he might have committed on shipboard that would need to be covered or explained "in case of detection," unless they were sexual, mutinous, or involved theft of cargo. Because Hill's autobiography was written at a moment of intense pious fear, it has the ring of a confessional, but still contains the stylistic artifice of a work of literature. He would not recount "thousands of Instances of depravity & folly" of which he had been guilty, he wrote, fearful that such a recitation "would be productive of more evil than Good, especially if it should fall into the hands of young persons."

But the anguish with which he returns again and again to the theme of necessary forgiveness, seems to argue that his transgressions were sexual. " O Merciful God!" he writes, "I have lived in Open Rebellion against thy known & established Laws, & that too against the light of my own conscience."

> Oh foolish & wretched man that I am, who shall forgive the multitude of my Crimes, who shall pardon so many Years spent almost entirely in the Voluntary Service of Sin in all its Varieties. Who Shall restore my mind to its ori[gi]nal peace & Serenity. ... Yet I must attribute to my own evil propensities the Chief if not the whole Blame of my Ill spent life, for I certainly knew I was doing wrong, & cannot plead even Ignorance in excuse.

If Hill as a young man had sexual relationships with older men on his ships, then Captain Robert Haswell is one candidate. The fact that Haswell invited Hill to live ashore with him in Batavia may have been completely innocent. In addition to being young and strong, Hill was smart, had excellent penmanship and a flair for turning a phrase; he would have made a fine clerk. There must have been many situations during Haswell's trade negotiations when an assistant like Hill would be handy to have around. Suspicion is raised, though, by that comment of Hill's, that on this voyage specifically he added to his stock of knowledge in the ways of iniquity.

Robert Haswell was already a very experienced mariner when Samuel Hill signed aboard his ship. Haswell had been on both voyages of the Boston ship *Columbia,* the first American vessel to go around Cape Horn into the Pacific and the first to circumnavigate the globe. The Columbia River was named after this ship by her captain, Robert Gray, when he sailed into it in 1792 with Haswell aboard.

As third mate on the *Columbia,* Haswell described a relationship with an older officer which may have had echoes years later in his own relationship with Samuel Hill. To have earned his rank, Haswell must already have been at sea for several years when he joined the *Columbia* in 1787, so he was not an innocent lad and it was a hard-bitten ship. Relief came from an almost instantaneous bonding with the first mate, Simeon Woodruff. Between Woodruff, a man of forty-four, and the nineteen-year-old Haswell, a close friendship developed. Each man found in the other a friend and ally in a troubled shipboard world.

Woodruff had been on Captain James Cook's third voyage to the Pacific, and was, consequently the only man aboard either the *Columbia* or her smaller consort, the *Lady Washington,* who had actually been around Cape Horn. The aim of the voyage was to explore the sea otter pelt trade on the Northwest Coast and the owners felt fortunate to have been able to sign Woodruff on the venture.

The captain was John Kendrick, a man who had been a professional mariner all his adult life. Between Kendrick and Woodruff there was "much discord," according to Haswell. By the time the ship had crossed the Atlantic to the Cape Verde Islands, Kendrick had demoted Woodruff and the latter decided to leave the ship. Haswell deeply lamented his loss.

> This Gentleman was of known abilities as a navigator and greatly experienced as a Seaman he had Commanded several Ships out of London. he was an officer under the Great Captain James Cook on his last Voyage to the Pacific Ocean.
>
> This Worthy Gentleman was my sincere Friend and the loss of him I regretted past expression.

Haswell was elevated to second mate and though he went at his job with a vengeance, he hated Kendrick for the rest of the voyage. Within six months he had transferred to the *Washington.* When Captains Gray and Kendrick exchanged commands on the Northwest Coast, Haswell transferred back to the *Columbia* with Robert Gray.

Though Haswell and Gray were able to maintain a working relationship on the *Columbia,* it was still an environment filled with anger and violence. Not only was the crew subjected to verbal tirades and physical abuse, but the violence was also directed out toward the Native people on shore as well. The lessons learned from Cook's narratives, and from the example of John Kendrick and others, was to take high-ranking hostages from the local Native community when trade lagged, or when slights were perceived, and to follow that quickly with gunfire if the situation went awry, which it often did.

When Hill went to the Northwest Coast for the first time as captain of the *Lydia*, he behaved in the same way. He had learned lessons from Robert Haswell on the *John Jay* that would influence him for the rest of his life. Haswell might almost serve as a template for Hill's angry and violent behavior on shipboard and his reckless and brutal dealings with Native people, yet both men were civilized enough at home. Haswell married when the *John Jay* returned to Boston, fathered two daughters, served for a few years in the U.S. Navy, and died at sea around 1801, enroute again to the Northwest Coast as master of the merchant ship *Louisa,* which was lost with all hands.

Though he was married for only three years and spent much of that time at sea, Haswell's widow and daughters mourned him for years after. Through the generations his family preserved a sentimental piece of mourning art, showing the mother and daughters at an empty grave, while a ship wrecks against a distant shore. Any dark side Robert Haswell might have possessed was washed clean by his death.

Upon his own return to Boston in January 1797, Samuel Hill immediately sought out another ship, and within a few weeks was bound to Hamburg, Germany aboard the brig *Lydia* under the command of Captain William Moreland. This was the vessel that he would come to know very well in 1804 when he sailed as her captain around the world, but on this voyage he was an Able Bodied Seaman earning eighteen dollars a month. (Though Boston ships went everywhere in the world, the community itself was still small enough that people in the seafaring trades moved easily from ship to ship and knew many of them in common. Moreland would take command of the *John Jay* for his next voyage, and had also captained another ship in common with Robert Haswell, the *Hannah,* which had been Haswell's first command.)

The *Lydia* made a direct passage to Hamburg in February 1797, riding the winter Gulf Stream across the North Atlantic. Hill had been much affected by his stay on shore in Batavia on his previous voyage and he decided to try to do the same in Hamburg. He asked Captain

Moreland if he might hire a local man to live on the ship in his place and stand his watch while the *Lydia* was unloaded and reloaded. This was a strange request for a sailor on limited wages, because it meant that Hill would get very little out of the voyage beyond the experience of Hamburg itself. To Moreland it made no difference who did the work as long as it got done.

As a den of iniquity, few ports in the world could compete with Hamburg. The waterfront district, the "Reeperbahn," was notorious for the variety of sexual experiences available. In describing his shore experiences twenty-two years later, Hill would write that what he really wanted to see was the world beyond the port. He was interested in learning languages and in meeting local people, especially women. He wrote that he "never took lodgings in a house with Seamen, nor frequented their Society."

> During the Intervals of my residence on Shore whether in Foreign Countries or in the United States ... most of my time was spent in the Society of Females, with them conversing. I forgot all time, & without them, Society was a Blank to me. This was a propensity which Nature had interwoven in my Constitution, & planted in my Heart's core, and that Levity of disposition, & Volatility of Sentiment, with feelings Spun in Nature's finest Web, which I inherited from the Author of Nature, was sure to gain their Friendship for me wherever I came.

As Hill remembered these sojourns in the romantic ecstasy of his religious conversion, the women he had encountered in his youth were not just prostitutes, and the relationships were more than sexual. From "an intimate and General knowledge of the Female Character," he wrote, "I am Convinced that the Female found in the undeviating principles of Modesty & Virtue is the most Inestimable Gift in the Creation of God." Hill does not say here that he actually spent his time among modest and virtuous women, and if he did, it is unlikely that he sought them out, or they him, in the precincts of the port of Hamburg.

The *Lydia* voyage was concluded in a matter of months, and Hill again spent only a few weeks in Boston before he signed on for another voyage, this time aboard a schooner bound to the West Indies. The *Polly* reached Martinique late in the fall of 1797 and took on a cargo of molasses, bound back to the rum distilleries of New England.

This was a perilous time for small American vessels running up and down the Atlantic seaboard. Both England and France were raiding American merchant ships for men. The U.S. Congress had just voided all treaties with France as the first step in a "quasi war" and directed the Navy to seek out armed French vessels. The *Polly's* captain, Oliver Appleton, had managed to make his way south without running into any French cruisers, but the crew was worried about encountering them during the run back northward. Consequently, after the cargo came aboard, the *Polly* waited while several other vessels finished loading, so that all the ships could proceed together in a convoy.

Captain Appleton was on shore making preparations for his departure when a hurricane burst with explosive force from the southeast. There were a number of vessels lying at anchor in the harbor at Port Royal and they were all swept together toward the mouth of the port. "The Night was dark," Hill wrote, "the wind was violent in the extreme, the Sea was high & dangerous, & the Rain fell in torrents, the Captain was on Shore & though Sent for did not Come on board." There was no choice but to cut the anchor cables and drive out before the storm. Hill would later describe himself as the hero of the day, the only one on the schooner who had any sense or courage.

I spent a night of extreme Solicitude, as the Vessel was in the greatest disorder & Confusion, the hatches open & with other loose things floating about the deck, the Sea frequently breaking over us. Mr. Barrett who was the mate & the only officer on board, was Sick & went to his Bed, and a Brother in Law of the Captain, as well as the Seamen & Cooper did the Same, & it was not without some entreaty that I prevailed on Some of them to awake & assist me at the pumps to prevent her from Sinking, of which I had Serious apprehensions.

In the morning, when the storm had run its course, Hill asked the mate (who would still not rise from his bunk), for permission to steer for home. "This was my first Effort in Navigating a Vessel," Hill admitted later. He then apparently single-handedly brought the ship back into Boston Harbor through a "long series of adverse Gales on the American Coast." The *Polly* arrived home in the spring of 1798 without the captain, the small boats, or the anchors. The schooner had also run out of provisions along the way, but the crew was "providentially relieved" by Captain Stephen Decatur of the U.S. frigate *Delaware*.

Hill was twenty-one years old. This was at least his fourth voyage and maybe his fifth. He had been at sea constantly for more than five years and still had not risen above the position of seaman. Despite the heroic acts he claims on this voyage—, his leadership in crisis, his navigational ability, his steadiness in storms, and even an encounter with the hero Decatur—, he was still not offered a position in the cabin. His schoolmates in Machias, without half so many miles under their keels, were very likely commanding schooners along the very route taken by the *Polly*.

Why hadn't Robert Haswell recommended him to a mate's position? Hill's chain of voyages does not seem to indicate that he had much ambition to advance at this point in his career. If he wanted to be a mate, he should have stayed on the ship in Hamburg and learned something about stowing cargo, as that was a principal responsibility of the chief mate. Had he done so, Captain Moreland might have recommended him to the *Lydia's* owners. But he immediately jumped to a new ship, a new destination, and a new captain.

Unwilling, it seems, to acknowledge the recklessness of his youth from the perspective of his middle age, Sam Hill disavowed the aimlessness of it as well when he wrote his autobiography more than twenty years later. He invested this voyage with actions that could be interpreted to his advantage across the haze of two decades. To accept his account as true we must also accept that the first mate would remain in his bunk through a hurricane and its aftermath in the absence of the captain, that the captain's brother-in-law (a likely investor in the voyage) would turn command of the ship over to a seaman, and that the sailor would then, without the assistance of either of the other two, navigate the ship along two thousand miles of coastline in storms and threats of war, into the safe haven of the home port. Upon the *Polly's* return to Boston there was no celebration of Able Bodied Seaman Hill's remarkable achievements on behalf of the vessel and her owners. There was no mention of it in the local papers.

Hill traveled from Boston to Machias—his first visit home to see his mother since he ran away to sea. He returned to Boston late in the summer of 1798 and signed aboard the ship *Franklin,* again as an Able Bodied Seaman. Strangely, of this voyage, which may have been his greatest and most significant adventure, he wrote very little.

Figure 7, American vessels *Franklin* and *Eliza* in Nagasaki Harbor, ca. 1799, by Shiba Kokan

Chapter III

✋

Franklin, 1798-1800:
Behind the Double Bolts

*How Sam Hill came to be the first American
to live in Japan.*

There were no seas to which Massachusetts ships would not venture in the decades that followed American Independence. In search of profit, Boston merchants were willing to speculate on almost any route and any cargo. What lay at the other end of the outbound voyage had the potential to bring riches or ruin, with a large range of mystery as to which it would be. A ship's orders were, consequently, accepted by owners, captains, and supercargoes to be a guideline for the enterprise, but they all knew that the power to make decisions for the success of a voyage had to lie ultimately in the hands of the men who were on the ship. What might happen on the spot in a distant port of call could not be predicted in advance.

In 1798 the owners of the ship *Franklin* of Salem, Massachusetts, thought that they could make a good profit on a straightforward voyage to Java and back with a load of coffee. The outbound cargo was simple enough, $32,000 in cash. The captain, James Devereux, and the supercargo, William Burling, were expected to buy as much coffee as they could for the cash on hand. If the price was high they would simply fill the hold; if the price was low, they would fill every inch of the ship with bags of coffee beans, including the cabins in which they and the other officers lived. (Boards to build a temporary deckhouse to accommodate them for the return voyage were provided.)

Samuel Hill signed aboard the voyage as a seaman that fall, and the ship proceeded around the Cape of Good Hope to the Dutch East Indies. The capital of the Dutch colony was Batavia (now called Djakarta), a thriving town on the northwest end of the long island of Java, and it was to that port that the *Franklin* made it's way, arriving in April 1799. For Hill, it must have been a pleasant return to the place where he had, three years earlier, added so considerably to his "knowledge in the ways of iniquity."

When Devereux and Burling went ashore to negotiate with the Dutch agents for the East India Company, they were made an unexpected offer. The Dutch had an exclusive monopoly on the European trade to Japan, but they didn't have a ship to send on their annual voyage. If the *Franklin* would make the voyage, the Americans would be paid thirty thousand piasters to carry a freight to Japan and another back to Batavia. The payment would be made in coffee, sugar, pepper, cloves, cinnamon, nutmegs, and indigo, in any combination. The outlines of the voyage were narrowly defined: the Dutch ships always left Batavia in mid-June to follow the seasonal monsoon winds, and they always left Japan near the first of December when the monsoon predictably reversed direction. The ship would be paid even if it were unable to enter Japan, unable to get a cargo once there, or even if it were wrecked along the way. The value of the silver piaster was not far off from that of the Spanish dollars they carried, so the ten-month round-trip to Japan would double the *Franklin's* buying power in Batavia. It was, simply, an irresistible offer.

The *Franklin* would not be the first American ship to enter the waters of what Herman Melville called "that double-bolted land, Japan." Two American vessels, the *Lady Washington* and the *Grace,* had attempted a landfall in

Japan in 1791, but were repelled by the locals, and the American-flagged *Eliza* had made the previous voyage for the Dutch, but was presently missing and presumed lost. For all other ships from the United States and Europe, Japan forbade entry.

It had not always been so. There was a time when the Japanese were interested in a wide range of goods and ideas coming from the outside, but the potent combination of guns and Catholicism was considered too great a threat to social order, and since 1639 the Japanese had worked hard to keep outsiders out.

The Portuguese were the first Europeans to drift into Japanese waters, arriving around 1543. Japan's ship of state was then battling mutinies from all quarters, as feudal warlords each sought to wrest control of his own region from the central government. The power of the Imperial throne had collapsed almost four centuries earlier, when the powerful military leader Yoritomo Minamoto seized control and declared himself Shogun in 1192. Control of the country shifted to the family of his wife in 1213, back to the Emperor for a short period in 1333, and then to the powerful Ashikaga family in 1338. From their palace at Muromachi in Kyoto, the Ashikaga shoguns ruled Japan for more than two centuries, honing samurai chivalry and the arts and philosophy that accompanied it.

Rival clans plotted against them though, and when the Portuguese arrived, guns became available for the battles that followed. A number of feudal warlords courted the Portuguese in the confusion that was then tearing at the fabric of Japanese society. The local daimyo at Nagasaki, Omura Sumitada, invited the foreigners to use his port beginning in 1571, and the deep natural harbor was the perfect portal into Japan. Trade and religious conversion both followed. As potent a force as firearms was St. Francis Xavier, one of the founders of the Jesuit order, who arrived shortly after the first ships. He was the first and most influential priest in Japan. He learned the language and converted a few hundred Japanese to Catholicism during his two years there.

Not all of the Japanese appreciated the impact of the Portuguese. Toyotomi Hideyoshi, a powerful feudal lord, consolidated power from the local daimyos and seized

Nagasaki in 1587, ejecting the Portuguese in the process. In 1590 he declared himself Shogun. Seven years later, still bothered by the influence of the Portuguese, and especially the Jesuits, he ordered the arrest of the priests and their Japanese followers in Kyoto and Osaka. In 1597, twenty-six Japanese Catholics were transported to Nagasaki and executed.

Hideyoshi was followed by another powerful shogun, Tokugawa Ieyasu, whose dynasty would rule Japan for over two and a half centuries from his new capital at Edo, the site of the modern Tokyo. Still plagued by the Portuguese, and now other Europeans, Ieyasu banned his own citizens from foreign travel and had an artificial island built in Nagasaki harbor to isolate Portuguese visitors in 1635. Two years later the local Christian population rose up in support of their priests, and in 1639 the shogun expelled the Portuguese entirely from Japan and began a period of virtual isolation that would continue until the United States Expedition under the command of Commodore Matthew Calbraith Perry arrived in 1853 and forced the Japanese to open their doors to trade.

There was only one exception to this self-imposed isolation: one or two ships sent annually by the Dutch East India Company were granted the right to conduct a limited trade. (In Dutch, the Honorable East India Company is the "Verenigde Oostindische Compagnie," commonly abbreviated as "VOC.") The Dutch had arrived in Japan in 1600, their fleet of five ships reduced to one survivor by terrible storms in the Pacific Ocean. Their pilot was an Englishman, Will Adams, who was begrudgingly befriended by the shogun and became his pipeline to information about European thought and technology.

In 1609 the Dutch received permission from Tokugawa Ieyasu to establish a small trading post at Hirado, not far from Nagasaki. In 1641 they were ordered to confine themselves to Deshima (Dejima), the artificial island in Nagasaki harbor that had been built for the Portuguese at the order of the shogun. There, the Dutch lived in a rigorously controlled environment, aimed at limiting their contact with and influence on Japanese people.

Despite the strict rules and elaborate rituals required to do business in Japan, which the Dutch often found petty and difficult, the trade provided them with access to silver and copper, which they could trade throughout Asia. In exchange, the men of the VOC brought their Japanese customers a range of textiles, principally silk produced in India, and spices from their great plantations in Indonesia.

The Dutch provided the Japanese with their only glimpse of the world beyond Asia. Gradually, the Japanese hierarchy eased restrictions on scientific books and by the middle of the eighteenth century Japanese scholars were seeking information through the Dutch connection at Nagasaki. Most of what was known of western products, technology, science, and medicine, was known through Dutch sources. Dutch maps provided a glimpse of the world; Dutch scientific texts provided a new understanding of the workings of the heavens, the human body, and the natural history of exotic animals and plants; and Dutch art began to inspire a new, more three-dimensional style of painting among a small school of Japanese artists.

By the end of the eighteenth century, however, the Japan trade was not an easy one to manage for the Dutch East India Company. The Netherlands was occupied by the French, the English were expanding their domain from India across the Indian Ocean to the Dutch territories in the Indonesian archipelago, and the VOC was collapsing. Unable to muster a ship to send to Japan in 1796, the managers of the firm in Batavia looked for a vessel from a neutral country to carry a cargo to Japan and return with copper.

A dozen years into independent trade, small American vessels were becoming familiar in the Indian Ocean and at the ports of the East Indies. For the Dutch, American ships offered a way to keep up their presence in Japan while avoiding entanglements with the English and French.

The first American-flagged vessel to make the voyage to Japan under the auspices of the VOC was the *Eliza* of New York, which was chartered for the first time in 1797 and after a successful venture was hired upon her return to Batavia to repeat it in 1798. On the unlucky second trip, the *Eliza* struck a rock and sank enroute from Japan to Java. Raised and repaired with great effort, the ship was subsequently dismasted in a storm near Formosa and limped back to Nagasaki. When the *Eliza* did not return to Batavia, the Dutch presumed she had been lost and, in 1799, looked for a second American ship to commission to make the Japan voyage. The *Franklin* proved to be the right ship in the right place at the right time, and consequently was offered powerful inducements to make the trip. For the Dutch, it was a last-ditch effort to keep their monopoly in Japan, as the rest of their great mercantile empire collapsed.

The VOC managers in Batavia gave Captain Devereux charts and instructions for the voyage to Japan, a Dutch flag to fly in place of the stars and stripes, and a young Dutchman named Hendrik Doeff, to manage the company's business on shipboard and to communicate with the company's employees residing in Nagasaki. The *Franklin* sailed from Batavia on June 17, 1799 with seventeen men on board, including Doeff and his Javanese servant.

Hendrik Doeff was a "junior merchant" of the Dutch East India Company and this was his first voyage to Japan; at twenty-two he was the same age as Samuel Hill. As Hill would describe it more than twenty years later, "during our passage this Gentleman became Somewhat attached to me." Hill's explanation for the attachment was that it was "probably owing to Some little Service I rendered in explaining his wishes & orders to his Malayan Servant, as he had not yet acquired the Malayan dialect," but the relationship became close enough that Doeff invited Hill to live on shore in the Dutch compound when the American ship arrived in Japan.

That Doeff, an employee of the Dutch East India Company, would not have been as fluent in the principal language of the capital of the Dutch East Indies as Hill seems a doubtful explanation. And Doeff would certainly not have needed Hill to serve as a translator for him in Nagasaki, where the Dutch agents and their Javanese employees could certainly converse with both Doeff and his servant. But Hill always tried to live on shore when he was in a foreign port, and his persuasion of Doeff to arrange it may have been due to nothing more than the Dutchman's kindness and good humor.

The *Franklin* proceeded without incident from Batavia to Nagasaki. As the ship approached the coast of Japan, Devereux was required to follow extremely precise written instructions, which he had received, in English, and transcribed into his shipboard journal. "When you get to the Latt. of 26° or 27° North," he wrote, "it will be Necessary to have every thing in readiness to comply with the Ceremonies which the Japanese are accustomed to see performed by the Ships of the Company." He then noted each item of protocol for entering Japan.

First: You will have all your Colours in order to dress the ship on her entrance into Port.

Second: There must be a table prepared on the Quarter Deck which must be covered with a piece of cloth & two Cushions for the officers to sit upon when they come on board.

Third: It is indispensably Necessary to have a list of all the People on board, Passengers & Officers their Stations & Age.

Fourth: All the books of the People & Officers Particularly religious books must be put in a cask & headed up, the officers from the shore will put their seal on the cask, & take it on shore, & on departure of the ship will bring it on board without having opened it.

Fifth: Before your arrival at Japan you must make the people deliver you their money & keep it untill your departure. This will not be attended with inconvenience as at Japan nothing is bought for Cash but they may ExChange their specie for cambang money & then make their trade, but this must be done by the Captain.

Sixth: When you are in sight of Japan you must hoist a dutch Pendant & Ensign in their proper places as if you were a dutch ship.

Devereux complied by collecting all the money and books onboard and sealing them into barrels. He made the required list of the crew and passengers. The ship was festooned with signal flags.

On the afternoon of July 18, 1799, the men aboard the *Franklin* caught their first glimpse of Japan. Two small fishing boats came alongside as the coast came into view, offering fish in trade. They were followed soon after by four boatloads of Japanese officials, demanding to know the identity of the vessel. When it was explained that they were the annual ship of the Dutch East India Company, the *Franklin* began to be processed for landing. Devereux and Doeff handed over the first of several lists of the names of the men on board.

On the afternoon of the following day, the *Franklin* came abreast of the opening to Nagasaki harbor and, as instructed, saluted by firing nine cannon shots. Two hours later they repeated the process when a Japanese official came on board, followed soon after by the resident agents of the VOC. The Japanese visitor sat upon the cushion prepared for him on top of the ship's table. Within another hour the ship was being towed into the harbor by eighty small Japanese boats, which Devereux called "prows."

Though the *Franklin* was not a large ship, it took several hours to tow it into the harbor. At ten that evening, under a nearly full moon, they passed a cliff called Takabokojima by the Japanese and "the Papenberg" by the Dutch. From that cliff two hundred years earlier, the converts of St. Francis Xavier had been thrown to their deaths. The *Franklin* again fired nine guns. At midnight, the ship passed the guardhouse of the Emperor's troops and fired another fourteen shots in salute. The Americans finally came to their assigned anchorage an hour later and fired another thirteen-gun salute. They fired another nine when more Japanese officials arrived shortly thereafter, and the same when they departed. In all, the ship fired more than seventy shots in eight hours, each carefully prescribed in Devereux's instructions. The Dutch had known that the *Franklin* would be surrounded by smaller Japanese boats, and Devereux had been told that he "must be very Particular in letting the boats round the Ship know when you are going to fire, as If you were to hurt any of them the consequences would be very Important."

At specified times the ship displayed large numbers of flags, hoisting additional pennants when officials came on board. By the time they reached the anchorage at Nagasaki, all the flags on the ship were flying except the Portuguese, Spanish, and American national flags. Devereux had been told that it was "immaterial" what flags he used, as the Japanese did not recognize the language in the signals, but he was reminded that he needed "to recollect that the Dutch colours must be always in their proper place as if the ship were of that nation."

After the persons on board were compared to the list, the barrels with the books and money were sent ashore, where a Japanese official affixed a seal. All the firearms on the ship were likewise sealed into barrels and sent ashore. The Japanese then searched the vessel. At that point Hendrik Doeff went ashore to take up his residence in the Dutch compound and Samuel Hill went with him. For Hill, this was an extraordinary opportunity. All the previous American visitors had lived aboard their ships when they came into Japanese waters. He was the first to live ashore in Japan.

The place in which he found himself, Deshima, was a fan-shaped island in Nagasaki harbor constructed for the Portuguese 165 years earlier. (Tradition says that when the workers building the island asked the shogun what sort of place he wanted them to construct, his response was to spread his fan and lay it before them.)

There were only two streets on Deshima. One ran from end to end along the middle of the island, following its bow-shaped curve. The other ran from the gatehouse to the middle of the island where it met the main street. Neither was very long. Engelbert Kaempfer, a German doctor who worked for the VOC on Deshima in the early part of the eighteenth century, wrote that the island was 236 paces long and 82 paces across.

There were about two dozen structures on the island, built of wood in the Japanese style. In addition to living quarters for the men, there were two warehouses and a small hospital. The Dutch had brought some furnishings to make themselves more comfortable, and had purchased chairs from the Chinese trading delegation who were their neighbors to the south and, with the Koreans, the only other outsiders allowed to trade in Japan.

Deshima had a vegetable garden with a dovecote for raising pigeons or squab. Goats, pigs, chickens, and cows, provided meat, milk, and eggs for the Dutch table. The animals were tended by servants brought from Batavia, who were called "boys" or "slaves" by the Dutch, and kurombô, or "black boys" by the Japanese. These young men did much of the housekeeping around the compound, though three Japanese cooks were trained to make dishes from Dutch and Indonesian recipes. There were other Japanese

Figure 8, Deshima in the late eighteenth century, by a Japanese artist

Figure 9, Portrait of Hendrik Doeff with a Javanese servant, by Shiba Kokan

residents as well. Two translators were always assigned to the island; there was household help and access to laborers when big jobs needed to be done; and there were women, assigned by the Japanese authorities to serve as companions for the visitors. The recreational center of the Deshima community was a pavilion in the garden, where the women lived when they were in residence. In paintings of Deshima made by a Japanese artist around the time Sam Hill was there, the Dutch men are shown playing billiards and eating lavish meals while their Indonesian servants play music on European instruments including violins, viola da gambas, and harps. The kimono-clad women talk and laugh with the Dutchmen and among themselves.

For Hendrik Doeff, Deshima was an unexpected challenge. He had gone there expecting to learn the business from the "Opperhoofd," the local head of the VOC. On his arrival he learned that the Opperhoofd was dead. To make matters worse, a fire the previous year had destroyed much of the Dutch compound. Because the *Eliza* had been wrecked and did not return to Batavia, neither of these facts was known to the management of the Company. (The *Eliza*, having recently been salvaged, came into Nagasaki Bay the day after the *Franklin* arrived—the first time it was seen by the Dutch that year.)

The highest-ranking Dutch person in Japan was now Leopold Willem Ras, who described himself in his daily journal as a "Bookkeeper/Scribe." The younger Doeff was Ras's superior in rank in the Company, being clearly in line for advancement to management, but he was completely inexperienced. Between them, Ras and Doeff had to figure out how to proceed.

The day after the *Franklin's* arrival, the ship began to be unloaded by transferring cargo and supplies onto Japanese prows and bringing them into Deshima through the watergate. These goods included not only the official cargo put onboard by the Dutch in Batavia, but dispensary supplies and some private ventures of Captain Devereux and his officers. As the *Franklin* was only about a third of the size of the usual Dutch merchantman, the Japanese were disappointed by the scanty choices available to them. The conflict with England had also prevented the Dutch from getting the best products on board. Sugar, the most abundant commodity currently available, had previously been transported to Japan in casks; now 250,000 pounds of it lay in burlap sacks in the hold of the *Franklin,* and the Japanese were clearly dissatisfied with the quality.

Worst of all, the *Franklin* did not have any presents for the shogun on board. This was a major breach of etiquette and Ras, his Japanese translators, and the local officials at Nagasaki were horrified. Where were the fine textiles—the striped silks from China, the delicate muslins from India, the European woolens? Ras immediately wrote a letter to the provincial Governor, Asahina Kawachi-no-kami. He tried to explain the situation in Europe, the loss of Dutch ships, and the war with England that prohibited their access to factories in India. The sea route from Holland was cut off, he wrote. He tried to pass off the American ship as a messenger, sent to bring the shogun information about the situation of the VOC abroad. Ras ended his letter by asking the Governor to put the best face on this information when presenting it to the shogun's court. As a postscript, Ras said that he would ask Captain Devereux if any of the private trade goods might make an acceptable gift for the shogun.

Over the next few days, in oppressively hot and humid weather, Samuel Hill settled into the house of the VOC carpenter, one of the few buildings still standing on Deshima. The ship continued to be unloaded, bag by bag, and box by box from the hold of the ship to the deck, from the deck over the side into the smaller Japanese boats, and then boat by boat to the watergate on Deshima: thirty thousand pounds of cloves, five thousand pounds of pepper, twenty thousand pounds of tin, two thousand pounds of ivory elephant tusks, and five thousand pounds of soft aromatic sappan wood.

A week into the process Ras was pulled aside by his interpreters. The unloading must stop. The governor was "greatly displeased and embarrassed about the fact that no gifts had been carried here," Ras wrote in his journal. Until they could solve the problem of the shogun's present, no further commercial activity was allowed. The Dutch were ordered to produce all of the potential gifts that were available among the property and private ventures of the crew for examination by the governor. Doeff and Ras went aboard the *Franklin* to beg or demand compliance and, in the presence of the officers, crew, and several Japanese officials, read and posted the rules of behavior for the Americans during their stay in Japan.

The best fabric available in the cargo were fifty-five pieces of "armozeen," a thin satin used by the Japanese as a lining for kimonos. Among the personal items on the ship, James Devereux had four pocket watches, which might serve as gifts for the shogun. These items were packed up, along with fifteen elephant tusks, and sent to the governor for his inspection.

The unloading of the ship commenced again, bag after bag of sugar, cloves, and pepper. Occasional thunderstorms hampered the process, but for a few weeks the crew of the ship, the Dutch from the Deshima compound, and Japanese and Indonesian servants, continued to transfer the contents of the *Franklin* to the warehouses onshore in the sweltering heat and humidity.

At the bottom of the hold were the elephant tusks, logs of sappan wood, and sheets of tin, on which the more fragile sugar and spices sat to keep dry. When they were unloaded, Captain Devereux asked for permission to haul his ship onto the shore adjacent to Deshima and careen it to scrape the barnacles off the hull that had accumulated during his voyage from Boston. Captain William Stewart of the *Eliza* was looking to make repairs to his ship as well, and asked permission to fell some trees to replace his masts. Both requests were granted, and for several weeks, the area around Deshima rang with the sounds of a shipyard as the Americans repaired their vessels.

After the initial thunderstorms that had greeted them soon after their arrival, the Americans found Nagasaki unbearably hot and dry. On August 10, Ras wrote in his journal that the "old Japanese are claiming that they have never experienced such a long period of heat and drought. It is the cause of many illnesses and deaths in Nagasaki."

Doeff and Ras were working well together, considering how to deploy the limited cargo available, especially to fulfill the obligatory gift-giving that would allow them to open trade negotiations with Japanese merchants. The armozeens had been rejected by the governor as too shoddy to serve as a gift for the shogun, and were now being recycled into the

Figure 10, Dutch Men with Japanese women and a Javanese servant observing a ship at Deshima, by Kawahara Keiga

Figure 11, The kitchen at Deshima in the early nineteenth century, by Kawahara Keiga

Figure 12, Dutch merchants sharing a meal at Deshima, by Kawahara Keiga

Figure 13, A game of billiards, by Kawahara Keiga

general stock. They did have some other fabric, especially chintzes, and these would serve as both gifts and stock.

By the middle óf August, the *Franklin* was back at her anchorage and the first export cargoes were being assembled on shore. The principal item sought by the Dutch in Japan was copper, smelted into flattened rods and packed into chests. On August 13, the first 250 chests of copper were weighed on shore and shipped out to the *Franklin*. The only break in loading the ship came a few days into the operation, when the Dutch and Americans paused to observe as the Japanese celebrated one of their principal holidays, O-bon, the anniversary of Buddha's enlightenment. Ras captured the essence of the commemoration when he translated it into Dutch as "Lampjesfeest," or the "lamp festival."

When the *Franklin* had been in Nagasaki for a month, the time came to display the cargo brought from Batavia and to invite Japanese merchants to examine and bid on it. The goods were displayed in a large courtyard at Deshima where, in addition to the sugar, pepper, cloves, and elephant tusks, the *Franklin* proffered silk thread and cotton yarn, chintzes (Indian patterned cottons), and the satin armozeens rejected by the shogun. Negotiations on which Dutch goods the Japanese would accept and the prices they would pay for them, and which Japanese goods would be made available to the Dutch, and what the cost would be, lasted for the next three months.

Goods were accepted, purchased, and often subsequently rejected and returned. Much of the bagged sugar had turned to syrup, and it was discovered halfway through negotiations that the wrong weights had been used to measure it. The Japanese officials continuously complained about the lack of presents for the shogun, and the problems that this horrendous oversight was causing up the chain of command.

As chests of copper were being loaded on the *Franklin,* they were simultaneously being unloaded from the *Eliza* where a leak below the waterline had been discovered, requiring the removal of a significant portion of the cargo. Captain Stewart rejected tree after tree as unsuitable for mast use and, as the trees were being cut from the garden of a temple, tempers were flaring on both sides. In total, more than twenty trees were felled to replace the *Eliza's* three masts, causing no end of consternation for Leopold Ras, who was negotiating between the testy captain and the monks at the temple. The sweltering heat made it all more difficult.

In the midst of all this activity, a fire in the city of Nagasaki destroyed some forty homes, and three earthquakes rattled the compound and rocked the vessels anchored in the harbor. Torrential rains finally began to pour down at the end of August with accompanying thunderstorms. Festivals came and went as the Americans settled into the rhythm of the Japanese working schedule. Samuel Hill, by his own account, "remained on Shore several weeks entirely unoccupied except a few days while our Cargo was landing, & the Copper for our return Cargo was weighing."

Hill probably spent some of his time consorting with the courtesans. The Japanese government went to some trouble to provide their European visitors with sexual partners. When the Dutch were still at Hirado, prior to their move to Deshima in 1641, several of them had married Japanese women, but Deshima was declared by the Japanese government to be exclusively a male enclave. The only women who were allowed on the island were a particular group of *yûjo,* or prostitutes, known as "Hollanda yuki" (which literally means "Go to Holland" or "Go to the Dutch"). These were young women from two towns in the region, Maruyama-machi and Yoriai-machi, probably the daughters of poor farm families who could profit more from the sale of their daughters than from their labor.

Hill also had an extraordinary opportunity to leave Deshima on one occasion and go into Nagasaki City. Two important officials from the shogun's court arrived during the second week of October, and Doeff, Ras, and Captain Devereux spent four days in the city to meet with them. Samuel Hill was invited to accompany them, giving him an unparalleled opportunity to observe Japanese life outside the controlled compound of Deshima though, unfortunately, he recorded no details.

As the time for the required departure approached, the two American captains, Devereux and Stewart, spent several days sounding around the harbor, hoping to identify the obstacle that the *Eliza* had hit the previous year. Ras and Doeff were simultaneously considering how best to finish up the business for the year and decided that they should consolidate the cargos of the two American ships. The *Franklin* was certainly contracted to the VOC for their exclusive use, but the situation of the *Eliza* was somewhat different, as the ship had never returned to Batavia to conclude the voyage of the previous year.

Ras began to be suspicious of Captain Stewart. He questioned if he had actually wrecked, or even if he was really an American. On November 12, the *Eliza* slipped away, Captain Stewart having refused to accommodate the Dutchmen in a deal that would remove any of the cargo from his ship. "May Heaven grant that this luckless ship reach Batavia safely," Ras wrote in his journal.

Between them, Ras and Doeff had also decided that the Company's managers in Batavia had to be told about the situation in Japan, and that Doeff should return on the *Franklin* to inform them. Thus it was that Hendrik Doeff and Samuel Hill again boarded the ship on November 21, having spent exactly four months on Japanese soil. In the hold of the ship were 2500 cases of copper, 50,000 pounds of camphor wood, and 1,700 empty boxes, being shipped back to Batavia to be loaded again.

Captain James Devereux and the supercargo, William Burling, each purchased a private stock of Japanese goods to bring back to Massachusetts, including lacquered tea tables, trays, and knife boxes—items made to meet Dutch tastes rather than local demands—and fans and kimonos. Before the ship left the harbor, the money, books, and firearms were returned, and there was a final period of less-controlled trade, when local merchants and craftsmen could approach the ship with handicrafts to sell to the sailors and officers. Certain items were completely forbidden in any exchange, including any image of the Emperor or his coat of arms, weapons, any representation of military men including dolls and puppets, models of Japanese watercraft, maps of the country, plans of castles or temples, and Japanese silks.

Devereux made a significant collection of souvenir items, including toys, small ceramics, and a number of woodblock prints, and it is likely that similar items were available to some of the crew before they left Nagasaki. The captain also managed to acquire a painting by the celebrated Japanese artist, Shiba Kokan, of the two American ships, *Franklin* and *Eliza,* in Nagasaki harbor.

The last person to board the ship was Leendert Geenemans, an assistant clerk of the VOC, who was being exiled from Japan for his violent abuse of the Japanese servants who worked at Deshima. It cannot have been a pleasant voyage. In addition to the ill-tempered Geenemans, Hill would later describe the *Franklin's* mate, James Gilchrist, as "guilty of some of the most barbarous & oppressive conduct to the officers & seamen Generally, during this Voyage" that he had ever witnessed. Though Hill noted that "it pleased the Almighty that I should escape through the Voyage without Suffering from his Brutality," the tone on board the vessel must have been bristling with hostility.

Leopold Ras watched the ship depart from Nagasaki harbor not knowing when he would hear again from his comrades in Batavia. His country at home was occupied by foreigners and his Company in Indonesia was largely cut off from supplies. Japan was the last outpost of the Dutch Empire and he must have felt very isolated as the Watergate closed. "Herewith I close this diary and heartily hope for a speedy peace," he wrote on the last page of his journal. He ended with a prayer "that the *Franklin* may travel to the capital of the Indies without encountering any disasters. ... May God grant her a safe passage."

The *Franklin* stayed in Batavia for three months, discharging the VOC's cargo and loading the coffee and spices bound for Boston. Sam Hill and Hendrik Doeff parted ways for the last time, Hill to return home in May 1800, and Doeff to return to Japan on the *Massachusetts,* the next American ship in the chain of VOC charters.

Hendrik Doeff's tenure at Deshima would prove to be the longest of any employee of the VOC, stretching over a period of eighteen years. He returned to Nagasaki with a new Opperhoofd, and gradually worked his way up to the position himself, taking charge of the Japanese operation in 1803. Though men usually served in the office for only a year or two, the Napoleonic Wars back in Europe devastated the VOC, and Doeff ended up commanding the outpost in Japan until 1817. During much of that period, he and his men were completely cut off from outside news, as no ships arrived to relieve them. The shogun continued to support the Dutch trading monopoly nonetheless, joining the small force at Deshima in beating off attempts by the British, Russians, and even the wily Captain Stewart, to establish new trading ventures in Japan.

Japanese copper was still an extremely valuable commodity in Indonesia, and when a neutral ship could be found to make the transit between Batavia and Japan, the Dutch were eager to take advantage of it. Fabric continued to be the most valuable cargo coming into Japan. When Doeff wrote about his experience many years later he reflected that it had been "extremely difficult to get cargos that were desirable to the Japanese."

> When I was Opperhoofd in Deshima... we had to create a demand for products.... Copper was needed in Java and could not be brought from Europe. Certain textiles, no longer desirable in Europe, were still popular in Japan, where tastes in fashion did not change as quickly. If I wanted to get a good cargo of copper, however, I had to sell the textiles cheaply.

Life within the walls of Deshima was not entirely a hard lot for Hendrik Doeff. He compiled the first dictionary from Japanese to Dutch, and he had a long-term relationship with a Japanese woman named Uriyuno. The couple had two children, a daughter who died in infancy, and a son, Jokichi, born in the winter of 1808, upon whom Doeff doted. Japanese regulations allowed the children of Dutch fathers at Deshima to visit the compound with their mothers until the children were six-years-old, at which point they were no longer allowed on the island. Doeff was able to extend this by a year, but after Jokichi was seven, their regular visits ended in November 1815.

Doeff stayed in Nagasaki for another two years. When he left in 1817 he had been there for eighteen years, almost half his life. He had held the fort for the Dutch through war and peace, on many occasions raising the Dutch flag over the small compound at Deshima when it was raised nowhere else in the world.

He asked for permission to bring his son Jokichi back to Holland with him, but was refused. He wrote to the officials at Nagasaki that he was worried about his son. It was not easy for a half-breed in Japanese society. He left a stockpile of sugar to pay for Jokichi's education, and asked the Governor at Nagasaki to arrange for him to enter into the service of the government when he came of age. To ease his way, Doeff and Uriyuno crafted a Japanese family name for Jokichi, taking the alternative sounds for the Kanji characters that spelled out Doeff's name in Japanese, "Dou" and "fu," to be read instead as "Michi" and "tomi."

Hendrik Doeff's plea found a sympathetic recipient in Governor Toyama Saemon. "I don't have any children in my own country," Doeff had written, "Jokichi is my only son." The Governor agreed to supervise the boy's education and employment and was true to his word. Michitomi Jokichi was nine years old when his father sailed away from Japan for the last time. When he reached the age of fifteen he was given the post of a junior officer with a salary paid from the receipts of Doeff's sugar.

In 1825 Doeff wrote to Nagasaki asking for news of his son. His letter was received by three of the translators he had known during his long years at Deshima. They did not have the heart to respond with the news that Jokichi had died that year at the age of seventeen. They arranged for him to be buried at the Choshoji Temple in Nagasaki, and had a stone carved to mark the site. On one side it bears the initials "HD" in script; on the other side is the mark of the family of his mother, Uriyuno.

When Doeff had been home in Holland almost twenty-five years, long settled with a new family and having gained a measure of fame for his service in Japan, he wrote a memoir of his experiences called *Herinneringen uit Japan* ("Memories of Japan"). Though he mentions the *Franklin* and other American ships, there is no mention of Samuel Hill, the American who was his friend. Nor does he acknowledge his relationship with Uriyuno, their dead daughter, or the son he loved so dearly.

***

The *Franklin* arrived back in Boston in May 1800, where the Indonesian coffee and spices were unloaded, along with the Japanese goods brought back as the private property of Devereux and Burling. Devereux proceeded to his home in nearby Salem, where he was a member of an organization of local captains who had formed themselves the year before into the "East India Marine Society." They were principally interested in the exchange of navigational information, and one of their members, Nathaniel Bowditch (who would gain fame as the author of the *New American Practical Navigator*), created a logbook form for members to fill out. Devereux's log of the *Franklin* was the first one entered into the collection.

Along with navigational information, the Society was interested in collecting curiosities for their museum. Bowditch had spelled out instructions for collecting in the logbook template, including "articles of the dress and ornaments of any nation." Devereux donated things he had brought back from Japan, including a kimono and several woodblock prints depicting Japanese women engaged in various daily and traditional activities. These were the first images of Japanese people ever seen in the United States.

Devereux also invited family and friends to his house to see the collection he had made. On June 23, 1800, Reverend William Bentley of Salem wrote that he had been to Captain Devereux's house and "received such things as he had lately brought from Japan."

He is the first person who has made a voyage thither from Salem. He exhibited such things as engaged his attention. The stuffed gowns, which on both sides silk, are filled with a very fine cotton, were luxuries. The Stone Tables, Tea Tables, Servers, Knife Cases, Small Cabinets, had no other recommendation than the excellent Lacquer gave them. Some were black & the best, others of a shining snuff colour. One Tea Board measured in its greatest length 3 feet 10 inches.

Bentley was especially impressed with the toy animals, several of which Devereux would later donate to the museum of the East India Marine Society.

The imitation of animals for toys were as good as hair could make them but have their best effect by candle light. The birds have their tails so balanced as to move easily, they are made from hair and not with feathers. The monkeys, dogs, mice, etc. were capable of answering their intent wonderfully.

It was the first glimpse for Americans into a world that had been made even more exotic by the isolation of the Japanese. Samuel Hill left the *Franklin* in Boston to drift onto another ship a month later. For him, the exotic had become the commonplace, and he never recognized the extraordinary nature of this particular voyage.

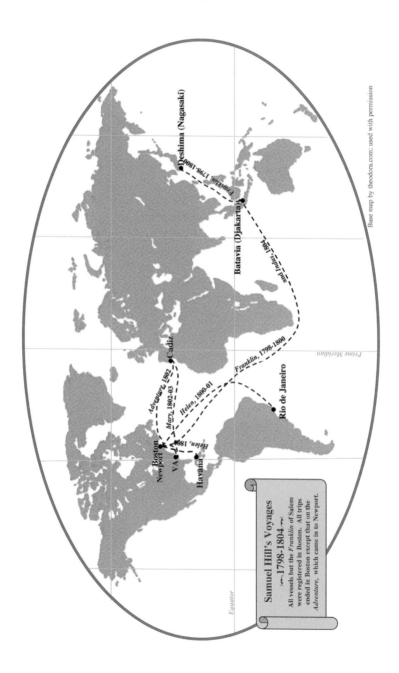

Base map by theodora.com; used with permission

Deshima (Nagasaki)

Franklin, 1798-1800

Batavia (Djakarta)

and Indus, 1804

Prime Meridian

Cadiz

Franklin, 1798-1800

Adventure, 1802

Mary, 1802-03

Helen, 1800-01

Rio de Janeiro

Boston

Newport

VA

Helen, 1804

Havana

Equator

Samuel Hill's Voyages
~1798-1804~

All vessels but the *Franklin* of Salem
were registered in Boston. All trips
ended in Boston except that on the
Adventure, which came in to Newport.

Chapter IV

❦

Helen, Adventure, Mary, Indus, 1800-1809:

Acquiring the Acceptable Accouterments of Adulthood

Sam Hill gets a wife, a house, and a child, and makes six more voyages.

When the *Franklin* returned from Japan in the spring of 1800 Samuel Hill decided it was time to marry. Though he stayed in Boston less than a month before returning to sea, it was long enough to meet Elizabeth Bray, a woman from Cape Cod. He sailed for Havana soon after they were introduced, but he seems to have decided to marry her either before or during the voyage, and may even have thought himself in love, because he set to work aboard the brig *Helen* with a seriousness and enthusiasm that he had previously lacked.

There is no doubt that Sam Hill had great potential as an officer. He was intelligent and wrote well, and he had a wealth of deck experience over several oceans. His calculations may have left something to be desired in his celestial navigation, but his coastal piloting skills were proven. The captain of the *Helen,* Andrew Harraden of

Salem, Massachusetts, was the first to notice. Hill worked hard on the voyage and when the mate died of yellow fever six weeks into the cruise, Hill was appointed by Harraden to fill his position. He finally had an officer's berth, and an arrangement was made for him to continue in it into the next voyage. It was the key to his being able to marry. When he returned to Boston in the late summer Samuel Hill proposed, was accepted, and married within a few weeks. He was twenty-three years old.

Elizabeth and her new husband moved into rooms on North Bennett Street in Boston's North End, a crowded waterfront neighborhood with a population of transient mariners in boardinghouses, longshoremen, small business that supported the maritime trades, and newly arrived immigrants. It was a part of the city where there were men and women of many races and tongues. For Elizabeth Bray Hill, who had been raised in the rural seaport of Yarmouth, on Cape Cod, it must have been somewhat unsettling to move into a multi-ethnic urban neighborhood and have her husband leave abruptly after only a month or so of marriage. But she was now settled into a home with a small but adequate income from the owners of the ship. If Sam continued up the chain of command, she would always have an income in his absence, and around her were other young women in the same position, with whom she could form a community.

It is unlikely that this was a love match. The newlyweds were all but strangers to one another, and they were about to settle into a routine that brought him home for relatively short visits in between long months and years at sea. Elizabeth certainly knew what was in store. Her new husband made no pretence that he intended to leave his seafaring career. On the contrary, he was committing himself to it with greater vigor.

For her, marriage to Samuel Hill provided a social station as a wife rather than as a spinster, and a more-or-less steady income, depending on his continued ability to get shipboard positions, which seemed good at the time. For him, marriage provided roots in Boston where he intended to build a reputation and eventually invest in property, someone to manage the property in his absence, and a reliable sexual partner when he was home.

Elizabeth receives only three mentions in Hill's autobiography, and never by name. The courtship and marriage are described in two sentences framing his voyages on the *Helen*. "It was during the Interval I remained in Boston after this Voyage that I became acquainted with the woman who is now my Wife," he wrote, describing his return on the *Franklin*. "It was shortly after my return from Havana with Brig *Helen*, I married my present wife," he adds later, almost as if she is the first in an intended chain of wives. If he had fancied himself in love, it did not last long.

In October, the *Helen* departed for the east coast of South America. Captain Harraden, a man with years of experience and a long family legacy of seafaring, was a good mentor for his mate, who already knew piloting and ship handling, and now wanted to learn the basics of celestial navigation. "The whole force of my ambition was now directed to the acquisition of a perfect knowledge of my duty, and to establish my character as an Active & Judicious Sea Officer," Hill later wrote of this voyage.

The Same Spirit of Ambitious Pride which had Stimulated me to become Superiour in the wages & Profligacy & Vice, had also induced me to apply myself at Stated Seasons with the most unwearied Assiduity to the Study of Nautical Science, & such had been my progress that I was competent to Navigate a Ship long before I was an Officer & this was well known both to my Officers as well as my Companions in the Forecastle on Several Occasions.

The *Helen* spent several months in Brazil loading sugar and did not return to Boston until the summer of 1801. Harraden was able to recommend Hill to his owners for another voyage. "I believe I gave him Satisfaction in the discharge of my duty as an Officer," Hill concluded of his relationship with Harraden.

Having been gone almost eight months, Hill now spent less than a month with his new wife before he left again for South America. When he got back to Boston early in the new year of 1802, she was well along on her first pregnancy. For the spring and summer of that year, Hill stayed on shore. It was one of the longest periods that he and his wife ever spent as a family. A baby daughter, Elizabeth, was born in the spring and if there was a great love in Samuel Hill's life, it was this infant. She died a year later while her father was at sea, and she is the only person mentioned by name in his autobiography other than captains, ship owners, or perceived persecutors. Elizabeth is the only child he acknowledges in the document, though there were three others living at the time he wrote it, and she had been dead for almost twenty years.

The fall of 1802 saw Hill again on the deck of a ship. He was chief mate of the schooner *Adventure,* bound to Cadiz, Spain for a cargo of wine and salt. This was a fairly quick trip by Hill's standards, directly from Boston to Cadiz, a rapid discharge and loading of cargo, and then home. In addition to the cargo of wine and salt, the *Adventure* picked up three "Gentlemen Passengers" at Cadiz, who quickly settled into a comfortable routine of wine and cards in the cabin with Captain William Miller. The vessel was left mostly in the charge of First Mate Samuel Hill.

It was late October when they came up from the southeast toward the Atlantic seaboard of the United States. Hill had tried several times to take a sighting of the noon sun, but cloudy weather obscured it and consequently he had no close idea of his position. A storm was looming to the northeast, and by the speed they had been making, he judged the coast of New England was not far off. Hill asked Captain Miller for permission to haul offshore as night approached. "He refused though I urged precaution," Hill wrote, and "positively Ordered me to Continue on."

On a stormy Halloween night, the ship struck the shoals near Nantucket Island, off the coast of Massachusetts. This notoriously treacherous patch of ocean had captured many vessels prior to the *Adventure,* and would ground many more to come. For Hill, the prospect was "truly alarming."

> The loss of the Vessel appeared inevitable; the passengers were in despair, the Captain was nearly intoxicated & incapable of giving any directions. He went to Bed. In this Situation I took the Command, & after a Night & part of a day of extreme exertion & fatigue, by the Peculiar Blessing of Divine Providence I Succeeded in

extricating the Vessel from her dangerous situation & arrived Safe in Newport, Rhode Island, with only a partial loss of Cargo, & some damage to the Vessel. In this undertaking I had but five men to Assist me, & the Captain enraged & mortified on my refusing to obey his orders any longer, threatened to Shoot me, which I think he might have attempted, had I not previously secured his Pistols.

As on his earlier voyage on the *Polly* (where he had similarly reported a more senior officer riding out a severe storm in his bunk), Hill was the only one to testify to his bravery. No owner was ready to discharge Captain Miller at the conclusion of the voyage and no testimonials to Sam Hill were made by the passengers. The local newspaper, the *Newport Mercury,* did not even report the storm as a particularly ferocious one. On Tuesday, November 2, 1802, the "Custom House" column included among the list of ships recently entering the port: "Schooner *Adventure,* Miller, from Cadiz," with no other details. But Hill was able to tell his version of events to one of the ship's owners, with whom he traveled to Boston by carriage, and before the end of the road trip he had been offered his first command.

A master mariner at last, Hill spent only a few weeks with the Elizabeths, mother and daughter, before going aboard the sixty-nine-foot schooner *Mary.* It was during this voyage, as he sailed south to Virginia, and thence across the Atlantic with a cargo of flour, that his daughter Elizabeth died. His wife was alone at home in wintry Boston while Captain Hill lived for two months in the home of a Spanish family "with a view, principally, of acquiring the Language." By the time Hill returned after seven months away, he and Elizabeth must have been almost strangers again, and the pattern that would see him away far more often than at home, was becoming well established.

Another command did not offer itself right away so Hill signed again as chief mate, for a voyage to Batavia in the ship *Indus.* This was his third trip to the capitol of the Dutch East Indies. His stock of navigational know-how, his gift for languages (of which he now had fluency in at least three), and his connections with Boston's merchant shippers were setting him up to be offered command of a vessel for a voyage beyond the Atlantic Ocean. After nine months away from home, he returned to Boston in the spring of 1804 with a cargo of Indonesian coffee and pepper and entered immediately into negotiations with Theodore Lyman "to command the Brig *Lydia* on a Voyage of three Years to the Coast of North West America to be employed in the Fur Trade."

This is the voyage that would first bring Hill some measure of notoriety. Because of the existence of testimony other than his own, it is the first time we know for certain the nature of his mistakes and crimes. And it was during this voyage that he first began to consider how he might reconstruct his history by parlaying his own version of events through the popular press to his neighbors and potential employers in Boston.

It is worthwhile here to consider the man who departed Boston as captain of the *Lydia* in August 1804. At this time, Samuel Hill's life was developing into three specific strands of expectation and behavior: his life at home, his life on shipboard, and his life on shore in distant ports.

At home was his wife Elizabeth, living in their North End rooms. The tie to respectability and a position in the community that his wife represented was obviously important to Hill. He would have enough money at the end of the *Lydia's* voyage to buy a house, and he would eventually acquire other properties in Boston as well. She became pregnant for the second time between Hill's arrival on the *Indus* and his departure on the *Lydia,* but may not have been not far enough along that he knew this when he left.

The way Hill's shipboard reputation was perceived by ship owners in Boston was mixed at this time. He was now twenty-seven, and though he had spent a dozen or more years at sea, he had only had one command. The owners of the *Mary* can not have been entirely happy with the time he spent ashore at Cadiz, well distanced from the work of the ship. That he did not receive another command in what was then a booming market and was obliged to travel again as mate is telling. Theodore Lyman, the owner of the *Lydia,* hired him originally to be both master and supercargo, but had second thoughts before the ship sailed and put Isaac Hurd on board to supervise trade.

The appointment of Hurd was a blow that undermined Hill's confidence. He saw it as a threat to his authority and thought that Lyman "had been prevailed on (by Some Officers or Self Interested Persons)" to appoint Hurd. "I foresaw it would be the source of much uneasiness to me," he wrote later, but by that time he had already invested in a stock of items to trade on his own account and had developed no other prospects to make a different voyage.

Hill's shipboard relationship with Hurd was devastating, as Hurd described better than anyone. Hill's behavior throughout the voyage showed a recklessness, almost a madness, that was frightening to everyone on board. Angry and petulant, Hill ended up taking out many of his frustrations on the men under his command. He had seen brutality among the captains and mates with whom he had served and he adopted the same violent tone on his own ship.

The time that Samuel Hill spent on shore in distant ports was the feature of his life that most differentiated him from other mariners. It was one thing for him to have moved ashore in Hamburg as a seaman aboard the *Lydia* in 1797. It was quite another to have done so in Spain as captain of the *Mary* in 1803. Unlike Captain Robert Haswell's move into shore quarters at Batavia to supervise the trade of the *John Jay,* Hill does not say that he was doing any business for the *Mary* in Cadiz. On the contrary, he specifically says that he took his "residence in a Spanish Family, in a remote part of the City."

In all the places that he had been prior to his second voyage on the *Lydia,* Hill's shore visits were very likely focused on consorting with prostitutes. It was an industry that few if any girls or women entered into willingly, though sailors liked to think they had. Coerced by poverty, family circumstances, or brute force into a life in the sex business, these women were, nonetheless, available for sexual intercourse with sailors on a commercial basis that had a well-understood meaning in the both the culture of the port and the culture of the ship. Girls who lived in the towns, villages, and rural areas beyond the port districts were generally not available for casual sexual contact. Relationships that might lead to pregnancy were carefully controlled within the social and cultural context in which they lived.

Once he rounded Cape Horn on the *Lydia,* Sam Hill found that everything had changed. In the Polynesian Islands of Tahiti, the Marquesas, and Hawaii, Hill's sailor predecessors had found sexual partners on an entirely different, seemingly casual, even "innocent" basis. Hill must have been thinking about this during the six and a half months that it took to make the voyage from Boston to Hawaii, because almost immediately upon his arrival there on March 5, 1805, he invited a Hawaiian girl of about fifteen years of age to come onto the ship for sex, and then sailed away with her across the Pacific. This is the young woman described in the shipboard diaries of Isaac Hurd and William Walker, and in the court testimony of James Bennett. All three men are very specific in their claims that Hill's relationship with this young native of the island of Kauai (commonly called Atooi in mariners' records of the period), dominated his thoughts and actions on the *Lydia,* to the detriment of the ship's business and morale.

The sexuality of Polynesian women had been described since the very first encounters by British mariners. Captain James Cook, and the men who served on his ships discussed it candidly in their published narratives, and Sam Hill wrote of having read "Cook's Voyages" while still at school in Machias.

American sailors consequently arrived at the islands of Polynesia with their heads full of notions of willing *wahines.* After months on a ship, where sex was a topic to think about and talk about, few young men attempted to restrain themselves when let loose on a tropical island. The problems of "ruining" a girl by using her to satisfy sexual urges without commitment did not exist on these islands, or so foreign sailors were eager to believe. Discussion of such a serious topic was impossible anyway; the only common languages were sex and trade goods.

The perception that there were no social standards governing sexual intercourse among Polynesians was widespread among American and European sailors in the eighteenth and nineteenth centuries. Whether this was true or not has been debated by Polynesian people, anthropologists, and historians ever since. There certainly were rigorous social standards regarding other behavior for women, including taboos against riding in canoes and sharing meals with men (both of which were observed and discussed by outsiders). That sexual intercourse should not receive the same parental disapproval as riding in a canoe dumfounded American sailors, who did not make much effort to understand the difference, although they willingly took advantage of it.

Anthropologist Marshall Sahlins argues that the Hawaiians mistook Captain Cook for their God Lono, because his appearance coincidently coincided with the most important elements of the myth cycle. By extension, if the visiting British sailors were Gods, then children fathered by them would inherit powerful *mana,* and Hawaiian women were consequently eager, even urged, to have intercourse with foreigners. Even if this supposition were true, however, the Hawaiians would certainly have begun to have serious doubts about the celestial nature of British and American sailors after a dozen or so ships had come into the islands, and yet the frequency of sexual relations did not diminish.

Historian Greg Dening says that for the Marquesans, sexual behavior was defined by a cultural code that outsiders simply didn't recognize. Most sailors did recognize differences in rank among Polynesians, however, and knew that higher ranking women were not available to them. In the Marquesas, the most readily available girls lived outside of the taboo culture, either temporarily, because they were going through a period of socialization that included sexual games and experimentation, or permanently, by virtue of their lack of rank, in which case a relationship with a foreigner might increase their status. In addition to being available, these women were also extraordinarily attractive to the eyes of European and American men. Ebenezer Dorr, who made a voyage to the Northwest Coast aboard the Boston brigantine *Hope,* wrote about a stop that his ship made in the Marquesas Islands in 1791 as they sailed north in the Pacific.

> The girls were permitted on board without any hesitation. They were in general small and young, quite

naked and without exception the most beautiful people I ever saw. Their shapes and features exquisite beyond description.... Their complection [sic] varied some of a Copper and others of as fine complection as any of ourselves. Their hair was of various colours long and fine wearing it flowing in its natural curls. ... On the whole their beauty and gentleness with the rest of their charms were such that but few could but admire them and none resist the impulse of the moment. They do not appear to have any idea of shame or criminality in their intercors with any and in that respect it seems to be nothing more thought of then mear cavilety [sic civility] to one another.

Dorr's opinion a few weeks later in the more northerly Hawaiian Islands was not so positive. "The women of these Islands," he wrote, "are not held in any great estimation if from what may be seen and heard be true. They do not scruple to give up their wives and daughters to any who may have a desire to gratify their inclinations." The crucial difference for Dorr was his perception that the Marquesan girls came to the sailors willingly, while the Hawaiian girls were persuaded, even prostituted, by their male relations. The latter case was thought to be a change from the Paradisical pre-contact period of all Polynesians, a devolution of culture as a result of encounters with foreigners, and though it made the sex more unsavory, it did not by any means diminish interest in participating.

Captain David Porter, who made a long cruise in the Pacific during the War of 1812 (and who would come to have an influence on Sam Hill's later career), defended the licentious behavior of his men during their passage through Polynesia. He wrote that critics of his actions, and of his descriptions of them in his published journal, made a mistake when they judged him by the moral standards of Anglo-American society, even though that is the society from which most of his men came. While he acknowledged that the commonly held social norms of right and wrong should govern the behavior of sailors when they were at home, it was precedent rather than precepts that established the moral code at sea.

"Man must have some standard of morality," he acknowledged, but "when placed in new and untried situations, beyond the sphere of the ordinary restraints of society, this standard is principally to be found in the conduct of those who have been placed in similar circumstances, and left behind them a character for justice and humanity." In other words, Captain Cook and his crews superseded the culture at large in determining acceptable behavior for men onboard ships in the Pacific Ocean. Whatever they did on their voyages would henceforth be considered the shipboard standard, and Porter felt that he had lived up to that standard.

Porter went on to give a number of quotations from British voyage narratives of sexual behavior in the South Pacific, specifically calling to his readers' attention, "the uniform mode in which all of these navigators have described the intercourse alluded to; the open and free, not to say licentious, terms they have used; and the omission on almost all occasions, to make any apology, either for themselves or the natives." These were probably the very passages most often turned to by those lusty lads who looked forward to the time when they might be the lucky recipient of an exotic beauty's erotic affection.

George Forster, on Cook's second voyage, had written with some enthusiasm on the subject.

> The simplicity of a dress which exposed to view a well-proportioned bosom, and delicate arms, might also contribute to fan their amorous fire; and the view of several of these nymphs swimming nimbly round the ship, such as nature had formed them, was perhaps more than sufficient to subvert the little reason which a mariner might have left to govern his passions.

Cook wrote about this at close to the same time, but did not see it with the same entirely innocent perspective.

> The ladies were very agreeable to our crews, who had no opportunity of indulging an intercourse with any other women since we left England; and they soon found out that chastity was not a distinguishing part of their character. Their consent was easily purchased—a spike

nail, or an old shirt, was a sufficient bribe. The lady was then left to make her man happy, and to exact from him another present for herself. We must observe, to the credit of some of these women, and the discredit of the men, that several of the former submitted to prostitution with much *seeming* reluctance; and they were sometimes even *terrified* into a compliance by the authority, and even menaces of the men.

The notion that the amorous favors of Polynesian girls was more prostitution than free love comes up again and again in the passages that sailors found so interesting. To the shame of all of the men involved, some of these sexual encounters were clearly rape, as Cook inadvertently documents in the previous description. The fact that there was a native man presumed to be the "father or brother" pimping the girl into prostitution relieved the foreigner of feeling responsible for his actions, and the women were treated like trade commodities. Porter quoted the following from the journal of Captain Samuel Wallis, which was published in the same volume as Cook's first voyage.

> The women, as we have before observed, do not consider chastity as a virtue; for they not only readily and openly trafficked with our people for personal favours, but were brought down by their fathers and brothers, for purposes of prostitution. They were, however, conscious of the value of beauty; and the size of the nail that was demanded for the enjoyment of the lady, was always in proportion to her charms."

When Tahitian women and their morals were compared by Cook to women back home, the women he chose in one instance were prostitutes, and that is the passage that Porter chose to quote in the second edition of his journal, adding italics for emphasis. "The *ladies* of pleasure in London," he wrote, "have not half the winning ways that are practised by the Otaheitean misses, to allure their gallants. With the seeming innocency of doves, they mingle the wiliness of the serpents."

The supposed willingness of Tahitian women to enter freely into a sexual relationship, especially when accompanied by their open and unembarrassed nakedness, led the British sailors first to distraction, and then to licentiousness. Among Cook's men, several were "punished severely for indecency in surpassing even the natives, by their shameless manner of indulging their passions." Cook began to notice another potential problem as well, one that would develop into a crisis during the next Tahitian visit of his navigator, William Bligh.

The longer a ship stayed, the more likely it was that a casual liaison would become a relationship. During the time that Cook's ship *Endeavor* was at Tahiti, there was "hardly a sailor who had not made a very near connexion with one or other of the female inhabitants." The officers were as likely as the men, though the inherent snobbishness of the English officer class led them to seek out women of higher rank "who were no less amorous and artful, though more reserved than those of the inferior orders." As the English sailors began to see individual women as their exclusive partners, the very freedom of sexual expression that had so beguiled them at first began to be perceived with jealousy, and two of the *Endeavor's* hands "went on shore, to terminate an affair of honour by the decision of their pistols."

As a Christian and as the captain of his ship, which carried with it a certain expectation of moral leadership, David Porter was forced to confront some of the conflict between his personal and cultural moral code and the way he and his men behaved among the Tahitians and Marquesans. If there was a crime at the base of this reckless sexual behavior, he wrote, "the offence was ours, not theirs; they acted in compliance with the customs of their ancestors; we departed from those principles of virtue and morality, which are so highly esteemed in civilization."

Porter allowed that for American sailors there was, at least, some measure of regret and responsibility in the *memory* of their actions in Polynesia, though neither the expectation of exotic lovers, nor the realization of those expectations, seems to have been much hampered by those same thoughts.

For Samuel Hill, his sexual encounter with the young woman from Atooi might, at first, have been justified in his own mind by the code that Porter used: if Captain Cook had not vigorously condemned such behavior among *his* men, then why should he not engage in similar actions? But when Hill sailed away from that woman's home with her on board, he departed from even the questionable standard that Porter used. What followed over the next year and a half included rape and violent physical abuse.

Hill's other crimes were mounting as well. He had, during the *Lydia's* voyage kidnapped Northwest Coast Indian men and held them as hostages, he stole furs, he cheated his Indian trading partners by watering down molasses and adding rope ends to gunpowder. He fired his cannons into villages without investigating the consequences, and he maligned and cheated his own countrymen, including the owner of the *Lydia*.

The ability to commit ever greater crimes increased with his level of command and with his distance from home, although the cruelty and recklessness that he displayed on the *Lydia* argues that he was not a novice at either. The fact that we have descriptions of his behavior from three other men casts the candor of his autobiography into question. By August 1806, when the *Lydia* departed the Northwest Coast for Canton, there is no doubt that Samuel Hill was a beast.

When he considered his behavior later, he would call this a "Voyage of much perplexity," but he did not take responsibility for his actions. In his autobiography he wrote that he had suffered "extreme Mortification" on this trip and blamed the "barbarous conduct & misrepresentations" of other Boston traders. When he arrived in Canton in November he suffered a complete collapse, brought on, he remembered, by those professional assaults, which had "gradually preyed upon [his] Spirits until no longer able to bear up against it."

I was Obliged to submit to its Influence & place myself under the care of a Physician soon after my arrival in Canton, but his prescriptions produced no favorable effect. He prescribed according to the rules of his art, but the origin of my disease was in the mind; and had I possessed a more intimate knowledge of the conduct of men when placed in Situations remote from Laws & the Observation of Society, especially when Influenced by

Self-Interested Motives I should have considered their conduct with that disregard which it merited. But I suffered myself to be alarmed for my Reputation at home, & as My Owner had no previous knowledge of my Character... my anxiety was extreme.

It is possible to read this passage in two ways. In his autobiography, Hill means his reader to understand that it is *other* captains from Boston who are being described when he talks of the "conduct of men when placed in Situations remote from Laws & the Observation of Society," but it may have been a way of justifying his own actions. The paralysis of "mental disease" which kept him from doing any of the ship's business during the whole of the period that he remained in Canton, may also have been influenced by guilt or regret.

He came back to the subject again, almost as if his pen hovered above the paper, ready to confess, but he was unable to acknowledge fully what he had done.

Thus ended a Voyage of much trouble & anxiety of mind, but during which I had acquired a very considerable knowledge of mankind in Various States & Situations, in Savage & in Civilized life, of men educated in Civilized Society, but placed beyond the reach of its Influence on their manner, & free from that restraint which Polite Law imposes on men. ... Teach me O Merciful Father to remember the miseries I have suffered from Others that I may Sympathise with the afflicted, & Compassionate & relieve the distresses of others.

At home waited the unsuspecting Elizabeth, and Frederick Stanhope Hill, the two-year-old son who did not meet his father until the *Lydia* returned to Boston in May 1807. Samuel Hill now had to leave the whole experience of the Pacific Ocean behind him. The violence, the erotic passion, the paranoia, the insensibility, all had to be hidden from his wife and child.

He set about repairing his reputation by publishing the article about his rescue of Jewitt and Thompson in the *Columbian Centinel*. He had made enough money from the voyage to purchase a house for Elizabeth and Freddie on

Myrtle Street in Boston, and Elizabeth quickly became pregnant again.

Hill clearly intended to take another ship to the Northwest Coast as soon as an offer might be made to him, and there were merchants willing to make such an offer. Neither his randy behavior nor his violent temper had prevented the voyage from making a profit for the owner. But the war between the British and Napoleon's France was sweeping across the Atlantic to dash his hopes. As he settled in to get to know his son, President Thomas Jefferson and the U.S. Congress were trying to figure out a way not to be drawn into the European war. Their conclusion was that Americans should halt all international trade and prohibit the importation of any foreign goods. During the resulting period of the Non-Intercourse Acts and the Embargo, Sam Hill was forced to stay at home.

***

Jefferson's decision to ban all foreign trade had not been reached without a great deal of provocation from outside the borders of the United States. Since the end of the American Revolution in 1784, the British had only nominally recognized the independence of American shipping. Combined with the depredations made by the French Navy on the neutrality of U.S.-flagged vessels at sea, American merchants had lost a significant number of ships and seamen to capture and impressment.

As the Napoleonic War heated up in Europe, both England and France found themselves desperate for sailors, and both turned to the crews of American vessels as a source of manpower, frequently stopping ships on the high seas and taking men by force. Any man who lacked a Seaman's Passport to prove his American citizenship was susceptible to forced conscription, especially by the British. Before the start of the war, some 10,000 men served aboard ships of the Royal Navy; by 1812 that number had rocketed to 140,000. The duty was miserable enough to make some 40,000 desert between 1793 and 1801. This, combined with constant casualties from persistent war, made the Admiralty even more desperate for men.

In addition to taking American sailors, both Great Britain and France passed laws to restrict free trade that were devastating to American commerce. The British passed an "order in council" in November 1807, which basically forbade anyone in the world from trading with Napoleon or his allies unless they paid a tribute to Great Britain. In response, Napoleon organized a "Continental System," which he announced a month later in Milan. Any vessel coming into a French or French-held port, which had previously been in any British port, would be seized.

Thomas Jefferson's response was that neutral trade must be defended, even if the cost of that defense was, for a time, the destruction of America's neutral foreign trade. Experiments in the "non-importation" of British goods had been tried over the previous year without any seeming impact on the British. Consequently, in December 1807, Jefferson urged Congress to pass the Embargo Act, prohibiting all foreign trade. In preparation for a potential war, American seamen were ordered to return home from foreign voyages to be prepared to protect free trade rather than practice it.

The Embargo Act was passed against the strong objections of the merchants of New England and New York, members of the Federalist Party. In favor were Thomas Jefferson's Republicans, who took advantage of the situation to try a bold experiment in self-sufficiency. It was a debate that went to the fundamental nature of how America would be defined as an independent nation. For the Federalists, a strong and immediate entry onto the world stage at the end of the Revolution was logically built on foreign trade.

During the Colonial Period, access to world products and markets had been strictly controlled by the British. Navigation laws prohibited colonial ships from trading outside the network of ports that flew the British flag—in the British Isles, the American and West Indian Colonies, and a few stations on the coast of Africa. Monopolies held by the British East India Company and British South Sea Company prohibited colonial trade beyond either Cape Horn or the Cape of Good Hope, where the most valuable commodities were to be had, and high taxes robbed merchants in Boston and New York of much of their profits.

Within these restrictions Boston merchants, especially, had built a network of legal and illegal trade around the Atlantic. With ships, navigational know-how, and a competitive entrepreneurial spirit, they prepared themselves for the moment when independence would allow them to burst beyond the Capes and trade everywhere around the globe. The period following the end of the war, commonly called the Federalist Period, rapidly saw New England vessels in every ocean and touching every continent.

The majority of the foreign shipping of the fledgling United States was concentrated in the hands of the Federalists. In the South, economic and political power was based on agriculture rather than trade. A farmer himself, Thomas Jefferson led a Republican party based on the wealth of agriculture. For them, the exposure to constant attack from the British and French was not supportable. American agriculture could make the nation self-sufficient. The debate over whether it was best to be isolated, insulated, and able to satisfy the needs of the nation without a dependence on foreign products (and the consequent foreign influence that came with them), or to attempt to send ships into the global marketplace before a fully-developed Navy could back them up, influenced the decision of a divided Congress to institute the Embargo in 1807.

For Boston shippers it was devastating. Ships near to being ready to depart were rushed to sea. If word could be got to ships already at sea in time, they were ordered not to return until the Embargo was lifted. Voyages to the Northwest Coast, Canton, and elsewhere were extended, often to extraordinary lengths. A number of the vessels already in the Pacific began to make patterns of cruises from Alaska to California, back to Alaska, then to Hawaii and Canton. Then, instead of returning to Boston they would return to the Northwest Coast and repeat the cycle. The Boston ship *Mercury,* which left home in January 1806, prolonged and prolonged and prolonged its voyage until it was captured by the Spanish on the coast of California in 1813, having been eight years at sea. (Captain George Washington Eayrs had, like Samuel Hill, brought a native woman onto the ship as his lover. When the ship was captured near Santa Barbara, the Spanish officials reported that he had a "family" on board, including a month-old daughter, and a young boy from the Columbia River, purchased there as a slave some five years earlier.)

In January 1809, Congress debated legislation to make enforcement of the Embargo increasingly rigorous. New England merchants led an attack on the legislation and ultimately defeated it. On March 1, 1809, three days before Thomas Jefferson left office, the Embargo ended. Another non-intercourse act was passed in its place, prohibiting American trade with Great Britain and France, but allowing for a resumption of trade to all other regions, including the Pacific Ocean.

***

Samuel Hill had now been required by circumstance to stay home for two years. Along the Boston waterfront, ships had been deteriorating, prohibited from returning if they went abroad. The national debate about global trade versus isolation was echoed in local discussions of mercantilism versus agrarianism and in individual conflicts between a life at sea and a life on shore. Hill clearly desired a life at sea. He had heard the siren song of the Pacific, and he had power on the quarterdeck that could not be replicated in town.

In a seaport flooded with out-of-work mariners, there had been no employment for Hill. When he became short of money he decided to sue Theodore Lyman for three thousand dollars, the amount of his commission from the *Lydia* voyage that he reckoned had gone to Isaac Hurd. As Hill had first been signed to be both master and supercargo of the *Lydia,* and was then replaced as supercargo by Hurd, he had a good case. The suit lasted several months and went through two courts. Hill was eventually awarded the sum he demanded from Lyman.

In order to get the money, Hill subjected his shipboard performance to scrutiny in open court. Depositions were read from Hurd and from the first mate, James Bennett. The fact that Hill had kept a Hawaiian lover on board for eighteen months was made public, though his other deficiencies as a captain were softened into acceptability by language that presupposed a certain amount of brutality as part of the job, and attributed his other bizarre behavior to illness.

For Elizabeth Hill, the public revelation of her husband's sexual escapades must have been humiliating. She had just accepted him back after almost three years absence, moved with him to a new home, and given birth to a second son, Charles. For wives at home, rumination on a husband's behavior at sea could easily lead to misery. The culture was permeated with imagery of sexual encounters between Anglo-American sailors and native women in distant ports-of-call, but it was very unusual for such specific evidence to be forced upon a wife's attention. There was no opportunity to hide or disguise what his actions had been.

Each of the Hills, husband and wife, was powerless to do anything about the situation through the whole of 1808. They waited through the Embargo hoping that Hill would be offered another job when it ended and, fortunately for them both, he was. When the Embargo was lifted on March 1, 1809, ships began to trickle, then to flood, out of Boston harbor and Samuel Hill was in command of one of them. It was the brig *Otter,* bound for the Northwest Coast and Canton. The principal owner was Thomas Amory, who had also owned Jewitt's ship *Boston.* Thus was Samuel Hill rewarded for the rescue of the captives and all his other sins of the voyage of the *Lydia* forgiven.

Chapter V

⌀

Otter, 1809-1812:
"Evil, Ill-minded, Mischief-making Persons"

Considering the lamentable fate of Robert Kemp, et al.

Given that Samuel Hill behaved erratically and violently as master of the *Lydia* on her voyage of 1804-1807, it might seem strange that two years after the end of that adventure he was once again on the quarterdeck of a Boston brig, bound for the Northwest Coast and Canton. That Samuel Hill was the *Otter's* captain can be traced directly to his rescue of John Jewitt and John Thompson of the ship *Boston.* Jewitt's journal of his captivity at Nootka Sound was just hitting the streets as the *Otter* voyage was being planned, and Samuel Hill, a minor hero of the story, was brought again to the attention of Thomas Amory, who was a principle owner of the *Boston* and who owned the *Otter* in partnership with Oliver Keating.

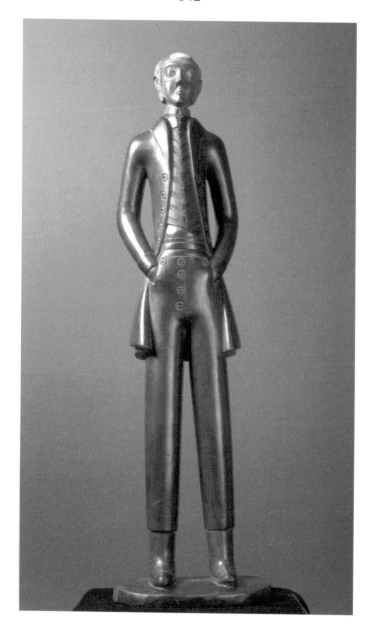

Figure 14, The Haida Indians of the Queen Charlotte Islands (Haida Gwaii), documented American mariners active in the sea otter pelt trade in a number of carvings in argillite, a stone indigenous to the islands.

Hill outlined the voyage in his autobiography, describing the by-now-familiar route around Cape Horn to the Hawaiian Islands and from there to the Northwest Coast where he traded until the middle of September 1811. He then "sailed from thence bound to Canton, having been Successful in my business Generally."

During the course of this "generally successful" voyage, Hill killed dozens of Tlingit Indians and buried five of his crew—two of them having been murdered. He had an altercation with the Russians that was reported to St. Petersburg and may have impeded the ability of Americans to trade on the coast of Alaska in the years to follow. For several decades the Chilkat people of Lynn Canal in Alaska threatened to take revenge on both British and American ships for Hill's actions aboard the *Otter.*

The voyage began well enough. At ninety feet, the *Otter* was slightly larger than the *Lydia,* and almost new. Twenty-five men and one boy were onboard when the ship left Boston at noon on April 1, 1809. Among the crew were three men who chronicled the voyage in shipboard journals: Samuel Furgerson, the carpenter; Thomas Robinson, the clerk; and second mate Robert Kemp, who "had not the least Inclination for such a long voyage" but was convinced at the last minute to sign on. He regretted the decision for every minute thereafter, until he was murdered on the *Otter's* deck on April 12, 1811. Kemp kept an anguished journal. Only a few months into the voyage he wrote:

There is Some verry Evil, Ill minded mischiefmaking persons on Bord of this Brig. Like unto Some physicians patient always Ready with open mouths to Receive a portion and [no] Sooner is it Swallowed then it is Immediately Evacuated and it has its Naturel Course throughout the Ship and it purges of and [spreads] Ill humours of the mind. It appears to me Like a person that toiled hard [to] gain the Summit of Some great mountain and when he is arrived at the Summit Some unknown Ill disposed person attracts him unperceived and the poor Labourer is overturned almost in a moment and Carreyd to the bottom where he Languishes away and dies for want of Justice & Judge.

His shipmate Thomas Robinson, the clerk, was a happier soul. He had been apprenticed as a clerk to a mercantile firm that dealt principally with the importation of English goods and was put out of business by the Embargo. Robinson landed on his feet, working as a sometime banker and scribe, and eventually obtained a short-term position with a merchant named Tuckerman, who was engaged to be married to Oliver Keating's daughter.

Sam Hill stopped by Tuckerman's shop one day and began to spin a yarn about his time on the Northwest Coast aboard the *Lydia*. Robinson was intrigued. "Capt. Hill being frequently at our counting room," Robinson wrote, "I took occasion to ask him if he thought there was any situation in a ship in which a young man could go a voyage to the coast." Hill answered that "he did not doubt but that there was," and if Robinson was interested, a clerk's position was available on the *Otter,* which was then being outfitted for a voyage. Robinson, with the blessing of Mr. Tuckerman, approached Oliver Keating about signing him on as supercargo, but was told that Samuel Hill was to be both master and supercargo. Robinson was offered the job of clerk and a short time later, "after consulting with Capt. Hill and viewing the vessel, agreed to go the voyage and do the duty of a clerk."

By insisting that he act as his own supercargo, Hill was obviously trying to avoid problems similar to those he had experienced with Isaac Hurd on the *Lydia*. Robinson, who had never been to sea, did not consult with any of the men from the *Lydia* and could not have known anything of Hill's behavior. Consequently a few days before the *Otter's* sailing, Robinson reported onboard and found his berth in the steerage section of the ship, not quite as far aft as the officers, but clearly separated from the seamen in the forecastle. Sam Furgerson, the carpenter, would have been quartered near him, and Robert Kemp was not far away.

One week into the voyage, Captain Hill tried to set a standard that he had neglected on the *Lydia*. The Sabbath would be observed on the *Otter*. There would be no work on Sundays other than that necessary to support the progress of the ship, and all hands were ordered to muster on the deck "to see that each man was shaved, washed and clean shirted." This was one of several occasions in his life when contemplation of his sins drove Samuel Hill into an obsessive show of religiosity. Nonetheless, the ship was not without sin. By week two, one of the seamen, Joseph Pierce, was "severely reprimanded by Capt. Hill" for unspecified "very improper conduct... in the gun room."

The ship made a rapid passage from the northern hemisphere, through the tropics and into the southern latitudes, moving from the cool spring of New England to the heat of the tropics to the frigid cold of the Antarctic winter in just over two months. By bad luck or bad planning, the *Otter* reached Cape Horn in the dead of the Southern Hemisphere winter. For the inexperienced Thomas Robinson, who had left Boston with notions of Polynesian adventures, this was not what he had bargained for and he was miserable. "Stiff breezes attended with thick rainy weather," he wrote on July 14.

> The winds variable, with heavy fogs and squalls of sleet which keep the decks constantly wet, of course the men are kept wet and some are daily complaining with the disorders naturally attending such exposures, as griping of the bowels, pain in the head and many biles forming on the legs, wrists, and arms.

That night one of the seamen, Tilly Hardy, fell from the rigging and was drowned. "As the brig was then going six knots under reefed top sails and a severe gale commencing it was impossible to save him," Robinson lamented. He had liked the guy, as inexperienced as himself when the voyage started, but "had already become a useful man onboard when his hard fate was determined by this unfortunate event." He was twenty-two years old and "his civil language and good conduct had procured him the good will of the officers and crew who sincerely lamented his premature loss."

As soon as the weather was calm and dry enough to permit it, Hardy's belongings were brought up on deck and auctioned among the crew. It was impossible on shipboard, and especially in the waters around Cape Horn, for the ship's company to pause and mourn the loss of their shipmate. Richard Henry Dana, Jr., who would lose a shipmate under similar circumstances in the same location thirty years later, described the paralyzing effect of public mourning. To stop and ponder would inevitably lead every sailor on the ship to the realization that it could as easily have been himself, and then it would become harder and harder to respond to every order to go aloft. Sailors joked their way through death when they were with their shipmates, but visions of Hardy's fall into the churning, icy waters must have haunted them as they stared into the darkness of bow watch. And every time his watch-mates mustered, Hardy's absence was felt.

Storms and fog prevented Captain Hill from taking any celestial observations either at noon or at night for days on end. His navigation was all by "dead reckoning"— determining the *Otter's* position by keeping track of direction, speed, and distance from the last known place and marking it punctually in the logbook. Over several weeks in stormy weather this was a tenuous predictor of location. On one day in late June, Robinson reckoned that the *Otter* had made 125 miles in the last twenty-four hours, so the ship was moving fast, but the direction traveled could only be noted hourly from the compass, and a lot was happening in the minutes in between.

When Hill finally determined that Cape Horn must be behind them, the worries of the crew did not end. They still did not know their exact position and the strong westerly winds that rushed toward the Horn from the Pacific could drive the ship in toward the South American continent. Robinson's fears of a violent encounter with "a hideous rocky Lee Shore" were not unfounded.

On Saturday, August 5, 1809, the snow, sleet, and fog finally broke. The sea was smooth; they had reached the Pacific Ocean. Hill ordered the men to bring their chests and bedding on deck, to clean and ventilate the forecastle, and to smoke out the vermin by burning gun powder on the floor of the spaces below deck. For Tom Robinson, this was a day finally to breathe easily after two months of anxiety and hardship. But Samuel Hill had unexpected plans for him.

At 8 A.M. while at breakfast Cap. Hill informed me that he had ordered the carpenter to knock up my Berth, which he had begun to do on the back side within the

Steerage, with a broad Axe and would certainly have cut my Bed Clothes all to pieces and split my chest if I had not immediately left my victuals and carried my things on deck.

Sam Furgerson was already hard at work demolishing Robinson's living space when Robinson arrived back at his bunk. Neither was given any reason for the action, they simply followed the orders of the Captain. Robinson's new quarters were in the "bread room" in the hold, which was also reconfigured by Furgerson, into a space that Robinson described as "Five Feet Seven Inches wide and Five Feet Six Inches high, situated exactly under the Break of the Quarter Deck, and dark as the lower Regions." Robinson shared this new cell with two other men, Timothy Pitman and Joseph Pierce, who had formerly been quartered in the gun room, where Pierce had committed the "very improper conduct" for which he received a reprimand in the first weeks of the voyage.

To make this miserable situation even worse, the new habitation was built into the companionway where the door to the mates' cabin was located. The first and second mates shared their own small space, and had to traipse through Robinson and company's new digs to get to it. William Hughes and Robert Kemp, the mates, had formerly used this space for storage, and continued to do so even after the three lower-ranking men moved into it. Consequently, Robinson reported, this small space contained two chests and a trunk, navigating instruments, "eight pairs of boots, four pairs of shoes, a large assortment of Books, Three hats, two large Bags for the purpose of stowing dirty clothes, three great coats, one box of Thread, sailors wet Jackets, Trowsers, Drawers, Vests, Shirts, Hose, Handkerchiefs, etc. etc. etc. and occupied by three men."

Why, in the first days of calm following a winter passage around the Horn, would Hill dedicate the efforts of so many to a task seemingly so trivial? Hawaii was still six thousand miles away. It is difficult to see why he would have orchestrated this uncomfortable shift in the accommodations except to break up a private liaison between Pierce and Pitman in their gun room domicile, or to exercise his power over the lives and comfort of his men as a reminder that he could do so at any time.

The relationship between Hill and Robinson does not seem to have suffered as a result of the shift. Robinson remained his affable self for the rest of the voyage to Hawaii. Hill made demands upon him and he cheerfully acquiesced. At one point, Hill told Robinson that he wanted his trunk "for the use of the Ship," and in exchange Robinson would get another one when they arrived in Canton. Hill showed him a sample of one model that might be available for him, and the young man agreed. It was a handsome leather-covered trunk, bound in brass with a nice oval space on the top where Robinson could picture his initials. He emptied his own trunk and delivered it to Hill, who put his books in it. Robinson then put as many of his clothes as he could fit under the mattress in his small berth, stowed those things he could find space for, and sold the rest of his clothes and possessions to the first mate. It would be more than two years before the ship reached Canton.

The rest of the voyage to Hawaii was mostly uneventful. The steward was found to be running a private store from goods he had brought with him from Boston, and Captain Hill demoted him to the forecastle. A number of Nantucket and New Bedford whaleships were seen as they passed along the coast of Chile and across the equator. The tropical weather made it possible to live largely on the deck, and the sailors spent their days making minor repairs to the ship and rigging. The armourer opened his forge and began to prepare for trade on the Northwest Coast. The carpenter got the small boat into good condition.

They arrived in the Hawaiian Islands in early October and met the ship *Hamilton* at Oahu, under the command of Lemuel Porter. The two captains had met many times before, most recently three years earlier on the Northwest Coast, when Captain Porter had just learned of the murder of his brother Oliver on the *Atahualpa*. They decided to proceed to the Northwest Coast in company and after less than two weeks in the Islands departed together on October 12, 1809. Thomas Robinson stayed behind to supervise the purchase and preparation of a cargo of sandalwood, so that the ship would not be delayed at Hawaii when they came through again enroute to Canton.

It took nineteen days to make the crossing east to the North American coast, and on the last day of October the southernmost tip of the Queen Charlotte Islands was sighted. In the early years of the trade, ships would have been leaving the coast at this time of year to spend the winter months in Hawaii, but the *Otter's* orders were to cruise along the coast throughout the winter. The Indians were already moving from their summer fishing camps to their winter quarters, in bays and inlets less exposed to the winter winds and waves of the coast.

Hill's plan was to spend the first few months in the Queen Charlotte Islands, visiting Haida villages that he knew from his earlier voyage on the *Lydia.* He approached each encounter expecting violence and ready to respond in kind. Nets to prevent Indians from boarding the *Otter* from the sides were stretched along the bulwarks, leaving only one opening at the gangway. As the principal members of a local tribe came onboard Robert Kemp and two men searched them for weapons. Half the crew manned the midsection of the ship to prevent visitors from going forward of the gangway. Hill and his first mate, William Hughes, were on the quarterdeck to manage the trade.

Hill's behavior toward the Indians is regularly described by the men under his command as condescending at best, violent at worst, and dismissive at all times. He showed no sensitivity to the social and cultural norms and expec-tations that were constantly on display around him. Even if he did not choose to behave well as a human being, it is surprising that he regularly showed very little sense as a merchant. A few hours devoted at the beginning of each exchange to the customary rites and rituals of the Indians would have brought him enormous advantages. Instead, his rude and crass behavior was constantly rewarded with animosity.

On November 18, for instance, having been in the Queen Charlotte Islands less than three weeks, Hill began to quarrel with Estakhunah, a man of very high rank in the village of Skidegate. This was one of the principal villages for trade and Estakhunah had relationships with the surrounding villages. Hill could have gained a great advantage by treating him respectfully, but Hill suspected that Estakhunah had come aboard the *Otter* armed and insisted on searching the chief in a rude, almost assaultive manner. Samuel Furgerson reports in his journal that this action "enrag'd him so that he alarmed the Indians who were all instantly in their Canoes and had their Muskets up ready to fire, but when they saw that we were all immediately in arms as well as themselves, they laid down their Muskets & paddled off with their Canoes."

The suspicious eye that Hill trained on the Indians turned toward the crew as well. In late November Robert Kemp reported that a dispute had arisen between Hill and his first mate "on account of Stories told from Some Ill minded person that he Encouraged the people to mutiny." Though the level of violence that had defined the *Lydia's* cruise on the Northwest Coast was never reached aboard the *Otter,* Hill began to demonstrate the same kind of paranoid fears.

It didn't help that trade was bad. The sea otter population had been dealt a disastrous blow by the trade of the last two decades, and what few skins were available could not be purchased with the cargo that the *Otter* was carrying. On Christmas Eve, 1809, Hill sold his washstand to one of the Haida chiefs. It was the only item on the ship that the Haida wanted with which Hill was willing to part. There was some demand for molasses, and Hill decided to extend the stock they had by diluting it with seawater.

To add to the frustrations of Hill and his company, the competition from other Boston ships had not declined along with the furs. In January, the *Otter* encountered the *Lydia,* Hill's old ship, now commanded by Thomas Brown, who had caused Hill so much anxiety on his previous cruise. Brown had left Boston a month after Hill, and had little new information from home other than that "many other Ships was Expected on the Next Season which gives us Every Reason to believe that the trade will be amazing Dull and great Scarcity of furs."

It was a bleak winter. Kemp lamented daily that he had ever come on the voyage, pouring his feelings into his diary. In the middle of February he noted that there had not been ten dry days in the last four months, and that they had collected only about sixty sea otter pelts. Tempers were easily ignited. The Indians were regularly accused of stealing. Samuel Hill was observed to be doing the same.

On one occasion, when the slave of a Haida chief was suspected of stealing a pelt, Kemp beat several of the Indian men with a rope as they left the ship because they did not leave the ship quickly enough when they were ordered off. Later they were "saucy" and the *Otter* was forced to move on. From the Queen Charlotte Islands, the ship proceeded north to trade among the islands off the coast of Alaska, but trade was no better there, despite having "run many hazards and Experienced a good Deal of hardship."

Short tempers were managed by moving men yet again within the cramped quarters on the *Otter*. Nathaniel Hall, the African-American steward, who had been moved forward in the ship seven months earlier for running his private store, was brought back to the aft cabin. His replacement, Thomas Sopp, was flogged for unspecified "misconduct."

By March 1810, everyone was truly miserable. The relationship between Hill and his mate, William Hughes, had irretrievably broken down. Kemp's homesickness and regret had reached its deepest stage. He reflected on the reckless life he had lived at home on Cape Cod, and gained maturity in his misery.

12 Months ago to day it was a bitter Snow Storm and I was at home at my own fathers house and now by the nearest Rout and best Calculation I am transported 25000 mi. from thence. When I was at home I was not Sensible of the Enjoyment that I had ought to have taken. As well as I Can Recolect the Evening was Spent By me and the Rest of my youthfull Companions at a publick house... It was a house by the Common Report of ill fame. With Shame I Rite this and with Sorrow will it be Read, but allowances must be made for Errors in youth. I was then in honey Moon and now I am in the midst of Despair but Every Man is in Duty bound as well as Honour to obey the Fluctuating and various Scenes of fortune which a man is Exposed to that travels the world. Every man had ought to have his desert whether old or young so I have no more to say on that subject.

Later that day, the ship grounded and the crew waited anxiously for the next high tide to refloat them. "We are now very unpleasantly situated," Sam Furgerson wrote:

On the one hand there is dangerous reefs of rocks that seem at once to threaten & defy us, and on the other an iron bound lee shore inhabited with merciless savages, who, if they knew our situation would be ready to seize upon us the moment the vessel should be driven on shore and revenge themselves on us for past injuries received from others.

Furgerson could not help but note that the very actions that Captain Hill was taking were inviting attack, if not for the *Otter*, then for the next ship. There were plenty of reminders all around them of violent acts of retribution for the actions of other ships. At the end of March they sailed into Milbanke Sound, where the *Atahualpa* had been attacked five years earlier. When the local chief, whom he called "Kyelte," came onboard, Kemp noted in his diary that it was he who had "So Inhumanely Murdered Captn Oliver Porter."

At this time they were sailing in company with the ship *Katherine,* also of Boston, under the command of William Blanchard. The *Otter's* boatswain had had enough of Hill by this point, and left to go aboard the *Katherine.* The next two months were spent going back and forth between the Queen Charlotte Islands and the mainland of British Columbia, often in company with either the *Katherine* or the *Hamilton.*

By 1810 it was clear that sea otters on the Northwest Coast were destined for extinction. Some American captains had begun looking for them elsewhere, and a place they were found in abundance was the coast of California. Unlike whaling and sealing, where American crews did the hunting and preparation of the prey, the sea otter pelt trade had always relied on Native hunters on the Northwest Coast. California Indians did not have the same hunting or ocean-going traditions, and so American captains began to engage Northwest Coast Indians or Aleuts and take them to California for the hunt. These hunters were transported with their native canoes or kayaks, on the decks of the American ships.

Aleuts lived within the boundaries of territory claimed by the Russians in Alaska, and consequently merchants from the Russian-American Company became partners of American captains in these ventures. The first of these voyages took place while Samuel Hill was on the Northwest Coast commanding the *Lydia.* By the time he returned on the *Otter,* they had become routine. Captain Blanchard of the *Katherine* decided to try his luck at one of these ventures, and headed north to Sitka, the Russian capital of Alaska. There he contracted with Aleksandr Baranov, the Governor of the Russian-American Company, to take a crew of Aleut and Kodiac hunters, with 50 kayaks or baidarkas, and hunt on the coast of California.

This trade was strictly illegal. California had been claimed by Spain for two hundred years before the Americans first arrived, and ordinarily captains from the United States were instructed by the owners of their ships to respect Spanish sovereignty. But the Spanish had only a very limited sea otter hunt and the resulting pelts were traded in Manila rather than Canton. With the animals becoming increasingly scarce on the Northwest Coast, the siren call of California was irresistible to both Americans and Russians.

The Russians would have preferred to run the California business without American assistance, but they were always short on ships. They contracted them when possible, but preferred to buy them if a captain was willing to arrange a sale, and usually paid in pelts. One of the first American vessels sold to the Russians was the *Juno* of Bristol, Rhode Island, a ship well known to Sam Hill from his previous voyage on the Northwest Coast. Captain John DeWolfe had, according to Hill, spoiled much of the trade by giving exorbitant prices for furs, as he dumped his remaining cargo before selling his ship.

On May 24, 1810, the familiar outline of the *Juno* hove into view as the *Otter* crossed Clarence's Straits. Now, of course, the captain was a Russian, Christopher Martinevich Benzemann. The *Juno* traveled in company with a Boston ship, the *O'Cain,* which was transporting Aleut hunters to California under contract to the Russian-American Company.

The captain of the *O'Cain* was Jonathan Winship, Jr. who had engaged in this business with the Russians before and was an old hand in the maritime fur trade. Winship and Benzemann departed from their usual practice on this particular venture. Instead of going directly south to California, they decided to have their Aleut hunters take sea otters along the coast of British Columbia as they passed through those waters.

The crew of the *Otter* knew immediately that something strange was going on. Furgerson spotted the kayaks before he saw the ships that had brought them. "Saw a number of Canoes of a different construction from any that we have seen upon the Coast," he wrote, puzzled by the light, skin-covered boats of the Aleuts. When the two ships were spotted Captain Hill "immediately concluded that they were Russians... who had brought these Asiatic Indians with their Canoes, or Bydarkies to kill Otter for them."

The *Otter* stood off as Hill tried to identify the ships, and he ordered his men to prepare the ship's cannons "to be ready to defend ourselves if occasion required it." A signal gun was fired and soon enough Jonathan Winship came onboard. He had, he reported, sold his Northwest Coast cargo to the Russians and was now sailing in company with the *Juno*. Baranov had furnished him with the hunters and the two would divide the proceeds from the hunt equally. A short time later Captain Benzemann visited as well.

Robert Kemp could clearly see what this meant for any success in trade the crew of the *Otter* might have hoped for in the Queen Charlotte Islands. Between them, the *O'Cain* and the *Juno* had 180 kayaks and 350 contract hunters, "which must be a great Damage to other Ships," Kemp observed.

More bad news was coming. Winship told Hill that the Russians were planning to extend their territory farther south and would be sending an armed force to control not only the Native people, but American traders as well. The main purpose was to prevent the sale of guns to the Tlingits, who vigorously fought Russian incursions into their territory, and with whom the Russians had already had two armed battles. Hill did not entirely trust Winship, and went aboard the *Juno* to speak to Ivan Kuskov, the

Russian supercargo. Kuskov reported that "he had not heard of the Russian Government's intention to interfere with American trade," though it was "no doubt contrary to their wishes for us to supply the Indians with muskets & ammunition," and they did, indeed, have plans to extend their settlements farther southward.

When Hill left the *Juno,* Kuskov presented him with one of the kayaks, which Furgerson, the carpenter and boat builder of the *Otter,* admired a great deal and described in his journal. "It is of singular construction," he wrote.

> They first make a very tight frame of wood in the Shape they think most convenient and fastens it together with whale sinew, it is then covered all over with Sea-Lions skins except on the upper part there is either one, two or three holes left large enough to receive a mans body, there they sit & paddle them along, and heave their darts with which they kill the Sea-Otter, Seal, Sea-Lion & c.

For a few days at the end of May, the three ships were surrounded by the Aleut hunters in their kayaks in the waters between the Queen Charlotte Islands and the mainland of British Columbia. When they parted company, the *Otter* was bound to the Haida village of Skidegate, but after learning from some Haida in transit to the mainland that the *Hamilton* had just been there, turned instead toward Milbanke Sound.

A report came to them just a few days later that the Haida had killed some of the *Juno's* Aleut hunters, but the details are unclear. Robert Kemp reported that the *Juno* and *O'Cain* were bound for the Nass River, where Americans regularly traded with the Nishga Tsimshian, and from there had gone further south, "the Indians not Suffering them to Remain in there former Station." Three of the contract hunters had been killed and decapitated, their heads "carried away as trophies" of the murderers' success.

Neither Kemp nor Furgerson reported any further knowledge of the incident, but Captain Benzemann, who retreated back to the fort at Sitka after the attack, reported to his superiors that Haida Indians had attacked his hunters, and that the attack had been instigated by Samuel Hill. According to Benzemann, the attack came at Dixon

Entrance and there were eight casualties, all Aleut men, who had been armed only with darts and spears for hunting sea otters.

Kuskov's written report about the incident was sent back to St. Petersburg. According to Kuskov, the Aleuts of his party were continually threatened by the Haida when they hunted in the waters off the Queen Charlotte Islands and he claimed that the *Otter* was in close proximity to them at the time of the attack. "At one time a multitude of boats with armed people surrounded our ships," Kuskov wrote, "and Hill on his ship tacked about at a little distance, being in readiness to cooperate" with the Indians.

Kuskov was an influential man in the Russian-American Company. Not long after the incident with Hill, he would sail south again to establish the Russian's California colony at Fort Ross, near Bodega Bay. His reports to Baranov and to the Company's managers back in St. Petersburg helped to turn the tide against Americans on the coast of Alaska. The original 1799 charter of the Company had claimed for Russia the territory down to the southern tip of the Prince of Wales archipelago, at 54° 40" N. By the time the charter was renewed in 1821, the claim was all the way south to 51°. At that time, Tsar Nicholas I issued an edict ordering American vessels off the coast, and sent naval vessels to enforce it.

***

After their encounter with the Russians, the men of the *Otter* took their vessel back to Milbanke Sound. Once again they met up with Captain Brown on the *Lydia*, who had had his own encounter with Russians, having rescued the crew of a Russian ship wrecked on the coast of what is now Washington State. Kemp reported that the Russians had all been "made Slaves to Indians and treated in the Most Inhumane Manner. Capt. B. was obliged to Buy them off the Indians at 5 Blankets apiece."

Despite the fact that that *Otter* had been within sight of land for many months, and that the weather was comfortable as summer approached, several men onboard were suffering from scurvy, especially the Hawaiians who had come onboard during the stop at the Islands. On June 17, the first of them died. The cold Alaska winter had been especially hard on these natives of the tropics. This man had lost four toes to frostbite several months earlier and had not been able to walk since. His shipmates carried the body ashore and Captain Hill read prayers as they buried him. The rest of the Hawaiians were, according to Furgerson, "all now lame with a swelling in their legs." Hill hoped to get them ashore at Nass, in the hopes that they could be cured, and soon after the funeral they set off. The Nass River region in June also provided an opportunity for Hill to take advantage of the annual fishing rendezvous of the local tribes, but aside from fish there was no trade to be had.

By September, the voyage was well on its way to becoming a commercial disaster. On September 8, Hill flogged three men for minor infractions: one had made a mistake in repairing the rigging, one had not sent a line to the deck from aloft to Hill's satisfaction, and a third was a Hawaiian who struck the bell eight times when it should have been seven. The *Otter* had now been cruising for almost a year up and down the coast, from the Straits of Juan de Fuca to Southeast Alaska and back, and from the Queen Charlotte Islands to the mainland and back, over and over again.

What little satisfaction Hill could get from the cruise came from seeing the misery of others in the same situation. Captain Brown had had an even worse time on the coast. When the *Otter* encountered the *Lydia* again in October, Brown was gone. He had traded commands with James Bennett, Hill's former first mate, and left the coast on another Boston ship. Bennett, like Captain Porter of the *Hamilton,* made "the same grievances that we do," Kemp wrote, "that there is no Furs to be found. One has collected 20 skins in 3 Months, the other about 100." With 200 pelts, Hill's meager lot was the best of the bunch.

It was a far cry from the trade of a few years earlier. Kemp noted that seven years before, 14,000 sea otter pelts had been traded from the Northwest Coast to Canton. In the last year there had "not been more than 8000 Collected by all the Ships on the Coast So it must be allowed that the Sea Otters decrease Verry fast."

Diseases carried by foreign visitors were simultaneously having a devastating impact on the Indians. Kemp noted that numbers of them were suffering from a disease he called "Land Scurvy," which "Renders them Compleately Incapable of Hunting." The coast was, he lamented, "as Silent and Solatary as the House of death and I wish that I was as Clear from it. I would take Verry good Care that no man Should Ever Catch me in this part of the world again."

On November 11, one of the Hawaiian sailors died suddenly and unexpectedly. A despondent Kemp described the scene as they sailed south along the British Columbia coast for the umpteenth time.

> Last Evening departed this Life very Suddenly, Woahiia, Native of Woahoo. This Morning the Sun Rose in Great Glory and Spread its Radiant Beams over the Surface of the Smooth and unruffled Ocean whilst the Luster of the Eastern Sky Covered the face of this Rude Country with the Richest glow. At 8 AM Every Body Repairing to the gangway the Service of the dead was Read over the Corpse and then Committed the Remains of the Body to a Silent and Wattery tomb.

By December, winter had once again settled on the coast with a vengeance. Trade was disastrous and Hill found someone to blame for it. Captain Lemuel Porter had decided to give a very high price for skins in order to obtain as many as he could quickly and leave the coast. On December 13, the *Hamilton* came into view and Hill went to visit. According to Robert Kemp, Hill behaved civilly. Porter was the villain in this scene, again near the Nass River.

> The Indians Expect more for there Skins then any tribe on the Coast in Consequence of Captn Porters giving them 5 fathoms of his thick goods and this he did through Envy to Captn Hill because the Indians was Inclined to trade with us. Captn Hill went on board of the Hamilton to Reason with Captn Porter and Convince him of the great Error that he was persisting and the Irrepairable Injury that he was doing himself and Every other Ship on the coast but he Received nothing but the groosest abuse. [Porter] immediately Ordered him out of

his Ship and attempted to Strike and Kick him. Captn H. made no Resistance to this But told him if he was a man to meet him on shore.

Though Kemp regularly reported having observed Captain Hill cheat the Indians by diluting molasses with seawater and gunpowder with rope fragments, he never seemed to hold him culpable for anything that went wrong during the course of the voyage. Unlike Sam Furgerson, who felt that Hill's violence against the Indians might lead to disaster for the *Otter* or some other American ship, Kemp didn't care. He had little sympathy for the Indians; they were part of a landscape that he despised. As the new year of 1811 dawned, he was in total despair.

January 1, 1811—... Reader Stop and Consider the Lamentable fate of a Sailor who is Exposed to the frozen Regions of polar Cold in the Latitude of 60 North and Longitude 135 West at this Insufferable Season of the year and if thy Heart is not Composed of flint or Something of a harder Composition thou wilt Easily be persuaded to Sympathize with us at our hard fate.

The whole northern region of the coast had descended into the coldest weather, with constant ice and snow. "We are Loseing ground all the time," Kemp wrote. "This is a Horrid Country for any man to Exist in. In my Opinion it is Neither fit for Habitation Cultivation nor Vegitation for any Human Beings."

On January 19, the ship struck hard twice on a rock and began to take on water. Men were required at the pumps through the whole twenty-four-hour day in order to keep up, and there was no prospect that the situation would change for several months, as repairs were impossible in the current location and weather. Down in the darkness of the hold, with freezing water covering their feet and lower legs, each of the common sailors had to spend a portion of his three watches each day grasping the cold wooden handle of the pump and repeating the motions that brought it up over his head, down to his waist, and then to his knees, again and again.

Kemp's diary speaks volumes about the tone of the ship.

> January 21st, 1811— I have no Idea of any Misery more Extreme than what the Natives of this Country do absolutely suffer there Suffering Certainly are Adequate to the Crimes that they are daily guilty of they are a terrible Savage Inhuman Race of Beings as Ever Existed. They have no Fortitude in bearing disappointments they have no Compassion nor Benevolence towards their Fellow Creatures they have no Sense of gratitude to Retaliate favours bestowed on them. On the whole they are hard hearted [and] Revengefull in Every Sense of the word.

> January 22nd, 1811— Commences on tuesday with Constant storms of Snow and hale and Every thing else that is Disagreeable. Winds Continuing from the Eastward which confine us up in this Horrid part of the World. There is Nothing to be done, no furs to be Bought nor no provision for the Ships Company to be had... they are all sick and unable to turn out in such distressing weather.

Adverse winds pinned the *Otter* to the northernmost part of their cruising track. Trade was nonexistent, in part because the Indians seemed just as bad off as the *Otter's* crew. For three months in the worst sort of winter weather, everyone on the coast, Natives and foreigners, hunkered down and survived as well as they could.

In April, the *Otter* sailed into Lynn Canal. This arm of the inside passage went as far north and east into the interior of Alaska as it was possible to go by water. It divided into two fingers at its end. In another century, the towns of Haines and Skagway would spring up at the fingertips, jumping-off points for the gold rush.

Robert Kemp was now beginning the final days of his life, and he would spend them in abject misery. He hated the cold. He hated the Northwest Coast. He hated the Indians. He seems to have been conflicted about how much outsiders, American traders especially, were responsible for the desperate situation of the native people, but he hated them nonetheless.

April 2nd, 1811—... The Natives here are poor and Destitute. No Furs nor no Inclination to Hunt any... Poverty Nakedness and distress seems to have visited by the directions of providence as a punishment for the horrid Crimes which they Hesitate not to commit But Study Every Method of Revenge Consistent with Interest. Their avarice Knows no bounds and they are always meditating Schemes of murder and Robbery on their Fellow Creatures. That Detestable practice of buying and Selling one another is So familiar that they seem perfectly Reconciled to it and I Cannot help think but the practice of Ships doing it and Coming at it has tended greatly to Irritate and Stimulate them to a thing so Contemptible and Contrary to the Laws of God and men.

April 8th, 1811— Bound up Lyn Canall as far as Chilkat. At the place we Left we were handy for trade with 3 tribes... but at present they are most wretched poor. However that ought to be Considered more of a misfortune than a Crime although poverty is not allways the Result of Misfortune. So Ends this frolix. Robert Kemp.

April 11th, 1811— We are now Laying at the Head of Lyn Canall as far as any Ship can get for Ice. ... This afternoon came on board Ziahduce & Kataneker the 2 principle Chiefs of this tribe who with the help of their Snow shoes Brought there Luggage over the Snow & Ice down to waters Edge & come over and Camp in shore of the Brig. It is very Surprising to me what Kind of feeling these people are possessed of for they go on Shore make a small fire on the Ice & then Sleep without the Least thing to Hang over them no covers but a piece of skin with the fur off & nothing to Cut wood with but a stone.

Robert Kemp was killed by the Chilkat Tlingit the following day. He was twenty-five-years-old, and a native of Wellfleet, Massachusetts, a small fishing port near the end of Cape Cod's arm. By the time of the incident, Sam Furgerson seems to have left the ship, though there is no mention of it in Kemp's journal. Robinson was in Hawaii, and so the only account we have of Kemp's murder is Samuel Hill's.

As he had done following the disasters of the *Lydia's* voyage, Hill seems to have been bent on controlling the way in which this tragedy would be perceived back in Boston. A few months later, as the *Otter* finally began the journey to Canton and home, Hill wrote a description of the events of April 11 for the Boston newspaper, the *Columbian Centinel,* which was published in the summer of 1812, a month after his return.

The article appeared on the front page in the left column. It purported to come directly from Captain Hill's "log-book account of the treacherous attack upon the brig OTTER, by the savages on the Northwest coast," and it described the calm heroism of Samuel Hill in the face of violent Natives and a treacherous mate.

Hill's description of the arrival at Chilkat is quite different from Kemp's. The situation of the Indians is one of power rather than misery, with the chiefs demanding high prices for furs. "According to my constant custom with these people," Hill wrote, "I did not urge the trade, not doubting they would accept of more reasonable terms in the course of the day."

As Hill waited patiently, the numbers of Indians onboard and alongside increased. There was nothing in their actions to raise suspicion. Hill had, he said, "visited and traded with them in the preceding autumn on the most amicable terms."

About noon a dog was observed swimming along side, and making the most dismal howlings imaginable; the poor animal had a large wound in his side, and as he attempted to get into the canoes the Indians beat him off. —I desired Mr. HUGHES to have the stern boat lowered down to take him up; —the boatswain and three men came aft to lower the boat; at that instant the Indians seemed to make a general move to go farther aft. I suspected some mischief, but on looking forward I observed our forecastle guard at their stations, and as I had no idea of the Indians having any arms on board I considered our situation as secure. I spoke to some of the Indians near me, and desired them not to go aft. When two of them instantly seized hold of me, and pressed me backward on the base of the after gun. I perceived an attack was their object, and not wishing to give a general alarm, I called for assistance in a moderate tone of voice, and was immediately relieved by Mr. THOMPSON, carpenter of the *Otter,* who struck one of the Indians that held me, and both of them let go immediately. — On looking around, I observed their daggers in motion on all sides, and some who stood abaft me brandished them in a menacing attitude. Mr. HUGHES, Mr. PIERCE, and the Boatswain, with two seamen, were several paces abaft me; they had lowered the boat halfway down and belayed the falls, two men were in the boat; my object was to gain a moment's time for those men to get forward before I should order our fire from the forecastle, otherwise they would have been exposed to certain destruction.

Hill calmly asked the Indians to explain the situation to him. He told them he "wished not to fight but to trade." As he spoke, he tried to subtly change his position on the deck but his action was discovered and the situation exploded. The first to fall was the boatswain John Smith, who was killed by a dagger to the head. Hill then "sprang toward the main deck, and ordered those aft to jump forward." He simultaneously shouted an order at the forecastle guard to fire into the crowd.

The fire took place instantly and did great execution on the quarter deck. I then ordered my men to advance upon them with their pikes, with the carpenter at their head; they advanced upon them on a full run; the Indians gave way in every direction; many of them who were wounded severely jumped over board, while others faced our men and contended until they had received two or three thrusts with our pikes. In five minutes after our operations commenced the decks were cleared, and in fifteen minutes the Indians were cleared from alongside, and I believe but one escaped on shore alive... and he had two balls in his body.

Lying among the dead and wounded on the deck was the body of Robert Kemp, killed in the first minutes of the attack. The first mate, William Hughes, was badly injured, as were five other men. There were at least twenty-five Indians killed, according to Hill, but by "their own account," he adds, their loss was "50 men, among whom they reckon thirteen principal chiefs." How Hill obtained this communication, he does not say. The Indians on shore "commenced a brisk and continued fire of musketry" following the battle, and he neither went ashore nor allowed any visitors to the ship before the ship departed from Lynn Canal. He did, however, repeat these figures frequently in the weeks and months to follow.

Within six weeks, he had perfected the story and told it to the crews of the *Hamilton* and *New Hazard.* The *New Hazard* log for May 10, 1811 says that the *Otter* "had a skirmish with the Indians... at a place called Chilcaht in which they lost their second mate and boatswain and six wounded. They killed 40 Indians, 13 of whom were Chiefs." On May 24, the log of the *Hamilton* notes that Hill "had been attacked up Chillcart by the Natives and unfortunately lost his second officer and boatswain but he killed 40 of the Natives, 13 of whom were Chiefs."

Hill does not claim all the glory in saving his ship. "Much credit is due to my men for their particular attention to, and prompt execution of my orders, on this occasion," he says with magnanimity. But who was to blame for the fiasco? The article is a masterpiece of storytelling. The Indians were clearly savages, as the readers of the *Columbian Centinel* had come to expect, but the piece needed a real villain, and Hill had one, in the person of William Hughes, his first mate.

> When I came to take Mr. *Hughes,* my first mate, below, in order to dress his wounds, he informed me in the presence of the carpenter, and several of the men, that he had expected the attack early in the forenoon, as he had then seen many of the indians with their daggers on board concealed under their left arm-pits. I was much surprised at this intelligence, and asked Mr. *Hughes* why he had not informed me of the circumstance, or made it known to some other person—he replied, *"If I live I will tell you; but if I die it is no matter!"* I knew not how to account for Mr. *Hughes'* strange conduct on this

occasion. His particular duty had been to attend to and examine the Indians, as they entered the gangway, in order to prevent them from bringing arms on board, ever since our arrival on this coast.

What motive Hughes might have had to support an attack on his own vessel, at the risk of his own life (as his injuries illustrated), could only be explained by Hill in one way: Hughes had hoped the Indians would kill Captain Samuel Hill. "Mr. *Hughes* very well knew," he wrote, "that whenever these people drew their daggers, I must certainly be the first and surest victim, as I was the only person who always necessarily remained in the midst of them on the quarter-deck to attend to my business of trade."

It does not seem that Hill thought this was a plot between Hughes and the Indians. Rather, it had occurred in a flash to Hughes, upon seeing that the Indians were armed, that they might kill Hill, and so he raised no alarm. What this said about Hill as a captain does not seem to have occurred to Hill the author. Where did his personal responsibility lie? Why *did* the Indians want to kill him? Why would his Chief Mate have been willing to have them do so?

Hughes was interrogated again, admitted again that "he had seen many of them armed... was very sensible that he had done wrong, but could not now help it, and on the whole said he was glad to be discharged from office." He was "accordingly discharged from any further duty on board."

The article ends with a description of the *Otter* going aground a few days later, just beyond Lynn Canal. When the tide turned, they hove off and "with a favoring breeze sailed for Hutsenhoo, where [they] anchored, and again commenced trade with the natives."

Hill came back to this episode eight years later, after his startling and deeply felt religious conversion. As he revisited that day in April 1811, he still felt no responsibility for anything that had happened on the *Otter,* but he also no longer felt it necessary to blame Hughes.

Previous to my leaving the N.W. Coast... The Indians, Natives of Lynn Canal... attacked me with their daggers in the most treacherous & unexpected manner. Treacherous because I had at all times treated them with kindness, & unexpected because I knew of no affront or cause of enmity between them & myself or my Ships Crew. About 50 Men of them were on deck for the purpose of Trade & with daggers concealed under their Garments they Commenced the attack by Seizing hold of me on the quarter deck. My Second Officer & Boatswain were killed, & six of my men dangerously wounded. Of the Natives I believe all that were on deck at the Commencement of the Affair except one were killed. —

At the Commencement of this affair, to all human appearance my Death was inevitable; Seized & held fast by two Stout men, & Surrounded by 48 or 50 more with drawn daggers, on the quarter deck; & the transition from this Situation, to that in which the charge was ordered, which terminated in their entire destruction, is extremely difficult to describe. Through the whole of that transaction with the Circumstances which preceded & followed it, the directing & preserving hand of the Almighty is apparent. May I render Unceasing Praise and Grateful Thanks, to his long suffering Mercy & Grace to an undeserving & Rebellious wretch like me, in thus permitting me to live and be made Sensible of the extreme danger of my Situation & of a firm belief in the truth & Efficacy of the Sacrifice Offered by our Blessed and Adorable Redeemer for Sinful Mortals, and I humbly hope I may yet feel convinced that his mercy may be extended to me & the multitude of mine Iniquities be forgiven, & whether it Shall please the Almighty Will, to forgive me or not, I am henceforth determined to obey the Divine Laws & Precepts, as nearly as my corrupt heart will permit me; and may that Grace & Assistance be given me, which has been so freely promised by our Gracious Saviour Jesus Christ, without whose assistance I must perish.

The hand of God had preserved Sam Hill. Robert Kemp, John Smith, and fifty or so Tlingit people were not so blessed.

The reasons for the Indians' attack on the *Otter* are nowhere in the record of the Northwest Coast trade. It is likely that Robert Kemp and his shipmates were the hapless victims of someone else's violence at the place earlier, just as their actions would resonate for years to come. Eleven years later, in the summer of 1822, the Boston ship *Rob Roy* was in the region and one of the influential chiefs, Shakes, told Captain Daniel Cross that he intended to take "the first vessel he possibly can to revenge the death of his wive's father who was killed by Capt. Hill of Brig *Otter* some time since."

As late as 1840, the story was still being told among the Chilkat, always with the name of Captain Hill attached. James Douglas of the Hudson's Bay Company, who set up the post at Fort Victoria, wrote that among all the Indians of the Northwest Coast "the only people from whom we have anything to fear are the Chilkats, who some 25 years ago, were defeated with the loss, as they state it of 100 men killed in an attempt to capture an American coaster, commanded by Captain Hill. ... They still preserve a bitter remembrance of this unfortunate attack and I am told have been using threats of retaliation on us for the very sound reason that we speak the same language as the Americans."

The *Otter* simply sailed away from the incident to continue cruising. In May, Hill met up with David Nye, his former first mate on the *Lydia,* now in command of the *New Hazard* of Salem, Massachusetts. In a circumstance that echoed that exchange of mates years before, when Nye came aboard the *Lydia* to replace James Bennett as mate, Nye took William Hughes onto his ship and gave Hill his mate, John Iverson.

Nye had learned well under Hill's tutelage. The *New Hazard* was a violent ship. Nye traded slaves, purchasing captives from one tribe and transferring them to others. He regularly beat his men; there had been more than twenty-five floggings on the ship by the time Hughes arrived. The *New Hazard* mates were brutes and Stephen Reynolds, who kept a journal of the voyage, was relieved to see Iverson go.

By the time the *Otter* left the Northwest Coast in September 1811, the ship and her sorry crew had been there almost two years. They had faced bitter cold, frustrations in trade, death to illness, death to accident, death to violence, and the departure of crew-members due to hostile and angry feelings. The ship had followed a seemingly endless track that took them repeatedly through the same waters. The legacy of the voyage would be felt for years, in U.S. relations with the Russians, in the relations of American and British ships with the Native people, and by the families of the dead crewmen in Hawaii and Massachusetts.

The ship arrived in the Hawaiian Islands in October. The *New Hazard* had beaten them there and William Hughes had already left that ship. He had exchanged one brutal captain for another and had been belittled and eventually demoted by David Nye. According to Stephen Reynolds, when Hughes asked for his discharge from the ship the "Capt. told him he never belonged to her—he might go to the Devil if he liked."

Despite Nye's reputation and Hughes's experience on the *New Hazard,* another man on the *Otter* asked to be transferred from Hill's ship to Nye's. He was a sailor named Williams, who had been elevated from the forecastle to the aft cabin after the loss of the first and second mate following the incident at Chilkat. Reynolds reported that after Williams moved to the *New Hazard,* he went with four men from his new ship back to the *Otter* to get his sea chest. "Capt. Hill got on board just as he was going away, ordered him back, his things on board again, gave him a severe caning, detained him all night but sent the boat back." The next morning, Williams returned to the *New Hazard* and entered a formal protest against Hill.

In a final action before leaving Hawaii, Hill went aboard the *New Hazard* and challenged David Nye to a fight. The two men "had a long talk and parted in anger." Hill collected Thomas Robinson and the cargo of sandalwood he had procured, and sailed for Canton. He made one stop along the way in the Marian Islands, where he found a small population of "white men & Natives of the Sandwich Islands, who had been brought thither by some of the American Trading Ships from the N.W. Coast" and abandoned. The perpetrators, Hill believed, were Captains Thomas Brown and Lemuel Porter, men he had never forgiven for what he perceived as plots against him. "These Poor People," Hill wrote later, had since "been all taken away by the Spaniards from Manilla [who] kept them as Slaves."

On December 14, 1811, Hill arrived in Canton. When his cargo was loaded and he was ready to depart, a passenger came onboard for passage to the western settlement at Macao. He was a British missionary, Robert Morrison, and Hill would later write that "Short as was our acquaintance it Shall never be forgotten, as I sincerely believe that through the Gracious Condescension of my Redeemer & Savior, he has been a messenger to me for good, and the means of opening to me the way to Salvation."

The *Otter* arrived home in Boston on June 14, 1812, having been away for more than three years. Not on board were: Robert Kemp, dead; John Smith, dead; Tilly Hardy, dead; William Hughes, discharged; Seaman Williams, discharged; Samuel Furgerson, fate unknown. Two Hawaiian sailors had also died on the ship. And the country was on the brink of war.

Robert Kemp's journal eventually arrived in the hands of his family on Cape Cod where the agonizing descriptions of his wretchedness must have been heartbreaking to read. That he died so far from home and family would have been saddening for them in any case. To learn that he had been so unhappy was cause to weep. As time passed, the book became more valuable for its stock of blank paper than for its sad contents. Nephew and nieces and great-nephews and great-nieces, scribbled in its pages, unaware of the tragedy that lay within.

Chapter VI

✍

Ulysses, 1813-1814:
Privateer and Prisoner

*Being an account of how Sam Hill spent
the War of 1812.*

Congress declared war on Great Britain four days after the *Otter* returned to Boston. Samuel Hill had certainly known that war was a possibility when he left Canton, but he had not received any news since he came around the Cape of Good Hope. His seafaring prospects were now limited, as commercial voyages were severely curtailed and he was disinclined to serve in the Navy. He decided to live at home for a while with Elizabeth and their two sons, seven-year-old Frederic and four-year-old Charles.

Their home on Myrtle Street was on what is commonly called the "backside" of Boston's Beacon Hill. At that time it ran down to an active waterfront, which has long since been filled. The neighborhood was slightly less transient than the North End where the Hills had lived when they were first married. Though there were still numerous mariners living in boarding houses, families, many of them African American, were beginning to put down roots.

Few options existed during the War of 1812 for mariners who wanted to avoid the conflict, and eventually it became clear to Hill that if he was to work at all during the war, he would have to engage in the risky business of carrying cargo through seas patrolled by the British Navy. Ten months at home was enough for him, and on April 9, 1813 he left Boston again, as captain of the brig *Ulysses.* "I was induced," he wrote, "though contrary to my own Judgement, to undertake a Voyage to France." This was not a last minute decision and Hill must have been planning his departure for several months. He owned the *Ulysses* in partnership with Oliver Keating, for whom he had worked on the *Otter* enterprise. The *Ulysses* was a new vessel and carried a substantial armament for its size. The cannons were for protection and to provide Hill with the option to attack English ships if they looked vulnerable enough to be taken. Permission to attack the enemy was provided by a special Congressional license carried onboard.

During the American Revolution, without a navy, a treasury, or even a reliable currency, the Continental Congress had depended upon private ships to engage in battles with British naval and commercial vessels. The benefit for the owners and crews was that captured ships and cargoes could be kept as prizes. The gains were substantial for the government as well. In addition to the benefit of having private vessels harass enemy ships, the government received a percentage of the prizes, while the private owners bore all of the costs of the vessel, its outfit, and its crew. Privately owned armed vessels that went out with the sole intention of attacking enemy ships were called privateers. Commercial vessels that would engage in such action if the opportunity arose, but were also in the business of carrying cargo were referred to by the license they carried, the "letter of marque." (Sam Hill referred to the *Ulysses* as a "Letter of Marque Brig.")

During the War of 1812, privateers and vessels carrying letters of marque were an important component of the United States' overall naval strategy. There were twenty-three ships in the U.S. Navy, which performed famously in ship-to-ship engagements, but which were no match numerically for the British. More than five hundred privateers and letter-of-marque ships added substantially to the potential for an American naval presence, especially in the harassment and capture of British merchant ships.

While the U.S. Navy captured 254 vessels, the number captured by private vessels was 1300. Without privateering, American commerce would have ground to a halt for the whole period of the war, as the movement of goods along the coast and to and from foreign destinations could not have been protected by the efforts of the Navy alone.

Thomas Jefferson wrote about the role of privateers and letters-of-marque ships on the Fourth of July, 1812. "What is a war?" he asked. "It is simply a contest between nations of trying which can do the other most harm." By the time he wrote this, as many as seven thousand American sailors had been pressed into the British Navy, and more than nine hundred vessels had been taken.

> What difference to the sufferer is it that his property is taken by a national or private armed vessel? Did our merchants, who have lost 917 vessels by British capture, feel any gratification that the most of them were taken by His Majesty's men of war? ... One man fights for wages paid him by the government, or a patriotic zeal for the defence of his country, another, duly authorized, and giving the proper pledges for his good conduct, undertakes to pay himself at the expense of the foe, and serve his country as effectively as the former. In the United States every possible encouragement should be given to privateering in time of war with a commercial nation. ... By licensing private armed vessels, the whole moral force of the nation is truly brought to bear on the foe, and while the contest lasts, that it may have the speedier termination, let every individual contribute his mite, in the best way he can to distress and harass the enemy, and compel him to peace.

The British took the threat of privateers seriously. They knew that these private adventurers could devastate their maritime commerce. A month before Jefferson made his statements about privateering, *The London Statesman* published an article on the subject, which reminded British readers of the success of privateers during the American Revolution, when the country "was in her infancy, without ships, without seamen, without money," and at a time when the Royal Navy "was not much less in strength than at present."

> The Americans will be found to be a different sort of enemy by sea than the French. They possess nautical knowledge, with equal enterprise to ourselves. They will be found attempting deeds which a Frenchman would never think of.

There were fortunes to be made in privateering, and despite the danger, it was not difficult to get crew members to sign on for a percentage of the prize money. From nearby Salem, Hill would have heard of the exploits of the privateer *America,* which captured six British ships in less than five months and earned more than $150,000 for her owners, officers, and crew. In total, American privateers and letters of marque brought English prizes into U.S. ports valued at almost $46,000,000.

Privateers could also earn a swashbuckling notoriety that must have appealed to the egocentric Hill. Captain Andrew Harraden of Salem, who had first promoted Hill from seaman to mate, and under whom Hill had served on two voyages, was the son of one of the most famous privateers of the American Revolution. Jonathan Harraden had commanded three different ships, the *Tyrannicide, General Pickering,* and *Julius Caesar,* and was a popular hero in New England for an astonishing, even dangerous willingness to take risks, and for having used a number of extremely clever ruses. It was said that he had captured more than a thousand cannon from British ships, most of which were larger and better armed than his own.

When the *Ulysses* left Boston, Samuel Hill must have known that he was taking a risk by trading in a war zone, but there was potential for money and fame beyond anything he had yet earned, and that must have appealed to him. It took only two weeks for the ship to reach Savannah, Georgia, where Hill took on a cargo of cotton, destined for France. The *Ulysses* sailed from Savannah on June 8, 1813, bound across the Atlantic to Bordeaux. Three weeks later, on June 30, she was captured by the British ship-of-war *Majestic.* There was no bloody battle, no famous encounter. The *Majestic* was almost thirty-years old and its rating in the Royal Navy pantheon had been reduced from seventy-four to fifty-four guns. Nonetheless, it was a big ship, more than twice the size of the *Ulysses,* with twenty times as many men. Hill would have been a fool to fight, and there was no shame in being captured under the circumstances.

The strategy for the naval actions of both the United States and Great Britain was to capture ships and men rather than destroy and kill them. Both had value. Ships could be sold for prize money or converted to naval use. Men could be persuaded to serve on ships for the other side, a tactic particularly important to the British who were desperately short of experienced hands for their battles in Europe. A sailor whose allegiance could not be swayed would sit out the war in a prison or prison ship, or be exchanged for someone equally patriotic on the other side— which was the usual practice with officers.

The victorious captain was Rear Admiral Edward Griffith. He put one of his men in command of the *Ulysses* and took Hill and his crew aboard the *Majestic.* The Americans were given the option of serving the rest of the war in the Royal Navy, or of being transported to a prison camp at Melville Island, near Halifax, Nova Scotia. By an extraordinary coincidence, Hill recognized the purser of the *Majestic* as John Miller, an Englishmen he had known in Canton on his previous voyage. "By the Politeness of Mr. Miller," he would write later, "I was Introduced to the Admiral, & all the Ward Room Officers, and received every attention & Politeness which my Situation would admit of."

The *Majestic* proceeded to Halifax where Sam Hill was allowed to live in the city while his men were processed into the prison camp. If a ship exceeded a certain size, then the captured captain was guaranteed a "parole," and it was customary on both sides to treat officers like gentlemen, while the men who served under them were treated like criminals. Even if they weren't eligible for parole, officers were granted extraordinary license and courtesy. The American ship *Diomede,* captured by the British in May 1814, was too small for the officers to be paroled, but they were allowed to hire a carriage to take them to prison, while their crew marched there.

Hill may have been treated even better than most because of the friendship he quickly developed, through John Miller, with some of the officers of the *Majestic*. "By a Continuation of the Same friendly conduct," he wrote, "they gain'd for me a favorable reception among the Citizens."

> Although I was detained as a Prisoner of War on Parole, near Seven Months, yet I enjoyed all the liberty in that Situation which I could reasonably wish for, & gained many Respectable & worthy Friends, among whom was John Lawson, Esquire & Family. These were Friends indeed, for I stood in need of friendship & they gave it me unasked.

The *Ulysses* followed the *Majestic* into Halifax where the cargo of cotton was discharged and sold. Though almost a new vessel, the *Ulysses* was condemned by the Admiralty Court; the British had seized so many vessels of its size and condition, that the market was glutted. One hundred and fifteen American ships came into the port of Halifax as prizes of the Royal Navy in the five-month period between April 20 and September 20, 1813.

Hill's men were now confined to miserable circumstances at the Melville Island prison, where more than eight thousand American sailors would be imprisoned during the course of the war. Earlier in the war, there had been a very active exchange of British-held American mariners for U.S.-held English mariners, but the sheer number of captives had begun to flood the system by the time the *Ulysses* was captured. Few men left Melville Island after that period, except to be transported across the Atlantic to an even more dismal prison at Dartmoor. Most of the men in the crowded camp had to wait until March 1815, three months after the peace treaty was signed, to be released. Four men from the *Ulysses* died as prisoners.

We know something of their life in captivity from the reports of two men who entered the Melville Island prison complex a few months after the men from Hill's crew. One of them, Ned Myers, had been a shipmate of James Fenimore Cooper when both were lads in 1806. More than thirty years later they met again and Cooper decided to chronicle his old shipmate's story "as a sure means of giving the public some notions of the career of a common sailor." The other was Benjamin Palmer, who kept a daily diary while in captivity.

Melville Island, where the prison was located, was about three miles from downtown Halifax. A garrison, built at the highest point near the middle of the island, had a commanding view of the complex and was well armed. The island was connected to the mainland by a narrow bridge. Another armed guard house was located on the far side of the bridge, with a view back to the prisoners' wooden barracks.

As the barracks were packed with prisoners by the middle of 1813, a number of men were kept on prison ships anchored offshore. Ben Palmer, for instance, lived aboard the *Ardent* for more than four months when he first arrived at Melville Island. In January 1814, four hundred men were already packed into the *Ardent,* but the guards were constantly trying to fit more in. "More Prisoners more Prisoners is the cry through out the ship," Palmer wrote, and "every man musters on deck to view their unhappy fellow sufferers."

> Negroes and Sailors, Fiddlers and Taylors 3 deep in the hole o God what reflections this sad night. ... Nothing but discontent reigns among the prisoners fearing that we shall have to stay here during the summer. if that should be the case I think a cargo of Coffins would pay a handsome freight, for it is my opinion that the most of us will make our exit and retire behind the scene of this world and become actors on the Stage of Death.

Some days they were served only peas, or "Bad Bread and little of it." Whenever they could, American merchants bought provisions for the prisoners to augment the English fare, and extras were available for men who had cash, but few did. Mostly, they were confined below deck and the hatches were often sealed for security or weather. The hold of the ship was a stifling, stinking place that could be cold and damp even with the press of bodies all around. Occasionally it became so noxious that guards would order the prisoners up by their mess groups to smoke out their quarters, or to clean them with buckets of lye. A guard ship circled the prison ship.

The prisoners' greatest amusement was fighting, and the English guards were happy to let them "flog each other pretty decently." Men died of pneumonia, tuberculosis, smallpox, and typhus, and were buried without ceremony in a plot nearby that came to be known as "Deadman's Island." Palmer watched one day as four bodies were carried there and wrote that he was "fearful a number of us will visit that place... if not shortly released."

News of the progress of the war was demanded of each new prisoner, and Palmer wrote it all down in his diary, though much of what he learned would prove to be false. In February 1814, an interesting rumor began to circulate among the men aboard the *Ardent*. The well-known American Commodore John Rogers was said to have taken the *Majestic* in a short battle. A few days later a disappointed Palmer wrote that "Rumour with her thousand Tongues has been very busy this day. The report of Rogers capturing the Magestic is reversed."

On April 15, 1814, a number of prisoners aboard the *Ardent* were ordered to prepare to disembark. The men began to dress themselves "as if they were a going ashore in America," wrote an excited Palmer. "We are to embark this afternoon to leave the Floating Hell that has held us in bondage... and now I HOPE to get home."

Palmer and his shipmates would be disappointed. Instead of home, their destination was the barracks on Melville Island. A large number of prisoners had been transported to Dartmoor prison in England, and the prisoners held on the prison ships were now being transferred to the prison on shore. On May 2, Palmer wrote in a shaky hand: "This day we embark'd for Hell."

At least on the island there were opportunities for fresh air and exercise, although the options for amusement were much the same as they had been on the *Ardent*— gambling, gossip, card games, backgammon, songs, and the endless mending of clothes. Ned Myers was already there when Palmer arrived, living in the barracks along with the crew of the *Ulysses*. Like Palmer, Myers had lived first on a prison ship before being transferred to the barracks and this was probably also true of some, if not all, of Hill's men.

Myers complained less about the quality of the food than Palmer, though there wasn't enough of it. The prisoners were fed "six upon four," which meant that six men shared rations designed to feed four. American sources were meant to make up the difference, but with twelve hundred men in the barracks, what additional rations were available were still too scanty. An American agent living in Halifax supervised the treatment of prisoners, and the men on Melville Island complained to him regularly about the food.

Within a month of arriving on solid ground, Palmer was in a state of despair.

> The Heavens wear a gloomy aspect. Nothing but vexatious disappointments seem to offer itself to the unfortunate prisoner. I almost seem to wish my dissolution to come. Day after day passes slowly on & nothing offers to animate our drooping spirits, worn out with afflictions confined within the dark walls of a prison with sickness and want presenting itself in every shape day after day rolls successfully on & nothing like Liberty appears. Hope! alass! even Hope has fled.

Ned Myers had relatives near Halifax who provided him with small sums of money, which he increased through gambling. He devoted most of his energy to planning escapes, and managed to get off the Island twice, though he was recaptured each time. After his first recapture his "treatment was a good deal worse" than it had been before his escape attempt. He was put in "the black hole" on bread and water for ten days. After his second recapture, the punishment was twenty days.

A "grand conspiracy" was formed in the fall of 1814, for the escape of a large number of men. By then, the prison population had grown to eighteen hundred, and at least fifty men joined Myers in an elaborate escape plot. An initial problem for the conspirators was that no officers were in-volved and sailors naturally looked to officers for leadership. As Myers explained, "There were a good many privateer officers in the prison, but they were berthed over-head, and were intended to be separated from us at night." This problem was solved by prying up the boards that separated the ground floor of the barracks from the floor above where the officers lived.

A passage was created in the opposite direction as well, down through the floor into one of the "black hole" cells. From there a tunnel was started that headed toward Halifax. Myers and his cohorts did not work out the details that would keep the tunnel from flooding when they reached the shore of the island, and they never had to. "One day we were all turned out," he told James Fenimore Cooper, "and a party of English officers, army and navy, entered the barracks, removed the mess-chest [that covered the hole], and surveyed our mine at their leisure." By the end of the week, almost half the men at Melville Island had been shipped to Dartmoor, including Benjamin Palmer.

Myers remained on Melville Island for several more months until one evening when the prisoners "heard a great rejoicing" from nearby Halifax. "A turnkey appeared on the walls, and called out that England and America had made peace! We gave three cheers, and passed the night happy enough." The prisoners were released the next day, March 15, 1815. At least 200 American sailors had died in the camp, including Perry Banser, Sam Oliver, Matthew Phipp, and John Webber of the *Ulysses.*

Their captain, Samuel Hill, had been more fortunate. He had lived comfortably in Halifax until Christmas 1813, when he was released in an exchange of prisoners—Hill for an English merchant captain held by the United States. In January 1814 he arrived back in Boston, where he sat out the rest of the war. His principal complaint about the adventure was that he had lost the whole of his investment in the *Ulysses,* about seven thousand dollars.

Hill was now at leisure to watch the progress of the ship *Majestic* as it stormed around the New England coast. After delivering the *Ulysses* to Halifax, the *Majestic* was the lead ship in a squadron assigned to blockade the Atlantic seaboard of the United States, preventing ships from entering or leaving the ports of New England and New York. It spent much of the fall of 1813 in the waters off Cape Cod, where it had a regular anchorage near Provincetown, Massachusetts. The local citizens there provided water, wood, fish, and produce, rather than be fired upon by the ship's cannons. When Hill arrived in Boston, the *Majestic* was still there.

A year later, in January 1815, the *Majestic* led the squadron that captured one of the prizes of the American Navy, the USS *President,* under the command of Commodore Stephen Decatur. Decatur (who had rescued a young Sam Hill in the spring of 1798, on his disastrous voyage of the *Polly),* became one of the great heroes of the War of 1812 as a result of his determined fight against four heavily armed British warships.

***

Almost a century after Samuel Hill's experience as captain of the letter-of-marque brig *Ulysses,* his grandson, F. Stanhope Hill, wrote a book called *The Romance of the American Navy as Embodied in the Stories of Certain of our Public and Private Armed Ships from 1775 to 1909.* Decatur was one of the great heroes of the book, but the author was also interested in acknowledging the impact of the private vessels that had engaged in the American Revolution and the War of 1812.

In view of the undoubted fact that our saucy American privateers were such an important factor in determining the result of the first two wars of this nation, and that so many of the officers and men who fought in these private ships made their first essays in naval warfare as privateersmen, it seems to the writer that, in this volume at least,—side by side with the record of the officers and men of the regular establishment,—should be recorded some of the brilliant deeds of those privateersmen, untrained in military science, who by their bravery, skill, and patriotism accomplished such extraordinary results.

Neither his grandfather nor his grandfather's ship received a mention in the book. The fact that both he and Stephen Decatur had surrendered their swords and their ships to the captain of the *Majestic* was not enough to earn Sam Hill a place in *The Romance of the American Navy.*

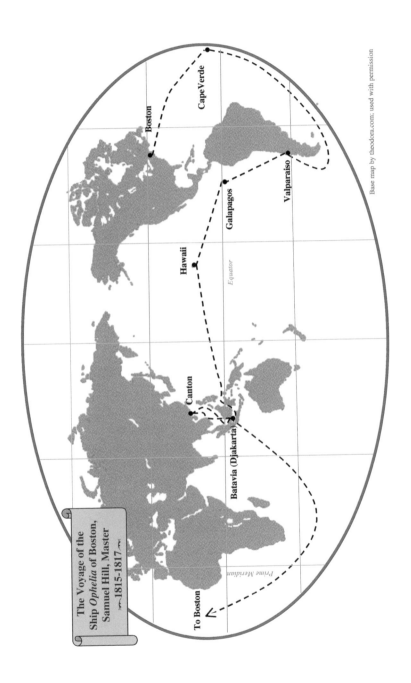

The Voyage of the
Ship *Ophelia* of Boston,
Samuel Hill, Master
1815-1817

Boston

CapeVerde

Galapagos

Valparaiso

Hawaii

Equator

Canton

Batavia (Djakarta)

Prime Meridian

To Boston

Chapter VII

~

Ophelia, 1815-1817:
Of Silks and Ships and Whales Teeth

*An unsuccessful voyage, which nevertheless proves
interesting because of a Revolution in Chile.*

Despite his disastrous experience as a privateer
captain on the *Ulysses,* Sam Hill was, according to himself,
offered a number of other ships for the same purpose "and
as often refused." His financial losses were ruinous, but for
more than a year he waited, hoping that the war would end
and bring him the possibility for another voyage to the
Northwest Coast.

By February 1815, he was forced to sell his house.
His family now consisted of three children—nine-year-old
Frederic, seven-year-old Charles, and an infant daughter,
Charlotte, conceived and born since his return from Halifax.
He took lodgings for his wife and children with a retired
captain, Abner Wheeler, who lived with his wife in
Framingham, twenty miles west of Boston.

Returning to Boston to arrange for the sale of his
house and furniture, Hill found the city celebrating; the war
was over. He took a room for himself near the waterfront and

celebrated for the next month. He needed to find a ship soon, or go into another line of work.

With the war over, many Boston merchants were anticipating a boom in shipping. Hill approached Captain William Sturgis, one of the most venerable Boston merchants. Sturgis had worked his way from foremast hand to captain in the space of five years, and had circumnavigated the globe four times under sail before he retired from the sea at the age of 28. With his business partner John Bryant, Sturgis controlled a significant portion of the Pacific trade. His relatives in the firm of James and Thomas Handasyd Perkins controlled much of the rest.

Sturgis and Hill discussed the possibility of a voyage to the Northwest Coast and Canton, with the firms of Bryant and Sturgis and J. and T.H. Perkins underwriting the cost of the ship. In April, they purchased a ship then under construction in South Boston and Hill signed on to supervise the rigging and outfitting in preparation for commanding a voyage much like those he had made on the *Lydia* and the *Otter.*

William Sturgis was an experienced hand in the Northwest Trade. He had made four voyages there himself (three as captain), and managed nine more. Among the men who considered him a mentor and friend was Richard Henry Dana, Jr., who made the voyage described in *Two Years Before the Mast*, in a vessel owned and managed by Bryant and Sturgis. Dana commented particularly on Sturgis's ability to "read" the men he hired, "for any one who has seen much of sailors can tell pretty well at first sight, by a man's dress, countenance, and deportment, what he would be onboard ship."

That Hill passed muster with Sturgis says something about the difference between the world afloat and the world ashore. The behavior of a captain on the deck of his ship was judged by a completely different standard from the behavior of a man in society. Even Dana, who described a horrific flogging he witnessed aboard the brig *Pilgrim,* could not bring himself to oppose a captain's right to use severe physical punishment, even though Dana considered it morally wrong. William Sturgis must certainly have heard rumors about Hill's behavior on the *Lydia* from Captains

Thomas Brown and Lemuel Porter, but Hill had prevailed in the lawsuit that followed the *Lydia* voyage, the *Otter* voyage had been a financial success, and Samuel Hill could be civilized and charming when he needed to be.

In early May 1815, just as Hill's new ship was receiving its final outfitting, three ships arrived in Boston after long voyages from Canton. They brought word of the collapse of the sea otter stocks on the Northwest Coast, and of difficulty procuring the few pelts that were available. The owners of the ship Samuel Hill was to captain, now named *Ophelia,* decided to abandon their plans for a voyage to the Northwest Coast and Canton, and try a new trade.

By that time, Thomas Perkins and William Sturgis had probably been considering a venture to Chile for several years. Closed to foreign trade by the Spanish colonial government, the ports of Chile were opened in 1811 by the junta that took control of the country in a revolution against the Spanish crown. The War of 1812 had prevented Boston merchants from exploring the trade fully, but new information was becoming available in 1814 and 1815 that made the prospects for success in Chile seem very realistic.

Captain David Porter, who had commanded the U.S. frigate *Essex* in the Pacific Ocean during the War of 1812, had returned to New York the previous summer, filled with enthusiasm for Chile and the prospects for trade there, now that the Spanish had been ousted. There had been several revolutionary factions and Porter had thrown his support behind the one led by José Miguel Carrera, a charismatic and handsome young man who was the second in a series of revolutionary leaders to seize control of Chile. In their fight for independence, Porter wrote, Chileans "looked up to the United States for example and protection," and he believed they should be supported.

Americans supported Chilean independence emotion-ally, philosophically, and, to a certain extent, financially. Not only did Americans sympathize with their brothers and sisters in the hemisphere who wanted to throw off the yoke of European control, but American merchants had been hampered by the Spanish prohibition of free trade in their ports. With independence came tantalizing opportunities for merchants like Perkins and Sturgis to tap the resources of South America.

In addition to news about Chile, Porter had valuable information about markets and sources of commodities for Americans seeking new options for trade in the Pacific. The Polynesian residents of the Marquesas Islands, for instance, had a great desire for sperm whales' teeth, and lived on the edge of great forests of sandalwood. In an extract of his journal that was published in October 1814, Porter wrote that "No jewel, however valuable, is half so much esteemed in Europe or America, as is a whale's tooth here: I have seen them by fits laugh and cry for joy, at the possession of one of these darling treasures." When his full journal was published a year later, Porter added a suggestion on how to capitalize on the market:

> Some idea may be formed of the value in which they are held by the natives, when it is known that a ship of three hundred tons burthen, may be loaded with sandal-wood at this island, and the only object of trade necessary to procure it, is ten whales' teeth of a large size; and for these the natives will cut it, bring it from the distant mountains, and take it on board the ship; and this cargo in China, would be worth near a million of dollars.

Porter shared some of this information with Boston merchants, including William Sturgis. No doubt part of the reason Hill's orders and destination were changed was to take advantage of this new opportunity. Porter even seemed to hint at where whales' teeth could be easily obtained—the Galapagos Islands. Even though he had taken a number of British whaleships there, he did not dispel a rumor that began to take hold in Boston in 1815 that sperm whales' teeth were lying in the shallow bays of the Galapagos Islands ready to be gathered up by the first ships that could get there.

William Boardman and Paschal Pope, owners of the ship *Sultan* of Boston, for instance wrote instructions to Captain Caleb Reynolds:

> At the great Albemarle [Galapagos Islands]... we are informed that Whales Teeth may be found on the Beach, buried in the Sand, from Whales that die in the Bay, & are driven on shore.— Or, if that source fails, you will no

doubt be able to obtain them from the Whale Ships you will meet about here [especially] from the English ships, which would not be so likely to know their value to you as the Americans, for the latter since the publication of Porters Journal, may estimate them at an extravagant price.

Consequently, the orders that Samuel Hill received for the voyage, included information about Chile, the Galapagos, and the Marquesas. The owners were clearly wary of the instability of the global situation and the potential inaccuracy of new information. David Porter was not above exaggeration, as anyone reading his journal could surmise. Perkins and Sturgis had both taken speculative risks in their time, but their enormous wealth was built, in large measure, on their ability to hedge their bets against failure and move quickly to the next venture, or back to a known enterprise even if the profits were smaller, such as the Northwest Coast fur trade. The instructions issued to Samuel Hill were extremely detailed, but provided option after option in case success did not come easily to hand. As summarized by Hill, the plan of the *Ophelia's* voyage was "to Carry out Seventy thousand Spanish dollars, with which to purchase a Cargo of Pig Copper at Valparaiso, or Coquimbo, and Proceed to Canton for a market, after which to be Subject to the orders of the House of Perkins & Co. in Canton respecting the further destination of the Ship."

David Porter's report on trade prospects in Chile was to be given a fair examination. In fact Porter had already negotiated a deal with the Boston merchants, as they informed Hill in his instructions.

You have a letter from Commodore Porter to Remigio Blanco, his agent at Valparaiso, in which the Commodore informs us, that he had given his agent authority to deliver to you, as Master of the *Ophelia,* such quantity of Copper as his funds in the hands...

Porter's particular friend in the Revolutionary government, José Miguel Carrera, had already been deposed by another faction in the independence movement when Porter left Chile in 1814, as the Boston merchants knew. That Valparaiso might not be open to free trade was clearly a possibility and in their instructions to Hill they tried to anticipate every situation that he might run into. They had heard that a few ships had already been able to purchase copper and that commodity, with cocoa, was what Hill should ask for. He would carry cash only and would not be permitted a private trade.

> You will have Nothing on board for trade Whatever, it being our express instructions that neither you or your Officers take on board any article of Merchandise, and as we send nothing in Cargo but Dollars, no Pretense can arise for alleging against you any disposition to violate the Laws of the Country by a contraband trade.

Upon reaching Valparaiso Hill was instructed to go ashore or send his mate to ask permission to get water and provisions and to trade for copper, and to ask for news about any Northwest Coast trading vessels that may have been in South American ports during the war. Hill was particularly instructed "not to violate any of the laws of any place you may be during the Voyage, but on the contrary Conform to all the Publick and Principal laws of the Several places you may visit."

Perkins and Sturgis had a price in mind for copper, but informed Hill that they would rather he pay a higher price than spend a long period of time in negotiations, and that he should "obtain such information in relation to future operations as will enable you to Prosecute another Voyage should it be desirable." On the expectation that Hill would procure a cargo of copper, the owners had put a "quantity of joist & Planks" on the ship to allow it to be stowed high up in the hold, protected from any water that might leak into the ship.

From Valparaiso, Hill was to proceed to Canton via the Galapagos Islands "for the Purpose of procuring whale teeth." He was provided with a chart of the islands, probably prepared by David Porter, marked with references to where whale teeth might be found. "Collect all of them you can find to be used in the Collection of Sandalwood," the owners wrote to Hill, "should you be unsuccessful in getting Permission to load Copper at Valparaiso." The whales' teeth were, of course, intended to go to the Marquesas to be exchanged for sandalwood, which would then replace copper as the intended cargo for Canton.

If both the Chilean and the Marquesan enterprises failed, Hill was instructed to proceed to Hawaii, where "we trust finally upon your Success in getting a load of Sandal wood at the Sandwich Islands, and which we presume will be readily Procured with Specie." If it happened that the "King of the Sandwich Islands" was inclined to trade sandalwood, but that it needed to be cut and transported, then Hill should take the intervening weeks and make a run to the coast of Alaska. At Sitka, he was to "pay a visit" to Aleksandr Baranov, the Governor of Russian America, "with the View of Purchasing Seal skins or other Skins — say Beaver & other land furs, to amt. of all your funds over what you may want to pay for your Sandal Wood." Sturgis speculated that Baranov might have more seals than Hill would be inclined to buy, in which case the Russian might try to get Hill to freight them for him. "We throw this out as a hint for you to reflect upon," Sturgis wrote.

If all other plans failed, Hill was instructed to go to Batavia for a cargo of coffee, or, potentially, to make a connection with his Dutch friends for another voyage to Japan. If he did that, he would still have his Spanish Dollars to trade in Canton, and would also collect a payment, in coffee, for freighting the Dutch cargo. In addition, he was told, "Japan Camphor is worth two dollars per pound here & takes but little room. You should stipulate that they should let you have a certain amt. in that Article."

That Hill would be responsible for making decisions on the spot was clear. The owners needed to depend on his honesty and his acumen. "We Point out some other objects which you will maturely reflect upon & act as you may judge best," they wrote. "You will ascertain Promptly what can be done at any of the Ports to which you go, & decide Promptly on the Course you are to Pursue." In the end, if he found no profitable trade in any of this transit around the Pacific Rim, Hill was to proceed to Canton and receive new orders from John P. Cushing, the nephew of James and Thomas Perkins, and manager of their operation in China.

As Hill was prevented any private trade on the outbound voyage, the owners were very specific about what his profits would be. On any cargo purchased with the Spanish Dollars, Hill would earn two and a half percent of the profits when sold in Canton. Once the sale of the copper, sandalwood, or seal skins, had been arranged by Cushing, Hill would be paid his commission. He could then purchase private goods, but only to the amount that would take up ten tons of measured space in the ship. As the *Ophelia* was a ship of 360 tons, this was a very small amount of space for the captain's privilege. The owners acknowledged this in their instructions. "You will perceive that the object of this plan is to have your adventure managed with the cargo & sharing the same fate," they wrote. His real profits would, consequently, come from the final sale of the Chinese goods in Boston, and not on private adventure.

Though Hill was to act as both the captain and supercargo, the owners clearly placed a great deal of confidence in the mate, John King. He had been to Chile before and presumably, like Hill, spoke Spanish. The son of the principal owner of the ship, young Thomas Handasyd Perkins, Jr. was going on the voyage as well, to learn the family business. Hill was told to give him "good advice & attention," for which young Perkins would, in return give "every aid in his power in effecting your business." That he might "feel an Interest in the undertaking," Perkins was allowed five tons of privilege. Hill was also instructed to "communicate with T.H. Perkins on the general objects of your Voyage, that in case of accident to you he may be enabled to take up our Ideas & direct the Prosecution of the Voyage."

The inexperienced Perkins was thus given a great deal of potential authority, which must have galled Hill after his experience on the *Lydia* with Isaac Hurd. If Hill were disabled or killed, the owners actually gave command of the ship to Perkins, rather than to the mate. Perkins was then to proceed to the nearest port, or if there was a Chinese-bound cargo already onboard, to "direct the Chief Officer to proceed direct to Canton & deliver the Property to Perkins & Co. for their Instructions."

Having laid out in detail the prices they considered reasonable for all of the goods described, and urging him the greatest speed on the voyage, the owner's instructions ended and Hill's journey began. On June 17, 1815 the *Ophelia* left Commercial Wharf in Boston and anchored in Boston harbor. Hill took stock of everything onboard. The legacy of the recent war and the potential for violence in Pacific ports-of-call required that the *Ophelia* be armed. The ship carried eight small cannons, 15 muskets, two blunderbusses, 12 cutlasses, 2 pairs of pistols, and 400 pounds of gunpowder and ammunition. There were also 15 boarding pikes. The crew had enough weaponry to defend against an attack by people without guns, but not enough to take another ship (or the *Ophelia* from Hill, if things went awry in that way).

Hill wrote in his logbook that the provisions of bread, beef, pork, etc., were "of the best Qualities for a Voyage of Eighteen Months, and our Lesser Stores was furnished for the Passage to Canton at least." His mate, John King, would provide important local knowledge in Chile. The other twenty men who made up the crew represented a variety of backgrounds and experiences. The *Ophelia* also carried two passengers. In addition to Thomas H. Perkins, Jr., whose father was one of the owners, there was ten-year-old Frederic Stanhope Hill, whose father was Captain Samuel Hill. The only cargo the ship carried was seventy thousand Spanish dollars.

On a bright sunny Fourth of July, the *Ophelia* was finally ready to sail. Only the entangling of the ship's anchor chain with a cable of the U.S.S. *Constitution* marred the glory of the departure. Once the *Constitution's* men had cleared the mess, the *Ophelia* got underway.

Hill made a good start to the voyage by reading and posting rules and regulations for the crew.

Rules & Orders to be observed by the Officers & Seamen of the Ship Ophelia during this Present Voyage from Boston to Canton in China, by the way of Cape Horn.

Whereas the custom of sitting or lying down & sleeping during the watch on deck, & also the custom of leaning or lying on the wheel while steering are deemed highly dangerous & improper, and as there is good reason to believe that many ships have been lost at sea by running against other Ships under full sail & sunk in a few minutes. Ships have been upset or dismasted in sudden squalls for want of timely execution by the men on decks, with many other evils too Numerous to mention, most of which may be fairly attributed to the dangerous Practice of Sleeping on deck, or to careless & Inattentive Steering. In order to prevent these difficulties as much as Possible & with a view of Preserving the lives of the men under his care, as well as the Ship & Property of the Owners, the Commander of the Ophelia has thought Proper to Issue the following Orders, Each & every person on board are hereby required to take notice & govern themselves accordingly. —

1st. No man shall be allowed to sleep during his watch on deck, or any person neglecting this order shall be sent to the mast head for two hours, and deprived of his allowance of grog the Saturday & Sunday following.

2d. The helmsman shall not be allowed to lean on the wheel, but when steering he shall stand up in such posture as to Command the Wheel, he shall pay a proper attention to the Glass & call out the bells & no man shall be allowed to stand at the wheel with dirty hands or a long unshaven beard.

3d. When the watch is called, the men shall be quick in coming on deck and the watch on deck shall not be allowed to go below untill the other watch are all on deck. When all hands are called every Officer & seaman will be quick in coming on deck. Should this order be neglected, the most efficient means will be used to prevent such neglect in future.

4th Every Saturday if the weather is good, the chests & bedding shall be brought on deck & aired & the men shall wash their clothes unless business prevents it.

5th Every Sunday Morning, if the weather be good, at Nine O'clock the Officers & Seamen shall be mustered on the quarter deck & their names called over. Every Person will appear Clean Washed, Shaved & Shifted, & no work will be done on the Sabbath day except such as is of absolute necessity.

6th No person Shall use Unnecessary Profane Language, Cursing, Swearing & C. Blasphemies are hereby forbidden, especially on the Sabbath day, & it will be pleasing to the Commander of the Ophelia to find that all such language be dispensed with.

7th Every Officer or Seaman, to whom the care of any business is committed or any charge is given, whether on board, or in boats, is strictly to attend to the same, & if by neglect or Carelessness any working tools, boats, furniture or other articles, be lost or stolen, the full amt. of such articles will be charged against the wages of those by whose neglect they were so lost or stolen.

Given on board Ship *Ophelia* at Sea

July 9th 1815

Saml Hill

The lax attention that Captain Hill paid to many of these very same behaviors on his *Lydia* and *Otter* voyages, would seem to indicate that he was making an effort to start this voyage on as promising a footing as possible. Or he may have been making a show for the benefit of Tom Perkins (and maybe even for his own son, Frederic).

The *Ophelia* headed east and south across the Atlantic to the Cape Verde Islands and then south and west toward Cape Horn. Approaching the equator, they encountered two British ships within ten days and each had important news. From Captain William Wilson, Hill learned that "the Political State of the Spanish Province of La Plata was very much disordered, that the republican cause was gaining ground, & that executions of the Royalists were frequent, & unless the Expected fleet & land forces from old Spain should arrive soon, the republican Government would be Permanently established."

From officers of the British East India Company Ship *Speke,* Hill heard about the Battle of Waterloo, but didn't believe it.

By the accounts recd from these Gentlemen, a battle had taken place in Flanders between the Troops of Great Britain & Holland on the one part, & those of France on the other, Lord Wellington & Bonaparte Commanded their respective Armies, & the French troops were defeated with the Loss of their Artillery. Such was the news detailed by the Officers of the *Speke,* but they shewed no Papers to confirm these accounts.

Hill found it more useful that the *Speke* had a chronometer, by which he could check his longitude against the elaborate tables he had been keeping of lunar observations. As he crossed the equator, his men "were indulged with Grog & allowed a holiday as usual. The Ancient Ceremony of receiving a visit from Old Neptune, & Introducing & Initiating the young Sailors, in the Mysteries of his Godship, was attended to, & Performed with all due Solemnity, to the no small satisfaction & amusement of the old sailors."

The days were filled with shipboard jobs, caulking the deck, repairing the hatch covers, sewing sails, and bending on a heavier suit of sails as they neared Cape Horn. Hill complained in his log that as his crew was composed of "a very Indifferent set of men, a very little progress was made."

For himself, Hill indulged in the practice of Natural History, which he knew well from his extensive reading of the narratives of James Cook, George Vancouver, and others. Hill was a keen observer and wrote evocative descriptions of what he saw. In mid-September along the coast of South America, he scribbled regular accounts of birds and fishes.

Many of the Southern Aquatic Birds began to Visit us, among which were the Majestic Albatross, the Monarch of the Oceanic feathered tribe, the larger & lesser Petrel, the beautiful Cape Pigeon, as it is commonly called, where neat little Profiles & fancifully disposed plumages exceeds for beauty every species of Oceanic bird with which I am acquainted. The sea hen, in great numbers and several man of War Birds were also Observed and as we approached that part of the Ocean where the Great River of Plate, or Rio de la Plata, Empties its waters into the Sea the Birds Increased in Numbers to a surprising degree. Flocks of Sea Gulls of Several Hundreds, Whitened the Surface of the Sea in Some places for many hundred yards & Immense Numbers of small fish were observed swimming in Shoals near the Surface. — Of the Amphibia, some Penguins of a dark Brown Color were observed. These frequently jumped above the surface like the fishes & the momentary appearance of the White space on the breast, made them appear like fish.

Hill tried to be a careful navigator, but whenever he had a chance to check himself against landfalls (often unexpected), chronometer readings, or soundings on a chart, he found he had miscalculated. His notes were obviously written so that future voyages or other mariners would be able to profit from his experiences. For example, he made comments about better routes and seasons to make a passage from Cape Verde to the Brazilian fishing banks.

The *Ophelia* rounded Cape Horn in the middle of October, and arrived at the Chilean port of Valparaiso on November 1, 1815. American sailors knew Valparaiso as a refuge after a hard passage around Cape Horn. Repairs and provisions, especially fresh fruit, had been available there since the 1790s, but there had been no real trade because of Spanish restrictions.

The *Columbia,* the first American vessel to go around Cape Horn, sought provisions and a place to make repairs there after the passage. Not knowing what sort of reception they would receive in Valparaiso, Captain John Kendrick decided to make a landfall at the Island of Juan Fernandez, 450 miles offshore. The *Columbia* remained there for two weeks in the spring of 1788, receiving the hospitality of the governor, Don Blas Gonzalez, who was later removed from his position for having aided the Americans.

Though there was no official trade, the long arm of Spanish law had become less and less powerful in the far-flung provinces of western South America, especially after 1796, when Spain was at war in Europe, and contraband trade brought needed hard currency into Chile. More than 250 American ships made their way through Chilean waters in the years between 1788, when the *Columbia* first entered, and 1815, when the *Ophelia* dropped anchor in Valparaiso Bay. During this period, copper discovered in the Andes provided Chile with a desirable high-value export.

The independence movement in Chile was tied to those in the rest of South America, and followed quickly on the heels of the Napoleonic Wars in Europe. When Napoleon first invaded Spain in 1808 and deposed the King in favor of his own brother, there was an immediate burst of patriotic outrage in Spanish America. It did not take long, however, for the Creole aristocracy in South America to see an opportunity in Spain's misfortune. This was not a revolution of the native people against Spanish oppression. As in the United States, it was the descendents of colonists who, generations removed from the motherland, now chafed against the control of a distant ruler. Unlike the British colonies in North America, however, the Spanish parties of exploration and colonization had been made up almost entirely of men, and the new aristocracy in Chile was descended from them and the local women they had married in the new world.

In 1810, revolutionary juntas took over, in quick succession, the governments of Venezuela, Argentina, and Chile. Chile's new leader, Juan Martínez de Rozas, was the most radical of them all. Within a year he had been deposed by another faction of the independence movement, led by José Miguel Carrera, who found an enthusiastic supporter in the influential Captain David Porter of the *Essex*.

When Porter arrived in Valparaiso in March 1813, he was prepared to declare himself and his ship "greatly in want of supplies of every kind" in order to gain access to the port. "I was induced to use this little artifice from a knowledge of the unaccommodating disposition of the Spaniards, and their jealousies respecting foreign vessels that enter the ports of their American possessions," he wrote. To his surprise, he was greeted with generous civility. To his even greater surprise, he learned that they had "shaken off their allegiance to Spain; that the ports of Chili were open to all nations; that they looked up to the United States of America for example and protection; [and] that our arrival would be considered the most joyful event." Porter praised the provisions. Fresh produce was abundant and excellent, there were plenty of hogs, and the "flour and bread were of a very superior quality."

One of the things that Porter had thought would make the Chileans uncomfortable was the war then being waged between the United States and Great Britain, an ally of Spain. Porter's mission in the Pacific was, in fact, to protect American shipping and destroy British commerce, which he proceeded to do with gusto upon his departure from Valparaiso. After capturing or destroying seventeen British vessels, he returned to Valparaiso early in 1814. There he found that Carrera had been replaced by yet another revolutionary leader, Bernardo O'Higgins, whose Irish-born father, Ambrose, had been the governor at Valparaiso two decades earlier. Porter also found the British Royal Navy pursuing him to the very mouth of the harbor. On March 28, 1814, Porter's *Essex* met the British frigate *Phoebe*, under the command of Commodore James Hillyar, accompanied by two smaller armed vessels. In a heated battle, Porter was forced to surrender with heavy casualties among his crew.

By July, Porter was back in New York, speaking and writing in favor of the ousted Carrera who had, in fact, returned to power soon after Porter's departure. The stage was thus set for Thomas H. Perkins and William Sturgis to consider backing a venture to Chile.

What the owners of the *Ophelia*, David Porter, and Sam Hill did not know was that the factional split between the revolutionaries in Chile had left them open to an invasion by Spanish forces. In October 1814 at Rancagua, in the foothills of the Andes, the revolutionary forces were defeated and the Spanish regained control of Chile. Bernardo O'Higgins fled to Argentina where he joined forces with José de San Martín, who was organizing revolutions all over lower South America.

When the *Ophelia* hove to outside the harbor of Valparaiso, Hill learned that all of the old Spanish trade restrictions were back in effect. He took a boat's crew and Tom Perkins into the town to ask permission to bring the ship into the port to procure water, of which, Hill says, they were "nearly destitute." Permission was granted and Hill was rowed back to the place where he had left his ship under the command of the first mate, John King. The ship was nowhere to be found. As Hill would describe the event in his logbook the next day, "Mr. King having made a long Stretch off the Land, I did not succeed in reaching the ship." There is no reference anywhere in the log, then or later, to suspicions of King's motives, though he would later write to the owners of a plot against him and their interests.

The next day the *Ophelia* returned and anchored in the Valparaiso roadstead. Around them were several Spanish merchant ships, an American whaleship (the *Charles* of Nantucket), and one of the vessels that had been captured by David Porter while on the *Essex* the year before. The officials told Hill that his men could have liberty on shore as long as they were back on the ship by nine o'clock each evening. He was ordered to surrender his instructions and log book, and any letters onboard that were addressed to persons in Valparaiso. Hill now had to surrender Porter's letter to Remigio Blanco and learned that Blanco had been arrested when the Spanish regained control of Chile and was imprisoned on the island of Juan Fernandez.

The Spanish position in Chile was still tenuous. Bernardo O'Higgins and José de San Martín were in Argentina planning another coup, Spain was still struggling to regain a solid financial footing, and the port of Valparaiso and the capital city of Santiago were a long way from the central government. On the expectation that his $70,000 might be valuable to the Chilean government, Hill tested the waters with the Governor at Valparaiso. Would it be possible for him to purchase copper while he was in the port? The Governor told him that permission must come directly from the President, Don Mariano Ossorio, in Santiago. That evening, Hill and Perkins had dinner at the Governor's house.

The next day another ship arrived from Boston, the *Beverly,* under the command of Captain Sam Edes. The Americans in the port now prepared themselves for an extended stay in Chile, and began a round of social encounters with the Chileans, both royalists and revolutionaries. Valparaiso, or "Valipo" as it was commonly known to sailors, was a charming and friendly place, rapidly developing from a ramshackle settlement to a world-class port. Though another port was developing further to the south at Talcahuano, Valparaiso was really the first place along the coast of Chile where it seemed natural to stop after coming around Cape Horn. It did not have a well-protected harbor, but it had a beachfront on a coastline surrounded by dramatic steep mountains.

Hill described the town upon his arrival.

The town of Valparaiso is Situated on a margin of uneven land, which extends along the shores of the bay and Part of the buildings are on the sides of the Hills which are dug away for that purpose. The chain of Barren Steep & Rugged Hills, which bind the Coast, rises very steep to a

Considerable elevation immediately behind the Town, and some of them almost overhang the Streets & houses. The Houses here are built with a kind of large square Brick made from the common red earth on the spot, and formed in Molds, after which they are dried in the sun and then used for building. The walls are afterwards Plaistered with lime mortar which gives them an appearance of Neatness. The roofs are covered with Tiles as in Europe.

When Hill had been in Valparaiso a little more than a week, Governor Villegas informed him that the purchase of copper, though "strictly prohibited by the laws," might be possible, given the current situation of the government. Hill decided to go to Santiago and press his application in person. Captain Edes, in Chile on a similar mission, asked to accompany him and the two men made plans for a venture by horseback to the capital. In the meanwhile, Hill spent most of his time on shore, having left orders with Mr. King for repairs to the sails, rigging, and hull of the *Ophelia* during his absence. Tom Perkins was not interested in accompanying Hill on his road trip and did not wish to remain on the ship, so he took a room in the house of Mrs. Blanco, and brought ashore his "box of Dollars," which Hill believed contained two thousand dollars.

On November 13, just before his departure for Santiago, Hill held a dinner party on the *Ophelia*. He invited several Chilean officials, and the officers of the nearby ships, including Captain Edes of the *Beverly* and his son Robert, who served as his first mate. Perkins had returned to the ship for the party, and in the course of the evening got into a fight with Captain Edes. Hill reported that "after hearing Mr. Perkins make use of very Indecent & abusive language to Capt. Edes, such as calling him a liar, and telling him he would deprive him of a living, and beggar him, by his father's Influence, that he was in his Power & he would make him know it," Hill "begged Mr. Perkins to desist and not make my Company unhappy."

Until this point, Hill had not said much about Perkins in his daily logbook. Now he began to complain about him, beginning with the fact that he had "directed the same kind of language" to Hill as he had to Captain Edes, and was asked by Hill to leave the ship and go to his quarters on shore. The mate, John King, also now came forward with a story about Thomas Perkins, Jr.

"The Day before this Fracas," Hill wrote, "Mr. King Informed me that some days Previous Mr. Perkins came onboard one evening when I was on shore and after walking the deck a few minutes he asked Mr. King to go in the Cabbin as he wished to talk with him."

> Mr. King went below & Mr. Perkins took out a Paper which he said was his Instructions for the Voyage from his father, and read some Parts of it to him. He then kicked a Box of Money which stood in his room & told Mr. King there was money for him whenever he wanted it. Mr. Perkins then Observed that it was believed on Shore that the Patriot troops from Buenos Ayres were coming in to Valipo & if he thought so he would order Mr. King immediately to cut the cables & Proceed to sea.

It is impossible to tell from Hill's manuscript logbook whether this entry was actually written at sea or if he recopied it after the voyage, which would have given him a retrospective opportunity to cast events in a different light. It seems unlikely that he would have given such free reign to hearsay testimony about the son of the owner of the ship in a document that he might later be asked to share with the owner. But it was clearly not long after the *Ophelia's* arrival in Valparaiso that Hill began to suspect Perkins of plotting against him.

> For some time past Mr. Perkins had conducted extremely Irregular & as related to me very unhandsome. Yet I had taken no further notice of it than to discontinue all Confidential Conversation with him, but still treated him with attention and civility. I had however for some weeks Past been convinced that a Serious Plan of Mischief had been meditated against me by Mr. Perkins, but I took no notice of it hoping he would one day open his eyes to reason & truth. Yet it gave me much Uneasiness, as the half confession of Mr. King showed that Private Consultation of a very serious nature had been held on board the Ophelia between Mr. Perkins & King.

Hill continued with his plans to travel overland to the Chilean capital of Santiago, and on November 18, departed with Captain Edes. Some twenty years before, Governor Ambrose O'Higgins had built a highway from Valparaiso inland to the capital, and it was along this road that Hill and Edes traveled, accompanied by several local guides and servants. Hill found the road impressive, a "most Stupendous Work, and considering the Country through which it passes, perhaps it equals anything of the Kind in any Country." For two days they traveled on horseback up and down hills, across plains and mountains. Hill was very pleased with the people he met, "who were very ready to give us anything we asked for and Seemed exceedingly Civil." They stopped one night on the road and arrived in the capitol in the afternoon of Monday, November 20.

Santiago proved a surprising treat for Hill, filled with elegant people and architecture. He estimated the population to be about 50,000—enough to support a cathedral, still under construction after more than sixty years. To his delight, "the Ladies in Particular [were] extremely Courteous, affable and engaging... very fond of evening Parties and dancing, and Scarce a female of any Class, but can Play on the Piano forte, the Harpsichord or the Guitar." Hill settled into the local schedule of a late breakfast, a morning of work followed by a meal, then a siesta, then another meal, then socializing with visits, music, and dancing, and then supper from midnight until two a.m.

There were, he complained, "no Decent Publick Houses in Chile where travelers can be accommodated," but "the Hospitality of the Chileans is Such that with the most Slight Introductions a Gentleman will be Provided with Apartments and every thing he may want for his Convenience which the Place affords." Hill had made several friends among the merchants of Valparaiso, and they gave him letters of introduction to their counterparts in Santiago. Through friends and relations of his Valparaiso comrades, he was introduced to "Don Felipe Santiago Solas, a Merchant of respectability," where he was received "with every mark of Politeness & attention & accommodated with a room ready furnished." Mrs. Solas was a beautiful young woman of around twenty-five years old.

As in Valparaiso, Hill settled comfortably into a round of socializing and business. He and Captain Edes were able to meet with President Ossorio almost immediately, and were advised to "Present a Petition stating in Short hand the reasons which Induced us to ask this favour, and the loss we must suffer by the Original Intention of the Voyage being defeated in consequence of our late arrival in China & c."

President Ossorio was frank about his need for cash to pay his troops. Seventy thousand Spanish dollars sitting in trunks on a ship in Valparaiso harbor was a powerful incentive for trade. But despite Ossorio's hopes and encouragement, it was not to be, he told the Americans. Such trade with strangers was prohibited by the crown and the Spanish authorities would not permit it. Ossorio was soon to leave office and consequently did not want "to Compromise himself," as he explained to Hill. The two Boston captains and their party returned to Valparaiso on December 13.

Everything seemed fine back on the ship. "Went on board where I found all quiet & regular," Hill wrote in his logbook. "I had been absent 25 days. Directions were immediately given to get ready for sea."

In subsequent documents, Hill would alter the timeline of events, making it difficult to pinpoint exactly what led to his accusation that his mate, John King, had tried to steal the ship while he was away in Santiago. After King had been discharged from the *Ophelia,* Hill wrote an account for the owners in Boston, saying that he had heard "shocking accusations" while he was in Santiago and had rushed back to Valparaiso. His daily log covering the ten days following his return to the ship, however, is silent on these matters.

How much of John King's history was known to Captain Hill prior to leaving Boston is unclear, but the merchants who owned the vessel certainly knew of his experiences on a previous voyage to Chile. King had gone to Chile in 1813 on a voyage of the *Pearl,* a vessel owned and managed by James and Thomas Handasyd Perkins. In the spring of 1813, the *Pearl* was leased, at Valparaiso, by the Revolutionary government of Chile to patrol the coast and keep Spanish troops and supplies from landing. In this venture, the *Pearl* (renamed *Perla* by the Chileans) sailed in company with another American ship, the *Colt,* which had been purchased for the same purpose. John King served as sailing master of the *Perla* under her new Chilean captain, José Vicente Barba.

At 200 tons, the *Perla* was not a particularly large vessel. Nonetheless, one hundred and twenty men were crowded aboard her, mostly Chileans hired to augment the American crew. On May 2, as the *Perla* and *Colt* sailed out of Valparaiso harbor, they were fired upon by the Spanish royalist privateer *Warren* and many of the Chilean crew of the *Perla,* in a pre-arranged plot, mutinied and surrendered the vessel. (The *Warren* was another American ship, which had been seized in 1807 by the Spanish for contraband trading on the coast of South America.)

Seeing that the *Perla* was going to be taken by the *Warren,* King jumped overboard and swam ashore. Too debilitated when he finally reached land to muster any forces before the *Colt* and *Perla* were taken off to the royalist port of Callao in Peru, King was at least able to report the plot and its aftermath.

One of the Americans on the *Colt* was Samuel Burr Johnston, a journalist who had come to Chile a year earlier and who wrote about conditions on the two ships after their capture. Johnston, who arrived in Chile with a printing press and two American partners, published a newspaper called *Aurora de Chile,* which openly promoted the cause of independence. He was, consequently, particularly worried about what his reception would be both on shipboard and by the Spanish in Callao.

The mutineers turned out to be no threat to him. They had been bribed by the royalists and were, he wrote, "the most unprincipled wretches, without any discipline or order amongst them." There was no acknowledged leader among the gang that now controlled the ships, he reported, "as the common voice prevails."

> Fore and aft are strewed buckets of spirits and wine, to which all have free access, and as soon as a bucket is empty, it is filled again. Gambling of all kinds is carried on with the money they have robbed us of, and riot, drunkenness, and every vice prevails.

On May 18, they arrived at Callao where the Americans were imprisoned under very harsh conditions. Though the government of Peru had no relations with the revolutionary government of Chile, they did have diplomatic relations with the United States, and even though there was no free trade with the Peruvian ports, a few American citizens were then residing in Peru. One of them was Samuel Curson, a merchant who often acted as an agent for the firm of Bryant and Sturgis.

Samuel Curson was an old friend of William Sturgis; the two had made their first circumnavigation together on the *Eliza* in 1798. After Sturgis became a merchant, he regularly hired Curson as a captain and later as a representative in Spanish-speaking countries, including Cuba. It was Curson who worked tirelessly on behalf of the American crews of the *Pearl* and *Colt,* finally getting them released after several months of imprisonment.

Back in Valparaiso, John King was commissioned by David Porter of the *Essex* to bring one of his prize ships, the English whaleship *New Zealander,* back to the United States. King sailed around Cape Horn and was within a few days of delivering the ship to New York when the British captured him and the vessel. (For a short period, he and Sam Hill may have been paroled in Halifax at the same time.) The date of King's release is not known, nor is the date at which he made himself available to the owners of the *Ophelia* in Boston, but by that time they had certainly heard about the misadventures of the *Pearl* and her crew in Chile. In addition to information shared by David Porter, Samuel Curson had probably written about the situation to William Sturgis prior to the *Ophelia's* voyage.

John King's presence onboard Hill's ship was, consequently, no accident. The owners obviously expected that his knowledge of both Chilean politics and the Spanish language would work to their advantage. That King sailed as mate rather than master is interesting. He was clearly qualified to command the *Ophelia,* though it is not clear that he was qualified to manage the business end of a voyage. Samuel Hill had already been hired as captain and supercargo of the ship before the Chilean venture had been solidified.

Little suspecting that they were playing to their new captain's paranoid weakness, the owners put John King onboard the *Ophelia* as mate under the command of Captain Samuel Hill, while publicly acknowledging that King had information and expertise that Hill lacked. Compounded by the presence of Tom Perkins, who had no defined position on the ship other than that of arrogant son of the principal owner, this was a recipe for disaster. Samuel Hill could see only one solution that would promote his own interests: King and Perkins had to leave the ship, and they did, at Valparaiso.

On February 28, 1817, more than two years later, Hill wrote a lengthy and elaborate letter to the owners of the ship describing why he had fired King. "It is reasonable to presume," he wrote, "that some confidence was reposed in that Officers ability to assist me at Valparaiso."

> I have therefore believed it my duty to lay before you the most full and satisfactory information relative to his conduct. ... I shall only remark that from a respect to the opinion entertained of that officers merit by my owners, as well as from a principle of Justice; I felt it my duty to conduct the examination of his conduct, with the utmost candour and impartiality."

The letter is filled with elaborate details, suspicions, suppositions, and foreshadowing, which Hill never hinted at in his log. By the end of the voyage, Hill seemed to remember that he had always been suspicious of King. He could report with surety that the incident on the *Ophelia's* first day in Valparaiso, when Hill returned to the ship and found it missing, had a very sinister aspect (though his logbook shows he thought only that the *Ophelia* was taken out of his reach by unfavorable winds on that occasion). Hill now asserted that he had always interpreted it with "extreme surprise and mortification." It was an event that had left him open to "a Suspicion of treasonable purposes," and had made him ever watchful of King's behavior. He had, in fact, been worried enough to ask port officials in Valparaiso to keep an eye on the ship while he was in Santiago. "I trust," he wrote to the owners, that "the necessity for such Precaution, has been Sufficiently demonstrated."

The two charges against King—that he had attempted to steal the ship and that he had been involved in revolutionary activities on a previous voyage to Chile—were dealt with separately. For the latter, Hill was assured, King would not be arrested if he did not leave the ship. If he should be found on shore, however, he would be apprehended and sent to Lima for prosecution.

Hill informed Sturgis and Perkins that he had inquired around Valparaiso and had learned "from the most respectable Gentlemen of those who were attached to the Patriot Party, that the conduct of Mr. King had been marked with extreme imprudence, and notorious improprieties, during the short time he was employed in Chili under the Revolutionary Government; and this information was corroborated by two American Gentlemen, who on seeing him onboard the *Ophelia,* inform'd me of the Circumstances above alluded to, and said they were present in Chile at the time of his employment there as aforesaid."

To determine the circumstances of John King's attempted mutiny, Hill held a drumhead court on shipboard. He explained the process in some detail in his letter.

Lest I might err in Judgment, I requested the attendance of Several Gentlemen of known discretion and ability; Capt. Fyffe of the Indefatigable is upwards of fifty years of age, and Mr. Colin Campbell, a very honorable Mercht. a Resident in Buenos Ayres, and having a family there and generally esteemed in Chile for his known Probity and exemplary Conduct, attended to explain in English, the evidence of the Commandant of the Port; lest I might be thought to give it wrong interpretation.

The other men in attendance at the hearing were Don Felipe Villaouinea, the Captain of the Port, Captain Edes of the *Beverly* with his son and first mate Robert, and Charles Brown, the supercargo of the *Beverly.* "Mr. Thos. H. Perkins Jr. was Particularly requested to attend, but he went on Shore and did not attend, or return on board untill next day."

King was allowed to make a statement at the opening of the proceedings, in which he reported a rumor in the port that Captain Hill had been arrested at Santiago and that the ship was going to be seized by the government. In consequence, he made everything ready onboard to cut the cables if necessary for a quick escape, and had the boarding pikes and guns put in readiness to repel any attempt to board the ship. Various members of the crew were called to testify as to King's actions. All agreed that he had prepared the ship to leave the harbor. That he *thought* Captain Hill might be a prisoner was also clear. But King did not, in fact, ever leave port with the ship. He was certainly arrested, but by that point, the two charges—of being a mutineer and being a revolutionary— seem to have become muddled in the minds of the port officials.

The whole of these proceedings may have been brought to a head by the arrival in port of the *Warren* on December 19, less than a week after Hill's return to Valparaiso. This was the very vessel that had taken the *Pearl* two and a half years earlier, when King was onboard. As he had escaped and stayed in Valparaiso at that time to report on the battle and on the traitorous conduct of several of the local crew, King must have found himself both recognized and unwelcome.

Also on the *Warren*, was the man who would replace Ossorio as leader of the colonial government in Chile, Don Francisco Marco del Pont. Whether the arrival of a new potential benefactor influenced Hill's decision to make public charges against John King, the known revolutionary, it now became clear that King could not stay on the *Ophelia*.

Hill asked Captain Edes of the *Beverly* if he would take him, but as three officers of the ship had been part of King's drumhead trial, it was clearly not a reasonable solution. Hill then asked Captain Page of the Salem ship *Indus*, which arrived in port on Christmas Eve, but was refused because "Doctor Frost, who was an agent or supercargo on board, and who had formerly known Mr. King at Coquimbo would say nothing in his favour." John King consequently spent the Christmas season in prison on shore.

Leaving his mate in a Spanish prison in Chile was certainly not going to look good to the owners, no matter how Hill explained it. King had been tapped especially for this voyage, and the Boston merchants were all in favor of revolutionary activity against Spanish colonial rule. Eventually, in late January, an English whaleship, the *Zephyr* of London, agreed to take King onboard and Hill made arrangements for his release from prison. Hill stated that his "principal object in this matter was a motive of humanity to Mr. King," which he "very readily approved of," and Hill waved a cheery good-bye as King was sent off on a multi-year voyage hunting whales in the Pacific Ocean.

Still onboard was the other obstacle to Hill's total control of the voyage: Thomas Handasyd Perkins, Jr. In both his logbook and his letter to the owners, Hill says that he wanted Perkins to back him in his prosecution of King, but Perkins would have no part of it.

> I think it would have been highly proper, that Mr. Perkins should have attended the examination, for which reason I very particularly notified him of it, and requested him to remain on board that morning, but he answered me by saying that he had nothing to do with it, nor did it concern him, and having breakfasted he went immediately on shore, and did not return on board untill the next day, when I immediately read to him the whole of the examination and evidence, to which he replied that he had heretofore believed Mr. King an honest man, but he now believed him a Scoundrel, and added that he supposed he had involved himself in difficulty, and wished to have some other person share the blame of it.

Hill seems to have regretted at that point in the proceedings that he had spoken so warmly about Perkins in his logbook and wrote a retraction of it. (There is also at least one page missing from the log during this period.)

> In Justice to Mr. T.H. Perkins Jr. I must remark that I am of opinion the Statement of King relative to the conversation held with him on the Subject of ordering the Ship to Sea, the offer of Money & c., was founded in falsehood, in part if not wholly; and intended to Justify himself: or if such a conversation was agitated it Probably arose from a vanity of Predicting what he thought would take place, or was dictated by a levity of

expression too frequently practised by that young gentleman; for which reason I did not propose the question which drew from him this statement, but it was I believe put by Capt. Edes. I had heard the story from Mr. King previous to my Journey to Santiago, and had paid no attention to it.

In June 1819, when he wrote his autobiographical statement, Hill would have worse things to say about young Mr. Perkins, but by then he was no longer hoping to get another command from his father. "The Eldest Son of T.H. Perkins Esquire accompanied me on this voyage as Passenger," he wrote, and "was the cause of some trouble, & much uneasiness to me." Perkins left the ship soon after John King and sailed home to Boston. Once again, as with the horrible events on the *Lydia,* Hill must have considered what sort of report of him would precede his return home. Neither King nor Perkins could have much good to say.

While King was still in prison, and with Perkins living on shore, Hill decided to make one more run at the Chilean officials to see if the transfer of power from Ossorio to Marco had created an opening for him to trade. He was, consequently, pleased to be able to place himself before Marco twice before the new President moved from Valparaiso to Santiago.

One of these opportunities was at a dinner party onboard the English frigate *Indefatigable,* which had come into Valparaiso while Hill was in Santiago. On December 22, Captain John Fyffe invited the captains of all the foreign merchant vessels, including the American Captains Hill and Edes, and the new Governor and local officials, for an afternoon of "festive Hilarity."

Hill and Edes attempted to press their trading interests, but were told that the new president was "unacquainted with the situation of the country, but after he arrived at Santiago he should be enabled to Judge of the Propriety of such a measure." The next day Marco left for Santiago and Hill and Edes decided to follow him and try again. Through the first weeks of 1816, Hill continued his application, until it finally became clear to him that he would not be able to purchase copper at this time in Chile.

The *Ophelia* had been in the bay of Valparaiso for more than three months and no cargo had come aboard. He wrote a melancholy "Review of Negotiations in Chile" into his logbook. "On Reviewing the Progress & results of my efforts for Procuring Permission to load at Valipo, I feel much mortified, and yet I have under all the Circumstances done what appeared to me to be my duty." The reasons for his failure were in part due to competition from Edes, whom Hill believed gave the government the impression that Bostonians were aiming for the Chilean port "for the Purpose of bringing correspondence to the Enemies of the Government," and the change of leadership which, unfortunately for Hill, was already in progress when he arrived. He believed that either Ossorio or Marco would readily have taken his cash to pay their troops, but neither felt himself in a strong enough position at that particular time. The real decision-making power had consequently fallen on the old guard, and their opposition to foreign trade was, Hill wrote, "easily explained." They were Spanish-born, and "the largest Capitalists in the Country." It was their intention to keep the people living in Chile poor and dependent, both to serve the Spanish Government and "at the same time advance their own Individual Interests." If peace returned to Europe, then it would be most profitable to ship the copper there to sell it.

Hill's best chance for success now seemed to rest on his ability to parlay information gathered on this voyage into profits on a subsequent venture. Two things about Chile were very clear to him: the Creole aristocracy had a desire for luxury items from Canton and the money to pay for them whether their country was independent or a Spanish colony; and Chile would not be a Spanish colony much longer. Anyone who could bring the right goods to Chile and have luck in the timing as it related to the transitory state of the government could make a fortune. To that end Hill laid out an elaborate scheme of contraband trading. In describing such a plan in great detail, he hoped not only to find sponsorship for his next voyage, but also to recoup something of his reputation at the failure of this one.

The following particulars will Perhaps Point out more Satisfactorily the reasons which induced me to Persevere so long in my attempt to gain Permission to load in Valipo and also the causes in part, if not wholly, why the attempt failed of Success. ... The high price which many articles of Merchandise would command at Present in Chile offers a powerful inducement to adventurers, but none can be Introduced except by contraband, or smuggling, and in this way I think a cargo of 50 or 60 thousand Dollars or even a much greater amount might be disposed of in Chile with very little risk and not much delay. In order to select a complete assortment of goods for the Market of Chile it will be necessary to include a variety of articles of the manufactures of Great Britain, France, Germany & c., but such an Invoice as can be made up in Canton will sell quick and pay a very handsome Profit, Say 200 p cent Clear of Charges of Selling and duties. See the following Schedule in which the amount in each Several kind of Goods is to be the amount Invested in Canton.

What follows is a remarkably detailed list of textiles: linens, silks, cottons, meticulously described with amounts in volume and value, for sale in Chile. Colors were specified, as well as quality. Hill described two grades of linens, for different uses in the Chilean marketplace, as well as the size, quality, and detailing of 3,000 linen handkerchiefs. He thought that at least ten thousand dollars should be invested in Silk Goods, "of which 1000 dollars should be in Silk Handkerchiefs and 1000 in Sewing Silks."

The residue in Lustings & Sarsenets for Ladies wear. Colors lively, say sky blue, Pale red, or Pink red, fawn color, White, Green, Pearl Color, Rose red, & c. a few Silk Shawls say five or six dozen, with raised flowers wove in the fabrick, the field or middle of one Color & a rich party colored border with a net fringe all round. Colors of the field: Sky blue, Rose red, Pearl, fawn and some few Green. 5 to 7 quarters Square. Also a few triangle Silk dress hkfs for the Breast of small size & Pick gaudy colors, with fringed borders — say 5 or 6 dozen.

Hill also recommended that a ship carry beads of glass and stone, and provided details about suitable colors, sizes, and configurations. He thought fifteen hundred dollars should be invested in chinaware, and the same amount in Chinese teas. He also thought that Chinese lacquered furniture, fans, and shoes would find a market.

The riches that were available in Chile had been tantalizing and frustratingly close during the months he had been in the country. Hill was chafing for the Chileans to recognize this and open trade.

> The kingdom of Chile is rich in Minerals of the most valuable kind and Contains not only Immense quantities of Gold & Silver, but also very rich Mines of Copper & Iron and Some tin. And when the Period shall arrive in which the Chileans shall rouse from that Lethargy which at Present Pervades the Inhabitants of this favored Clime and assert those rights which their Situation entitled them to, when a just and equitable Government is formed by the native Inhabitants of the Soil, and free from those wretched Minions of the Kingdom of Old Spain, then, and not till then, Chile will become a great and a Powerful Country, and the Introduction of commerce will give them all which they want to make them a happy, a brave, & generous People.

After three months in Chile, Hill was forced to admit, "much to [his] mortification and regret," that he had failed to crack the market. As he left Valparaiso, his reputation was in some danger, not only from the report he would get from Tom Perkins and John King, but from the final outcome of the voyage, which did not look promising. He now depended on the accuracy of David Porter's questionable whales' teeth proposition to make the voyage a success and he was rightfully dubious about it. Without whales' teeth, the Marquesas were out. Without a cargo onboard, even Hawaii was not a good prospect. Neither the Hawaiians nor the Marquesans had any interest in or use for his Spanish dollars. They had no place to spend them.

At this point, however, Hill had no choice but to continue west and northward toward the Galapagos and Polynesia. The *Ophelia* weighed anchor and sailed from Valparaiso on February 6, 1816. "The Object of my Visit to the Galapagos Islands," Hill recorded, "is to Procure Whales teeth which are Said to be found in great numbers... and if successful in finding a sufficient number of these teeth to proceed with them to the Marquesas Island to Procure Sandal wood by Purchasing it with the teeth." The Galapagos Islands were sighted on the afternoon of February 24, and numerous whaleships were in the vicinity. The *Ophelia* log records five American whaling vessels sighted in the first two days.

Hill found the sailing difficult. This was a "very confused irregular sea," with strong currents. He quickly lost his position and devoted page after page in his log to mathematical calculations, trying to determine his longitude by the lunar distance method.

On his second day in the area he spoke to Captain Caleb Reynolds of Boston, sent on the same errand as himself aboard the ship *Sultan*. Reynolds' orders were specific about the whales' teeth. Like Perkins and Sturgis, the owners of the *Sultan* were depending on David Porter's report. Reynolds and one of the whaling captains told Hill that in this season the winds and currents made it difficult, if not impossible, to get into Narborough Island's Banks Bay, and Reynolds was obviously beginning to have the same doubts as Hill about the whole venture.

In respect to the whales teeth they would not be Positive, but doubted if there were many to be found at this time as they were of Opinion that nearly all of them had been taken away some time since and they doubted if any whales had been killed lately to Produce more. Added to this the demand for them in Nantucket Previous to their Sailing had been such that they were of Opinion most of them would be Preserved by the Whalers instead of throwing them to drift ashore in the Shelters as formerly.

On February 26, Hill "got within five miles of the North West Point of Narborough Island," and "considered it as certain that I should get into Banks Bay with ease before night." But the winds died, the current proved stronger than expected, and he found himself drifting rapidly in the wrong direction. For eleven days he fought the winds and currents, moved in close to the islands, was swept back out to sea, and lost and regained his position.

Through it all he saw numerous ships. On March 1, there were six ships in sight. From one of the captains he learned that they had been fighting much the same battle. They "had been endeavoring to work up against the current for three weeks, & had not yet been able to effect it. Their object was to get into Banks Bay in the hope of finding whales there. ... They stated that they had never experienced the currents running so strong as for several weeks past."

For almost two weeks the *Ophelia* struggled to enter Banks Bay without success. Finally, Hill's expectation that there were probably few teeth there, compounded by his inability to get at them anyway, led him to abandon the effort. This was certainly the right decision. The rumor of whale's teeth lying in the sand of Banks Bay would prove false, and the numerous Yankee whaleships cruising in Polynesian waters were bringing sperm whale teeth directly to the Marquesas anyway, making them available there in ever greater numbers. Tahitian and Marquesan men were also beginning to sign aboard American whaleships for Pacific cruises and could bring back teeth on their own. It was inevitable that the valuable market in whales' teeth described by Porter would collapse.

On Thursday, March 7, 1816, the *Ophelia* turned toward the Hawaiian Islands, some four thousand miles distant. Three weeks later brought the crew in sight of the east point of Oahu.

***

Hill did not have high expectations for success in Hawaii though he was, for the first time on this voyage, in familiar trading territory. On March 30, he learned from islanders at Waikiki that the Hawaiian King, Kamehameha (or Tamahahmaha, as Hill wrote it), had moved his court from Oahu to a village near Kealakekua Bay on the big island of Hawaii. This was a location well known to Americans and Europeans as the place where Captain James Cook had been killed in 1779. The *Ophelia* proceeded there and arrived four days later.

Hill had spent significant time in the Hawaiian Islands on the voyages of the *Lydia* and *Otter*. The king, wrote Hill, "immediately recognized me and seemed glad to see me." In the course of the day Hill introduced his business. Would the king provide him with a cargo of sandalwood in exchange for Spanish Dollars? Kamehameha was doubtful. He had none cut, he explained, and his people were unwilling to go to the mountains to cut it because they had not been paid by the last two Boston captains who had come through the previous year.

Besides, what Kamehameha wanted was not dollars but ships. He had already purchased three from Americans, the *Albatross, Lydia,* and *Cleopatra's Barge,* and he had a small schooner built for him by Americans in 1805, which he named *Tamana* after his Queen. He used it to upgrade to a larger vessel, the *Lelia Byrd,* which was purchased with the *Tamana* and a cargo of sandalwood.

Kamehameha's current dispute with two Boston captains, William Heath Davis and Jonathan Winship, Jr., was over the *Lelia Byrd.* Davis and Winship had sold their vessels, the *Isabella* and the *O'Cain,* to the Russians at Sitka in 1814, and had then taken passage on the Salem ship *Packet* to Hawaii, where they negotiated a deal with Kamehameha for a cargo of sandalwood. Having no ship of their own on which to transport it, they had "borrowed" the *Lelia Byrd,* and Kamehameha wanted it back.

Hill explained that he "was totally unacquainted with the business of Captains Winship and Davis" (though he certainly knew Winship from his previous voyage). He was very sorry if they had "ill treated him," but it was not in his power to remedy it. Kamehameha and Hill discussed paying the dollars for sandalwood, but the king's price was too high. The party moved from shore out to the *Ophelia,* where the king visited with a large party, but as Hill "did not furnish them with Strong Spirits in Sufficient quantity to make them Intoxicated, they made but a short visit."

For several days negotiations alternated with eating and drinking until finally Hill began to lose patience. Kameha-meha "would talk of nothing but a Brig or Schooner in exchange for Sandal wood," Hill wrote, and "as this was an article which I could not furnish him it appeared to me useless to talk more on the Subject."

In going over the entire inventory of the ship, which had been purposefully kept clean of useful cargo in order to avoid harassment by the Spaniards in Chile, Hill found little that would serve to open serious negotiations. The only thing in the hold was the wood to build a base, on which the Chilean copper would be sitting had they actually procured any. In a flash of inspiration, it occurred to Hill that he could build boats out of those pine planks.

He tried to convince Kamehameha that a few good boats would be of "infinitely more service to him than a large Vessel," but the king was unmoved. The Hawaiians already had their own outrigger canoes which were well suited to inter-island travel. Furthermore, Hill soon learned that Captain Ebbets of Boston was lying at Oahu with the brig *Forrester,* and might be willing to sell it.

Hill then tried to get the Hawaiians to give them some pigs and produce, but as the *Ophelia* carried no small trade goods, they were refused even that. "The King only sent me one Indifferent Hog, & about two Bushels of Vegetables, which was all I could have," he lamented.

The only glimmer of good news that came in this part of the cruise was obtained from Captain Isaiah Lewis of the Salem brig *Panther,* who had come to Hawaii from the Marquesas Islands. "The eagerness with which those People formerly had sought for whales teeth had almost entirely subsided," Lewis told Hill. "Firearms and ammunition were now the articles most in demand." At least Hill had not wasted more time pursuing the empty promise of Porter's Marquesan scheme.

On April 6, Hill ordered the anchor weighed and headed to the island of Kauai, or Atooi. This was the home of the unfortunate girl he had abducted and taken on the *Lydia* on his first voyage in the Pacific. Like Kamehameha, the King at Atooi, Kaumualii (called "Tamooerea" by Hill), "seemed Indifferent to any kind of barter for Sandal wood, except a Brig or a Schooner of 180 or 200 tons burthen." Also like Kamehameha, he complained of "fraudulent treatment from the Messrs Winship and Davis."

Hill now abandoned hope of purchasing a cargo of sandalwood. Seriously in need of fresh provisions, he cruised from island to island selling his pine planking for pigs and produce, and carrying native passengers between the islands. It was almost a month later that he was finally ready to proceed on the voyage. Now he would sail "with all Possible dispatch" for Batavia, to see if he could find any business with the Dutch. This appeared, he thought "the most advisable Route both in compliance with my Instructions and for the Promoting my owners Interest, as my arrival in Battavia, if I should be able to effect nothing there, the Season would be such that we should arrive in China in Sufficient time to Profit of the favorable Monsoon for the Passage to the United States, should that be the determination of my owners, or their representatives in Canton."

***

Hill could not leave the Hawaiian Islands without commenting on the changes that had occurred in the native people since his last visit there, on the *Otter,* six years earlier.

> This ended our transactions at the Sandwich island, and from my Observations while among them I am decidedly of opinion they have degenerated in Character, Conduct & Morals, within the Last Six Years very much. Indeed many of them acknowledge the fact, and as men ever Seek some excuse for what they know to be wrong, these say that it is owing to the Faithless & deceptive Conduct Practised among them by the White men. ... How far these Assertions may be true I am not to decide, but the whole of the Inhabitants of these Islands taken as a People are certainly more depraved than when I last visited them.

Among the white men mentioned by name were the by now familiar Davis and Winship. That Samuel Hill himself might bear any of the responsibility he never acknowledged. He had certainly matched any American or British captain in his mastery of deceptive practices when trading with Hawaiians and Northwest Coast Indians on his two previous voyages. And yet, when Sam Hill explains why Hawaiians now seem so degraded, the answer is found more in their own weaknesses. "At Present both the males & females give themselves up to an Immoderate use of ardent Spirits, and make a Point of getting Intoxicated whenever they can obtain a Sufficient quantity of Liquor," he wrote. "They also make use of an Immense quantity of tobacco."

These practices, in addition to a diet where dried salted fish was replacing fresh fish, produce, and pork, had also made them less attractive in Hill's eye. Especially among "those who reckon themselves as Chiefs," a number of disgusting maladies were common, including blood-shot eyes, and "cutaneous disorders & Eruptions such as the Itch, Scab, & a humour resembling St. Anthony's fire." It was "now a rare thing to see a fair smooth skinned Islander except among the Farmers who live at a great distance in the Country."

Kamehameha he acknowledged to have been a good leader, but Hill did not find his son promising. "Rehu Rehu, the Kings Son who is heir to the Sovereignty of these islands," Hill noted, was "about 20 years of age, about 5 feet 8 Inches in height and rather Stout, in Proportion to his height." Among other improprieties witnessed by Hill, Liholiho (Hill's Rehu Rehu) had brought the old art of stealing to new heights. When he came aboard the *Ophelia* with a retinue, they pilfered a number of objects. "From all I have seen of this young man's conduct I do not hesitate to give it as my opinion that whenever his Father dies, and he succeeds to the Sovereignty, there will be many Irregularities Committed."

Disappointed and disgusted, Hill left Hawaii on May 7, 1816. Two courses were now open to him: proceed directly to Canton, where he would turn over the business to John Cushing, the nephew of Thomas Handasyd Perkins, and the manager of his firm's business in China; or to Batavia, on the Island of Java, to do business with the Dutch.

By choosing to go to Batavia rather than to Canton directly, Hill played a hand that still gave him a good measure of control over the outcome of the voyage. If he was successful in carrying a cargo for the Dutch, he would be able to gain an advantage for the owners that they were unlikely to have with any other captain. Hill presumably spoke some Dutch. He certainly spoke Malay, and he had experience with the Dutch trading company. The disadvantage of going to Batavia rather than Canton was that it forced the *Ophelia* to cross through the more dangerous and complicated waters around New Guinea.

Hill's approach to Batavia took him on a southwesterly course from Hawaii toward the Solomon Islands. The great

Malay Archipelago, which lies between the Pacific and Indian Oceans, is a scattering of islands that stretch from Australia north and west to Asia. Sumatra is on the western extremity, and geologically one might consider the Solomon Islands as the eastern edge. This was where Sam Hill made his approach. Even as late as 1858, *Lippincott's Gazetteer* acknowledged that most of the thousands of small Malaysian islets had never been surveyed or charted and were, at any rate "studiously avoided by European navigators, who dread not only the hidden dangers of coral banks and islets, but also the piratical habits of those who dwell upon them." In addition they warned that the territory appeared to have "been raised from the ocean by the agency of subterranean fires."

The Indonesian island of Java, where Batavia served as the Dutch colonial capital, lay in an arc along the southern edge of the archipelago. To approach it, Hill could go either north or south of the big island of New Guinea. The southern passage would take the *Ophelia* along the northernmost point of Australia, which was separated from New Guinea by a number of islands. A navigator could choose to pass through either the Torres Strait or the Endeavor Straits—named for Captain James Cook's first ship. Hill rejected this southerly route as too dangerous.

He planned instead to travel along the northern edge of the island of New Guinea, but he overshot his mark somewhat, arriving at the end of May at the eastern edge of the Solomon Islands, far south of his intended route. Hill was now obliged to make his way back to a more northerly latitude along the southern coast of Bougainville island and through a narrow passage that lies between the islands of New Ireland and New Britain. At each island that he passed he observed and wrote elaborate descriptions of the flora, fauna, and native people.

On June 8, as if to announce that he had now crossed the great tectonic line that separated the Pacific plate from that on which Australia and the Indian Ocean sit, Hill felt "a Severe Shock of an Earthquake... which continued for nearly one minute & a half, during which the ship was very sensibly agitated and a confused rumbling noise was heard at the same time." It was another two weeks before he saw familiar waters, from his voyage on the *Franklin* seventeen years earlier. Navigation was extremely difficult through this period and Hill's logbook has page after page of calculations as he struggled to determine his position. They struck a reef, had limited charts, and he had "not an officer on board in whom the Smallest Confidence can be Placed not even to keep the Run of the Ship" on their intended course.

On July 11, the *Ophelia* entered the approaches to Batavia, and the crew began to see both British and Dutch warships. The Netherlands had been occupied by Napoleon's troops in Europe, and the British had seized the Dutch possessions in Indonesia. An agreement had been reached to return the islands to Holland, but the official transfer had not yet happened. The Dutch authorities, Hill wrote, "were waiting in daily expectation of it being given up to them."

Five Dutch naval vessels were in the harbor, prepared to land troops when the transfer came. A British man-of-war, three East Indiamen, and a number of smaller merchant vessels lay ready to receive the departing Englishmen. And several American merchant vessels waited to see if there would be any trade. For Hill it was another disappointment in a voyage filled with commercial disappointments. "The very great Scarcity of Coffee, Sugar, Pepper … and the high Prices at which those articles were selling induced me to give up all thoughts of loading the Ship at Batavia," he wrote. "The English Merchants or Officers of the Government being the Greatest holders of Coffee chose rather to Ship it than sell it," and though the Dutch were willing to sell him coffee if he would wait two months, the price at which they offered it was prohibitively high, and their gaining control of the trade again in a timely fashion was by no means certain. There would be no trade for the *Ophelia* at Batavia.

For Hill, who had spent an extended period at Batavia on the *John Jay* voyage twenty-one years earlier, and who had visited on several occasions since that time, the alterations in the city were almost as disappointing as the lack of trade. "The Canals, Roads, Bridges, Walls & c. are broken down or choaked up in many Places," he wrote. After a week, he weighed anchor and pointed the *Ophelia* for Canton. Had he been able to secure a cargo for Japan, he would have found his old friend Hendrik Doeff in control at Deshima.

As they left Batavia, Hill hoped to get a glimpse of a nearby volcanic island, which he called "the Triton," but missed it and blamed his crew for not keeping a vigilant enough lookout. The island was Krakatoa, and it would erupt in 1883 in one of the most powerful explosions ever recorded, killing more than 35,000 people and destroying over 150 coastal villages.

The *Ophelia* arrived at the Portuguese-held port of Macao on the last day of July. It was the only European outpost in China, and from there Hill dispatched a message to John P. Cushing at Canton. The nephew of James and Thomas Handasyd Perkins, and the agent for his family's firm in China, Cushing would now relieve Hill of responsibility for making decisions about the *Ophelia's* business.

Trading in China involved an elaborate dance through regulations and connections. Unexpected rejection of incoming cargoes, willful withholding of promised commodities, and bribes were common. Like the Japanese, the Chinese rulers had sought to cut off contact between the Chinese people and outsiders in the seventeenth century. Unlike the Japanese, the Chinese had realized that a tightly controlled foreign trade could still bring enormous wealth and an extensive list of desirable products into the country. What Deshima was to Japan, Canton was to China: an exclusive trading center for foreigners, in which Chinese rules and regulations governed trade. However, in Canton the Chinese conducted trade on a much larger scale and many more nations were involved than were permitted at Deshima.

Canton was a bustling port with a sizeable foreign population. It had two ancillary outposts, an anchorage downriver at Whampoa, where European and American ships remained with their crews while cargoes were shipped up the Pearl River to Canton; and Macao, which had been provided in 1557 as a settlement to the Portuguese and had become an important European outpost over the next two hundred and fifty years.

All trade at Canton was handled through the "co-hong," a group of merchants assigned by the Chinese government to deal with outsiders. The most successful foreigners were those who had long-term relationships with one of these "hong" merchants. With such a relationship, the China Trade could provide huge profits; without it, trade could be frustrating and financially disastrous. The Boston firm of J. and T.H. Perkins had been particularly successful in China because they always kept a family member posted there, and put a high priority on developing relationships within the Chinese merchant community.

In John Cushing the Perkins's had an agent of particular intelligence, resourcefulness, and tact. He lived in China for a number of years, spoke Cantonese, and developed and maintained connections with both local and foreign traders. Ten years Hill's junior, Cushing was, nonetheless, Hill's superior in business acumen and connections, and Hill never referred to his "much esteemed Friend John P. Cushing Esqr." without some obsequiousness.

On August 5, Cushing arrived at Macao to visit the *Ophelia* and take stock of the venture. Within a week the ship was moved to the anchorage at Whampoa and within days after that, Cushing had arranged for a place to make repairs and to begin removing ballast and replacing it with cargo. Deep in the hold were stacked bags of saltpeter, a primary ingredient of gunpowder. On top of that were placed boards, then lead-lined boxes of tea, then porcelain wrapped into straw packaging, some Chinese-made furniture, miscellaneous items, and finally, bolts of silk. It took six weeks to prepare the ship to go to sea again. On September 24, Hill reported that "we finished the Stowage of the Ship, having filled up all the State Rooms & Store rooms with Cargo & Stores, the magazine, Sail room, & c. & c. being all stowed with cargo."

Just before the ship left Canton, Cushing arranged for a passenger to return to Boston with them. It was James Bennett—now Captain Bennett—who had been Hill's mate on the *Lydia* voyage and who had left the ship thoroughly tired of Captain Hill. Bennett had been one of the men to testify on behalf of the *Lydia's* owners in Hill's lawsuit against them, and had mentioned Hill's distraction with his "young Hawaiian girl." On being asked if Hill was a good captain, Bennett had responded "when he was well," choosing not to elaborate on Hill's maniacal behavior. That was ten years before, and now Hill clearly seemed more rational to Bennett, who generously offered to take charge of one of the watches. Hill acknowledged that this "relieved me of a very considerable degree of fatigue & care which I otherwise must have Suffered by being deficient of a first Officer."

As the ship left China on September 30, 1816, Hill wrote a "memoranda" which he tucked into his logbook about who was onboard. It was a company of twenty-three, "including Capt. Bennett, & Frederick S. Hill." It is the only time he acknowledged his son's presence onboard. In fact, it was the only time he ever mentioned his son by name in all of his voluminous writing and he spelled his name wrong, adding a "k" at the end that Frederic never used.

***

As the *Ophelia* headed to the Sunda Straits, a narrow passage through which most American ships bound between China and the Cape of Good Hope passed, Hill rescued three Malays from pirates, and off the coast of New England he rescued nine Boston mariners from shipwreck. He described both incidents in his journal, and when he remembered the voyage years later in his autobiography, it was defined by these two events. He described the first in great detail.

On Halloween night, 1816, in the Banca Straits, he and his crew were "alarmed by the hailing of some men from a canoe a Short distance from the ship." As Hill spoke the Malayan language, he was able to learn their story.

They were two Malay men & a boy Subjects of the Sultan of Bantam, that about a year since they had been captured while on a fishing excursion... by some Pirates of Jambee, ... that they had been sold to Slavery & had remained in that condition ever since, until about a month from this date when they had found means to desert or escape. ... They stated they had suffered much... and finally entreated me to receive them on board & relieve them from their Present distress. ... They were received on board & treated with kindness.

Hill was able to learn something of the regional culture and political situation from his passengers during the week they were onboard. One of them could speak and read Arabic as well as Malay, and he and Hill discussed languages and religion. He also learned about the political conflicts between the people on either side of the Sunda Straits. Having brought the two men ashore with him to help with negotiations for water and wood, Hill was surprised to find that they "would not trust themselves with the Malays of Sumatra beyond the reach of our Muskets."

> Although they speak the same language yet they Shewed no inclination to converse with them & on being asked if they would go on shore & remain there, they replied that they would Sooner remain in the Ship at my disposal even if I thought Proper to keep them as slaves, but I informed them that we kept no Slaves.

On November 7, Hill dropped off his passengers at a place he called "Pulo Menaar," and described their departure.

> No language can describe the expressions of Gratitude which these good People Manifested on being thus Placed among their Friends again. They would fain have kneeled & kissed my hands, but it was not Permitted. I can truly say that I felt a Sincere Pleasure in having it in my Power to assist their return to their native home. The Inhabitants of the Village on Shore received them with expressions of Joy, & would have loaded the Boat with Cocoa Nuts & Plantains but the Officer whom I sent in the Boat was ordered to return immediately & of course declined their liberal offers.

The passage across the Indian Ocean and around the Cape of Good Hope had more than the usual heavy weather of that time of year. Hill had never, he noted, in all his "numerous Passages around this Cape ... ever experienced so long a continuance of adverse winds nor such very sever Gales."

On Christmas Day, the Island of St. Helena was sighted. Having heard but disbelieved the British report of

Napoleon's defeat at Waterloo in the first weeks of the voyage, Hill did not know that Napoleon was now finally exiled on this remote rock in the Atlantic as the *Ophelia* passed by a year and a half later. He marked the New Year of 1817 with the entry "Time Rolls its ceaseless course," and three days later noted that in passing over the meridian of Greenwich, had the ship had "Compleatly Measured 360 degrees of Longitude" during the voyage.

On Valentine's Day, they encountered the brig *Waterloo* of Saco, Maine, named in honor of the battle that first brought Napoleon to his doom. The vessel was dismasted and wallowing with three feet of water in the hold. The small crew of captain, mate, and seven sailors were exhausted from working the pumps and Hill took them onboard.

Sam Hill turned forty years old in a raging gale on February 20, and the *Ophelia* reached the Gulf Stream. The storm continued for over a week as they made their way past all the familiar landmarks and into Boston harbor. On February 28, 1817, Hill wrote a final entry in his logbook: "Thus ended our Voyage after an absence of twenty months from Boston harbor which by the Blessing of Divine Providence we had been enabled to finish with Safety and Success."

The voyage was a success, in that the owners made money on their Chinese goods. The failure of the Chilean portion of the trip was not the fault of Samuel Hill. He had followed the instructions of the owners and they knew the risks attendant on testing new mercantile relationships, trade routes, and commodities. His inability to purchase copper in Chile was the result of the unstable political situation, the whales' teeth gambit would not have paid off even if the *Ophelia* had made it into port in the Galapagos Islands, Spanish dollars were essentially worthless in the Hawaiian Trade, and the ongoing transfer of Batavia from the English back to the Dutch at the very moment he arrived there was just bad luck.

Nonetheless, certain things that were within his power had also gone wrong. The firing of John King had no real evidentiary foundation, despite Hill's efforts, in a letter written to the owners at the end of the voyage, to convince them that it did. King had been a protégé of the owners and his dismissal looked suspiciously like a sacrifice to the unpopular colonial rule of Spain.

Hill had socialized with the right people in Chile, scrutinized the market, and correctly predicted political changes. But while he could be an intelligent and charming companion in the short term, he was an obsessive, autocratic, and irritating commander on his ship. That Thomas Perkins, Jr. left the ship in Valparaiso would speak volumes about Sam Hill to the young man's father. And young Perkins was due to become influential soon enough. In January 1817, the firm of James and Thomas Handasyd Perkins became Perkins and Sons.

Samuel Hill's logbook was passed down to his son, Frederic Stanhope Hill, who had made the voyage with him. Frederic gave it to his daughter, who gave it to her husband, who gave it to the New York Public Library in 1926. By then, Hill had been dead for over a hundred years.

In 1937, a historian named James W. Snyder published extensive excerpts of the log in an article in *The New England Quarterly.* Snyder described it as "the account of a voyage to Canton in the early days of America's China trade." The "romantic story" had been told before, Snyder wrote, "but seldom are the actual incidents related by the trader himself."

Samuel Hill would have been pleased to know his account would be taken at face value. That was his intention every time he took up his pen.

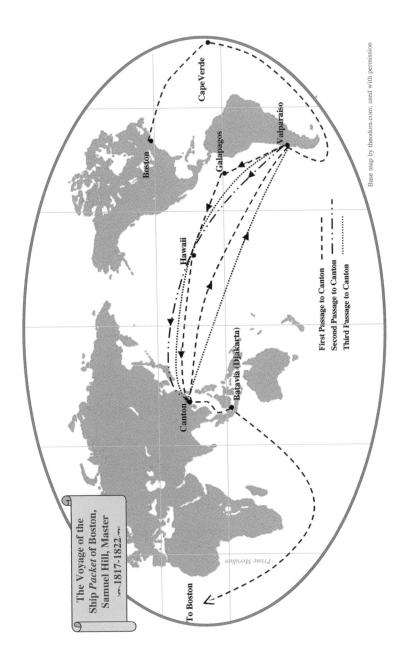

The Voyage of the
Ship *Packet* of Boston,
Samuel Hill, Master
1817-1822

First Passage to Canton
Second Passage to Canton
Third Passage to Canton

Boston
Cape Verde
Valparaiso
Galapagos
Hawaii
Canton
Batavia (Djakarta)
To Boston
Prime Meridian

Base map by theodora.com; used with permission

Chapter VIII

ༀ

Packet, 1817-1822:
Of Handkerchiefs and Revolutionaries

*A voyage, the success of which would be
debated for years, that includes another Revolution
in Chile, the death of the King of Hawaii,
and Sam Hill's thoughts on Religion.*

Although he had been away from home for three
months shy of two years, Sam Hill did not spend much time
with his wife before planning his next venture. After only a
month in Boston, he approached the *Ophelia's* owners with
a new plan for the Chilean trade.

In Chile, the situation was changing rapidly. Hill
must have nearly crossed paths with José Carrera who,
having been to New York seeking support for his cause,
sailed south in December 1816 and arrived at Buenos Aires
as the *Ophelia* was sailing into Boston harbor. Almost
simul-taneously, Bernardo O'Higgins returned from
Argentina to Chile with José de San Martín, to lead a
decisive charge against the Spanish at Chacabuco and
bring the revolutionary government back into power. Hill
would return to Chile in time to witness the rest of the
major events of the revolution that would bring Chile, once
and for all, into the community of independent nations.

Engraved by Jenkins from a Painting by Chinnery in the Possession of Mrs Morrison.

Figure 15, Reverend Robert Morrison with Chinese students

He did not, of course, know these things as he went, hat in hand, to the office of Thomas Handasyd Perkins at the conclusion of the *Ophelia* voyage. Perkins was singularly unimpressed with Sam Hill's first voyage in his employ. His son, Tom Perkins, Jr. had no doubt told his tale around the office where he had, a month prior to Hill's return, become a managing partner. The firm, wrote Hill, did not "seem to entertain that confidence in the voyage which it appeared to me to deserve."

One of the Perkins's competitors, however, was interested. Israel Thorndike, a wealthy Boston merchant, was willing to take advantage of the experiences and connections that Hill had gained in Chile, and back him on a voyage. There was no love lost between Thorndike and the Perkins family. Thorndike was the owner of the ship *Beverly,* which had been in Valparaiso with the *Ophelia.* Captain Edes, who had tangled with young Mr. Perkins, was an employee of Thorndike.

Thorndike pledged "a capital of fifty to Sixty thousand dollars, with proposals to receive on Subscription a further sum to make up a Cargo of one hundred and fifty or more thousand dollars." The seven-year-old ship *Packet* was purchased in May 1817, and Hill supervised the necessary repairs for a voyage from Boston to Valparaiso to Canton and back to Boston.

This was to be an eighteen-month voyage, for which the profits to be made by the owner, the captain, and the investors were clearly spelled out in advance. Hill noted all these details at the beginning of his shipboard logbook.

> On Compleating the Cargo, the amount of Goods Shipped by the Honorable Israel Thorndike amounted to about One hundred thousand dollars, and the residue being that of the Shippers Goods to about Seventy thousand dollars, making an aggregate of one hundred and Seventy thousand dollars, besides the Ship and outfits being about twenty five thousand dollars more, which with private adventures made the whole exceed $200,000.

With thirty-one men packed tightly into the 95-foot ship, Hill left Boston on July 5, 1817. After his unfortunate prior experiences with meddlesome mates, supercargoes, and sons-of-owners, Hill was very clear in his agreement with Thorndike that he should have "the entire control & management of... the business of the voyage from the commencement to its conclusion." His reason "for insisting on this Point," Hill wrote, "was to prevent future difficulties, which experience & observation had taught me, too often arose from imprudent & assuming young men being selected by owners to go abroad with their Commanders in the capacity of clerks & assistants."

Thomas Robinson, who had served as Hill's clerk on the *Otter,* was convinced to take that same position on the *Packet.* Robinson had, since the conclusion of the *Otter's* voyage, been working as a merchant in Boston. He had witnessed some of Hill's peculiar management style on the earlier voyage, but had remained in Hawaii during the ship's entire two-year sojourn on the Northwest Coast.

Hill certainly had a plan in mind when he approached Thorndike, and Thorndike seems happy to have let him manage the details based on his experience in Chile.

> The Owner's Goods, as also the Goods of the Shippers which composed our cargo, outward, was wholly selected by myself, agreeable to Samples brought by me from So. America, and conformable to what I conceived to be the General Style & taste of the Inhabitants of Chile and Peru, and no one article of Goods was Received from Shippers, without first having been examined and approved of by me.

Hill was feeling magnanimous as the ship pulled out of the harbor. In celebration of American Independence, "a full allowance of Grog was served to all hands, with fresh Beef & Puddings for Dinner." He seemed happy enough with his mate, Mr. Crocker, as the voyage began. Once the ship was safely out to sea, he sat with his logbook and carefully copied into it the letter of instructions from Israel Thorndike.

He was instructed to keep his destination and trade a secret from any other Boston ships he might meet along the way. If asked, he was to report that he was bound for the Northwest Coast. Both the owner and the captain hoped that the ports of Chile and Peru would be open and independent when the *Packet* arrived, but if they were not, Hill was to smuggle his goods into the ports as best he could, "taking care never to anchor in, or approach any Port so near, as to be within Cannon Shot of any forts or Battery, or so near the shore, if you can possibly avoid it, as will expose you to be annoyed by Field pieces that may be transported to the Spot for the purpose of attacking you."

Thorndike expected Hill to proceed directly to South America, to load the ship with copper "so deep as to sink all the wales in the water except the upper one," and to proceed directly to Canton without stopping "unless absolutely necessary for the preservation of the Ship, or health of your Crew."

Thorndike gave Hill details on how to pack the ship, how to keep records, and he made it clear that he wanted to know about the state of the markets at every stage of the voyage. Once Hill arrived in Chile, for instance, he was to find out the types of textiles that were considered desirable there and depict the patterns "with marginal marks, describing the length and breadth of each kind of Goods, with such explanations & remarks as... will enable me to form a correct Judgement of the Trade, & of the Goods suited to the market." In order to receive it as expeditiously as possible, Hill was told to send the information home, not in a letter, but to ship "one of your trusty, Intelligent, confidential men" home on one of the whaleships he would inevitably find on the coast of Chile. As captain and supercargo, Hill would make twenty dollars a month in wages, receive a two and one-half percent commission on the sale of the outward cargo and the Chilean cargo in Canton, have all of his shore expenses paid, and have six tons of "privilege"—space in the ship's hold to carry cargo for himself back to Boston.

If the situation in Chile had changed enough to bode well for a return to South America from Canton, Hill was instructed to send the China goods home as freight on another ship and return to Valparaiso with a cargo "to an amount not exceeding fifty to Eighty thousand dollars." From there he would go back to Canton and home unless, Thorndike specified, "you Should meet one of my own Ships that can take all my Stock on board, and that has my orders to you to make another trip."

The *Beverly* would follow the *Packet,* and Hill was instructed to "leave a letter at Valparaiso, carefully sealed, in the hands of some trusty confidential Person, directed to the Captain or Supercargo of the Ship *Beverly* from Boston" in which Hill would share what he had learned, and enhance the *Beverly's* prospects of a profitable voyage.

The *Packet* made good time across the Atlantic to Cape Verde, and from there was on the east coast of South America by the middle of August. A month later, on a clear southern hemisphere spring day, they saw the big rock of Cape Horn. While calm weather and seas made the passage around the Horn much easier than it had been on his previous passages, Hill's health deteriorated as the ship came into the Pacific. "From the time we Left the Land of Tierra del Fuego," he wrote on October 11, 1817, "I was most of the time very unwell with a dangerous Inflammatory Sore throat, until we arrived at Valipo."

A welcome sight greeted him as he dropped anchor in Valparaiso in October 1817. As the "breeze freshened from the S.W., the Patriot flag was plainly perceived to be flying on the Forts on Shore." Chile was once again in the hands of the independence-minded revolutionaries. An armed brig approached on behalf of the new government. It was the *Eagle,* purchased from her American owners, and still commanded by her American captain, patrolling the coast looking for Spanish cruisers.

The next morning, Hill met with the local officials and began to negotiate for permission to trade. There were three other American ships in the harbor, not counting the *Eagle* and the *Pearl* or *"Perla"*—former American vessels now owned by the Chileans. (The *Perla,* on which Hill's former mate, John King, had served, had been recaptured for the revolutionaries from the Spanish by the *Eagle.*) There were also two British vessels at anchor, the naval frigate *Amphion,* and a merchant trader.

Hill wrote immediately to one of the merchants he had met during his previous residence in Santiago, a man by the name of Solar, and asked him to come to Valparaiso and act as his local agent. Solar arrived a week later and the two men began the process of selling the *Packet's* cargo, though "the duties imposed by the Government were very high" and "the prices of Goods was low," and expected to go lower when the cargoes of the captured *Pearl* and the ship *Lion* of Providence, Rhode Island, which arrived a few days after Hill, were sold.

Armed Spanish ships were patrolling the coast, and Hill and Solar determined that it was better to remain in Valparaiso and sacrifice some profit, than run the risk of proceeding up the coast to the Peruvian port of Callao. Valparaiso and Santiago were in the hands of the revolutionaries, but Spain still controlled other parts of the coast. Just that week, two American ships, the *Beaver* of New York, and the *Canton* of Salem, had been captured farther south at Talcahuano, where, according to Hill, "they entered Voluntarily, having been deceived by the patriot Flag hoisted on the Forts."

Hill began to discharge his cargo, first to the custom house storage facility, and from there, by mules and carts to Santiago. He gathered information on the progress of the revolution and the state of trade from both Chileans and Americans, of whom a number now lived in Valparaiso. Henry Hill, who had come to Chile as the supercargo of the brig *Savage* of New York, had set himself up in business there and was a valuable source of news and local knowledge.

By November 6, Sam Hill was ready to go to Santiago to sell his cargo. He took Thomas Robinson with him and the two proceeded on horseback, arriving three days later.

It did not take Hill long to begin negotiations. On November 17, he made a sale to a consortium of Santiago businessmen for $60,000, to be paid in thirty days. These men "were Considered among the best purchasers in the City for Ability and Punctuality in payment," Hill wrote with satisfaction. Ten days later he made another significant sale of $20,000.

What began as a very promising stay in Santiago was, however, doomed by the political struggle unfolding around him. By early December, word began to circulate that Don Mariano Ossorio, who had been the President of Chile on Hill's last visit and was now General of the Royalist forces, had already left Lima with an army to invade Chile. "It was suspected," Hill wrote, that "their orders was to attack the Port of Valipo by Sea and land." In charge of the revolutionary or "Patriot" forces, as Hill and other

Americans called them, were Generals José de San Martín and Bernardo O'Higgins. San Martín was marshalling his forces even as Hill traveled from Valparaiso to Santiago.

Had Hill been carrying guns rather than fine textiles, he would have found the situation very profitable. As it was, trade was entirely at a standstill, and he had made his two lucrative deals for credit rather than cash. On December 18, he made a memo on the situation in his logbook. "Almost an entire Cessation of Commerce," was at hand, he wrote.

> The State of War had hitherto Changed the State of Government so often, that most of the merchants and traders, and indeed a great portion of the Population of the Country, viewed the result of the approaching crisis as a matter at least extremely uncertain, and instead of encouraging each other to a determined resistance, they were busied in Plans, and arrangements to save their necks from the halter, and their cash & valuables from Pillage, and such was their mutual distrust of each other that each one adopted his own private method, and this pernicious policy & foolish mode of Conduct extended even to some of the members of the Government.— Some got all the effects they could converted into Gold, and Secured the means of Conveyance for it themselves across the Andes to Buenos Ayres. Others buried their Cash and Valuables, in secret places under ground. Others Still more impolitic, & these were not a few, Sought Friendship and made their peace with the Gostros as they are called, I mean that Class of beings whom we denominated Tories, or friends to their Royal Master, these Gostros were very numerous, & some of them were wealthy and those Chileans who were imprudent enough to unfold their doubts in the ability of the Patriot Government to defend the Country, to this Class, produced more mischief than all the rest. ... In Such a State as this it was not to be expected that the trading Class would take the hazard of purchasing Goods at any prices, & consequently there was but a very few purchasers, and those only on a Limited Scale, barely sufficient for present Consumption.

It was clear that all attempts to trade during the crisis were stymied and there was no chance to leave the port while a battle by land and sea was imminent. Since his cargo had already been cleared through customs, transported to Santiago, and stored, Sam Hill sat back to observe the progress of the war. He was a keen observer of the progress of the Chilean Revolution and met most of the key players during his time at Santiago and Valparaiso on this voyage. Beginning in December 1817, he wrote a detailed account of the movement of the troops, the capture and execution of enemies, the coming and going of American diplomats, and the removal and return of Creole families.

He made a trip back to Valparaiso in the second half of the month, to check on the *Packet*. There he found that most of the ship's crew had deserted to join "the several Privateers then fitting out under the Patriot flag, and such was the Inducements offered to Seamen that almost every Ship in Port had lost nearly all hands by desertion."

At the end of December, the British frigate *Amphion* returned from a cruise to Lima with confirmation that the "Royal Expedition for the Subjugation of Chile" had sailed and was bound their way, though there were no details of where or when they could be expected. A month later an American naval vessel arrived. It was the sloop-of-war *Ontario,* bound to the Columbia River to ensure that the trading post at Astoria, taken by the British during the War of 1812, was returned to American hands. Onboard was an American jurist, John B. Prevost, who had taken passage to Chile to observe the situation for President James Monroe.

On January 31, 1818, Hill and Prevost traveled together from Valparaiso to Santiago. Along the way, they stopped at Orego to pay "a visit of respect to General San Martín, where he was at that time encamped with the main body of the Troops."

He received us very politely, and after a Short Conversation we sat down to Breakfast with him & his aids. He Conversed on Various Topicks, in all of which I thought he displayed a great share of liberality and Good Sense, especially in his remarks on the illiberal prejudices of the Chilean People, arising from an improper education, the unbounded & tyrannical Influence of the Church, and a want of Intercourse with the world. In his Observations on these subjects and the means of remedying them, he displayed more knowledge of men and of General Principles, than any Inhabitant of South America which I have yet met with. ... On the whole I parted from General San Martin with impressions very different from those I had before formed of him, and very much in his favour.

Unlike the vast body of the Chilean population, whose behavior in the current situation was viewed with contempt by Hill, San Martín and his troops stood out as admirable. "Amidst all this Vacillating Conduct of the Inhabitants Generally the Soldiery remained firmly attached to the cause of Liberty, or what they believed liberty to be," he observed. Much of the credit went to San Martín, who trained them with "rigorous discipline." They followed his personal example and "patiently submitted to hunger & fatigue in long & rapid marches under a burning atmosphere." On them, Hill concluded, rested the hope for a free and independent Chile.

On February 12, 1818, Generals José de San Martín and Bernardo O'Higgins officially proclaimed Chilean independence. O'Higgins was named "Supreme Director" of the new independent nation. Hill was in Santiago to witness the proclamation and the celebration that followed, and wrote a vivid description of the events.

On this day the Publick Celebration of Chilean Independence Commenced and Continued Six days. ... It was observed with Publick Shows, Grand parades of Infantry & Cavalry, both Regular & Militia, Salutes of Artillery, Grand Balls, Fire Works, on a very Superiour Scale, Grand Civic Processions, and Solemn Religious Processions, General Illuminations, those of the Public Squares, Edifices of the State and Churches, were very Splendid and arranged in a very Elegant Style. Paintings and Inscriptions were placed on all the Publick Buildings fronting the Squares, among these, on the west side of the Plaza or Principal Square, was a large painting on a frame of woodwork, representing the Glorious Liberty rousing Old Lautarro from the Tomb, to behold the darling object of his wishes accomplished viz. the downfall of the Spanish Tyranny in America and Liberty restored to his

People. This was executed in a Superiour Style, and as large as the life.

Of the Processions, that which presented a column of fifteen hundred Chilenian Youths, Mechanicks artisans Labourers & c. from 12 to 17 Years of age, all from the Common Class of People, Marshalled & Conducted in Perfect Military order—in double file, & dressed in white trowsers and a white robe tied about the waist with red & blue Sashes, & Caps of Liberty with wreaths of Flowers—marched to military musick & paraded on the four Sides of the Great Square fronting the Palace. This was the work of Captain Bertrand formerly a Priest, but now a Military officer, and Commander of the Arsenal or State Armoury. The Fireworks were also executed & conducted by him. ...

Considerable Sums of Money were expended in Entertainments given to the Poor in the Streets, and much money was thrown into the Squares among the Crowd on various occasions. — The Royal Colors of Spain with the Crown on them was Spread on the Ground at the Base of the Pillar of Liberty, for the Populace to tread on, and a very severe Sarcasm was levelled at the Pope & his Inquisition, by the figure of an Ancient Priest, dressed in his official habit, with much of the Ludicrous, and an affected Shew of Sanctity & Gravity. The whole figure was a severe cut at the main prop of the Catholick church.

Hill hoped to take advantage of the largesse and spirit of the day and visited all of the merchants who had contracted to buy his stock, pressing them to make their promised payments, but they all complained that they would be unable to sell the goods at this time at anything like the prices they had agreed to pay him. Two made partial payments, totaling about $15,000. The rest asked for more time. They were still fearful that the government might change yet again.

The day after Independence Day, San Martín and O'Higgins marched their troops south to Talcahuano to meet Ossorio and the Royalist army. Ossorio's forces were impressive. He had almost six thousand men, half of whom were experienced soldiers from the recent war in Europe.

For the next month, the population in Santiago and Valparaiso waited anxiously for each piece of news that came in—"Ossorio had crossed the River Maule," "San Martín with the main body of the Patriot Army was advancing to form a junction with O'Higgins' Division," "The Royal Army was Intrenching in Talcahuano."

On March 21, the most disastrous news possible reached Santiago. The Patriot troops had been defeated. According to a source that Sam Hill thought reputable, "the Country was Irretrievably lost to the Patriots, and the Royal Army was advancing Rapidly towards Santiago." The next day, he wrote that "the Confusion and despair in the City was extreme. Many of the most Influential men sent off their wives & families, and were preparing to follow themselves across the Andes toward Buenos Aires, all the Shops & Stores were shut, and Several Officers of the Government set out on their Journey to Abandon Chile."

Hill was inclined to be more optimistic. He had such a high opinion of San Martín and the troops he had trained that he believed they would surely rise again. "That the finest Army which Chile ever saw, & which consisted of 7000 regular Troops... had been thus entirely destroyed, and rendered incapable of making any further resistance against the advancing Enemy, was a Story that appeared to me incredible," he wrote.

Nonetheless, he sent Robinson back to Valparaiso with the cash he had collected and the most valuable of their trade goods, to make the *Packet* ready to go to sea instantly if Ossorio's army approached the port. Most of the foreign merchants had already left. All of Hill's countrymen who were in Santiago made a beeline for Valparaiso and departed. Mr. Solar took his family and headed for Buenos Aires, "among the rest of the fugitives." He had not settled Hill's accounts before leaving, but he left a stock of goods as security for any losses that might accrue to Hill and the *Packet*.

Bernardo O'Higgins returned to Santiago on March 24. He had received a wound in his arm, but seemed anxious to demonstrate that he was still the head of state. San Martín arrived the next day and began to reconstruct the army. Hill was impressed that he was able to display "the greatest activity, and a perfect Self Command & Cheerfulness.... in the Short Space of Nine days he had an Army of near five thousand Bayonets, ready to march, with about 1500 Cavalry, and 8 pieces of very light Brass field Artillery, Six of which were the same which were brought across the Andes, and used in the affair of Chacabuco, on the 12th of February, 1817."

On April 1, the Royalist army was reported to be at Rancagua and advancing toward Santiago. It was at Rancagua, less than fifty miles from Santiago, that O'Higgins and his forces had been defeated three and a half years earlier—the action that had brought the Royalists back into power and had led O'Higgins to join forces with San Martín.

The two generals marched with their troops to meet the enemy, and saw them the next day. On April 3, Hill reported that "most of the Females took their residence in the Convents, and a great number of Families moved their effects on Mules towards the Andes." On April 4, San Martín "put his Army in motion ... and publick anxiety was on the Stretch to know the result of their operations."

At noon the next day, the battle began at Maipu, on the outskirts of Santiago. Both sides "fought with great Obstinacy," Hill reported. After three and a half hours, San Martín's troops broke through the enemy line and the tide turned in favor of the Patriots. The Royalist troops lost their artillery and the lives of about 1000 men to San Martín; another 3700 were taken prisoner, among them "nearly all the Officers except General Ossorio who it was said had left the field of Battle some time before the Charge was made, and with a few Companions made his escape."

It was a decisive victory, from which the Spanish would not recover. Chile was now irreversibly independent. The next day a victorious General San Martín marched into Santiago, driving his prisoners before him. "This was a proud Day for the Inhabitants of Santiago," wrote a happy Sam Hill, "when they had the Satisfaction of beholding the Chiefs and leaders of that Army which had for Several months been their terror & dread, in the humiliating Situation of Prisoners."

San Martín left for Argentina on April 13, and the citizens of Santiago began to settle back into the routine of business. Early in May, Hill found a replacement for Solar when Don Manuel Ramirez Arillano agreed to act as his agent in Chile. He now began a round of business and social engagements, as both residents and foreigners returned to the capital. A number of parties and balls celebrated the victory at Maipu.

Hill returned to Valparaiso at the end of May. The *Ontario* was there and her Captain was helping with negotiations between the Royalists from Peru and the Chilean government to exchange prisoners from the recent battle. It was now winter in South America and Hill began to feel the wet and cold, especially on the three-day journeys on horseback back and forth between Valparaiso and Santiago. During June, Robinson was laid low with smallpox and Hill managed the business at both ends of the highway. On one of his transits, between the July 6 and July 10, several severe earthquakes rocked the ground beneath him, but Hill had, by that time, become almost accustomed to the active earth of Chile.

As July turned to August, the new Chilean Minister of Revenue turned to Sam Hill. The state was in urgent need of funds and the customs duties on the *Packet's* cargo had not been paid. Hill's excuse was that he had not yet been paid in full by the merchants who purchased his cargo. He negotiated a settlement, to be paid from the subsequent sale of the remaining goods still stored in Santiago.

It was time for Hill to think of proceeding on to Canton, even though his Chilean cargo had not been sold or paid for and he had not, to this point, purchased the copper that was to make up his Chinese cargo. He decided to leave the recovering Robinson in Chile to manage the rest of the business there, and prepared for departure to Canton. Hill planned to stop first at the southern port of Coquimbo where he hoped that the copper he sought might be more readily available.

It was necessary to hire a whole new crew at Valparaiso to replace the men who had deserted upon arrival, almost a year earlier. Though Hill makes no mention of it in his logbook, Chilean customs records tell us that on the night of August 22, 1818, before leaving Valparaiso, Hill sent several men sneaking on shore with bags and chests that had not been declared to or examined by Chilean officials.

Their destination was Hill's lodging at the home of some local women.

The furtive actions of the *Packet* crewmen raised suspicions at the guardhouse and two men were dispatched to investigate. "Just dirty laundry," was Hill's explanation. The next day, Chilean officials made another visit to the residence and found two boxes containing eighty felt hats, twelve pairs of silk stockings, six silk handkerchiefs, and enough material for three dozen more. Such a small portion of his cargo, all presumably from Hill's private venture, made little difference amongst the larger losses of the venture thus far. Hill did not bother to remain in Valparaiso for the hearing on his case. On September 10, 1818, after a very dramatic eleven months lying in the harbor of Valparaiso, the *Packet* weighed anchor and sailed. A month later, the local judge declared that Captain Hill had smuggled in the last of his cargo "with malice." The goods were seized and Hill's landlady was fined for his transgressions. Robinson was still in Santiago recovering from smallpox.

***

As the *Packet* sailed south, Hill brought his records up to date, noting in meticulous detail the prices and customs duties of all the products available for sale in Chile, including tallow, hides, almonds, aniseeds, cocoa, chin-chilla and vicuna skins, tin, copper, wheat, and hemp. He also listed all of the vessels that had cleared into and out of the port between February 1817 and the week of his departure in September 1818. The information predates his own arrival in Valparaiso by eight months, so Hill must have obtained it from port officials or the captains of other American ships.

During the nineteen months documented in his list, an astonishing array of goods came into Valparaiso. Most of the vessels were American—thirty-two merchant ships, six whalers, and the sloop-of-war *Ontario*. There were ten British vessels, two of them warships. There were also two Prussian vessels, a Swedish ship, and numerous Chilean-owned vessels. The latter were all employed in the war effort, and many were American-built.

On these ships came Peruvian bark, rice, and alpaca wool; wines from Bordeaux; silks from Canton; flints and corks from the Mediterranean; nails, iron hoops, and canvass duck sailcloth from the Baltic; long underwear and "demijohns" from England; tobacco from the United States; "Segars" from Cuba; and paper, twines, oil, cotton, gin, sugar, textiles, hardware, cutlery, glass, crockery, liquor, jewelry, tin plates, and, of course, weapons.

Several American vessels had come directly to Chile with guns to support the independence movement as soon as word reached the United States of the victory at Chacabuco in February 1817. Within six months, the brig *Adeline* of Philadelphia had arrived with 4510 muskets, gun screws, and other items, including the vessel itself, which became the Chilean Privateer *Chileno* under an American captain.

Hill had arrived in October 1817, with a cargo of textiles and other high-end goods aimed at the Creole aristocracy. After eleven months, he had sold little of his cargo. The Philadelphia ship *Bengal,* which arrived that same month with "67 Boxes of Muskets, 1580 Kegs of Powder, Swords, Pistols, Musket balls, Flints, Tar, Crockery, Dry Goods, Tobacco, Nails, Rum, Chairs, Iron & c.," departed after seven months with the cargo of copper that Hill had hoped to obtain.

Other vessels with arms for sale had similar luck. The *Rhea* arrived in January 1818 with "870 Muskets, 400 Kegs of Powder, Flints, Pistols, Drums, Knapsacks, Cannon Balls, Glass ware, Furniture, Rum, hard ware, wooden ware, Saddlery, Crockery, Dry Goods and c.," and left for home six months later loaded with copper, cocoa, almonds, hides, and tallow.

The journey south from Valparaiso to Coquimbo took just four days, and there Hill found many of the merchants he knew from Santiago. Within twenty-four hours it was clear that he would get no copper at Coquimbo. "This Port is the great mart of Chile for Copper," he wrote ruefully, "but at this time it was very scarce and dear owing to the unsettled state of the Government of this Country for three years past."

When he left Robinson at Santiago, Hill had already decided to return to Chile from Canton. His reasoning was that copper would become more available as time passed.

The mines, which had been largely shut down during the war, were increasing production levels and Hill was convinced that they would be producing enough copper to export when he returned. He stayed in Coquimbo for a few days, just long enough to find a ship to take letters back to Thorndike and the other owners in Boston and to feel two earthquakes, one big enough that it "moved the Ship very sensibly, and was accompanied with a sound like that produced by a Ship running over a Shoal or bank without stopping her head way."

Once again, Hill gathered information on the vessels and cargoes that had come into and out of the port over the last year, wrote detailed sailing directions for entering the harbor, described port charges and customs expectations, and took his leave. The *Packet* arrived at the Hawaiian Islands in the last week of October to obtain wood, fresh water, and "a few of the most miserable pigs" Hill had ever seen, and then pushed on to Canton.

***

The coast of China came into view in early December 1818, and for the next week Hill worked his way up the coast to the anchorage at Whampoa, where he left his ship before continuing up the Pearl River to Canton, where all trade in China was conducted. On his previous voyages to China for the firms of Lyman and Co., the Amory brothers, J. and T.H. Perkins, and Bryant and Sturgis, Hill had turned over the business of the ships to resident managers of the Boston firms when he arrived in Canton. Unlike his Boston competitors, however, Israel Thorndike, the owner of the *Packet,* did not maintain an agent in Canton. Consequently, though Hill had been in Canton many times since his first visit on the *Lydia* a dozen years before, this was the first time he managed his own trade there. Benjamin Wilcocks was serving as the American Consul in China, and for five hundred dollars he arranged for a space for Hill to conduct business and store cargo in the American *hong* or "factory." These large buildings, which stretched along the Pearl River on the Canton waterfront, provided lodging, warehouse space, and business offices for foreign merchants.

Hill read the letters from Thorndike that were waiting for him regarding "the State of the market" in Boston, and "lost no time in Issuing orders for the Silks wanted both for the home Market & also for South America." Two members of the co-hong, Puqua and Namchong, facilitated his order. By the end of February, the silks that Thorndike wanted most urgently were paid for and delivered to a Boston-bound vessel, to be freighted at eighty-five dollars per ton.

Samuel Hill took great care to get just the right things for the Chilean market. He believed that if he could just once be lucky enough to be the captain who arrived with the right cargo at the right moment, he could make a killing in Valparaiso. To this end he had, during his months in Santiago, observed and talked to women about fabric, sketched out designs for patterned silk, noted colors that were popular, and differentiated between the finest fabrics desired by the rich, and the lesser goods that the middle class would buy.

Once again, his plans were disappointed at several steps along the way. "In Canton there are but two men who can design & draw the figures for the Silk weavers, when any new European figures are wanted," he wrote. "Of these Het Fo is the most Capable & is most sought after." To Hill's chagrin, it was a lesser artisan, Ching Shing, who was employed by Namchong for Hill's commission. The special order was due to be made and delivered to him in early March, but Namchong was dissatisfied with the results. By the time Hill learned of this, "it was too late to remedy the business by ordering Goods of another kind" and he was "obliged to determine either on leaving my Goods, or wait & have them finished according to the patterns given." Namchong took Hill on an expedition to see the weavers in early April and Hill "determined on the latter, and the only Consolation to be derived from this tedious delay, was that of having the wind & weather more favorable for my passage."

Hill spent some time consulting with John Cushing, with whom he had worked on his last voyage. Hill negotiated with Cushing to deal with Namchong and Puqua on his behalf, and left additional orders and twelve thousand dollars for the purchase of tea and silks, so that he would not be delayed as long on his next visit to Canton.

On May 7, Hill was finally ready to return to his ship at Whampoa and go back to Valparaiso. As was his custom, he prepared an extensive report on the goods that had come into and left China during his residence, and on the current prices, as told to him by John Cushing. Hill noted the prices being given on copper from Chile, gold, American ginseng, sandalwood, Indian cotton, opium, and sea otter pelts. Of opium, he noted that since it was "strictly prohibited," the amount introduced annually into China could not be known with authority, but he did know that the Indian opium brought by the British was considered superior to the Turkish product smuggled by the Americans, and that the former had sold for as much as fifteen hundred dollars per chest.

Northwest Coast sea otters had almost entirely collapsed as an available commodity because of over hunting. In the years that Hill had been most active in the trade, American ships brought an average of 12,000 sea otter and 320,000 seal pelts annually to Canton. For the current year of 1818-1819, only four thousand pelts of each species were delivered to the port.

Among the goods exported from China, teas were still at the top of the list, and Hill wrote down the grades and prices on gunpowder tea, imperial, hyson, young hyson, hyson skin, souchong, souchong inferior, bohea, and congo. Silks and cotton textiles were listed by grade and color, including "nankings," lightweight cottons made for the British East India Company in yellow and blue. There were also crepes—soft, crinkled, light-weight fabrics designed for the American market, crepe shawls, embroidered shawls, silk handkerchiefs, "Sarcenets, Florentines, light and heavy Sattins," and damask.

At some point during his stay in China, Hill met again with the English missionary, Robert Morrison. When, five years earlier, Morrison had taken passage on the *Otter*, Hill had not appreciated the possibility that Morrison might serve as "the means of opening to me the way to Salvation," but, reflecting on it now, he felt it necessary to apologize to the cleric for "some indecent Rudeness" he had been guilty of on that earlier journey. "I was happy to find," he wrote, that Morrison "freely forgave it or even seemed not to remember it."

Morrison gave Hill a number of books, and as the *Packet* left Canton in June 1819 and began the Pacific crossing back to South America, Samuel Hill underwent a profound evangelical conversion experience. He did not write about it in the shipboard logbook, but did write a long declaration of his new faith elsewhere in the form of an autobiography. In typical sailor fashion, he signed it with the date and his position: "on board the Ship Packet at Sea, in Latd 33 deg north, Longd 179 deg. East from Greenwich, June 14th 1819."

The books from Morrison were a key factor in Hill's awakening, especially a volume of lectures preached by Morrison at Macao, including an "Address to Seamen," which could have been written directly to Samuel Hill. It addressed an audience that had been exposed "to the perils of the ocean; scorched by the hot rays of a vertical sun; and in danger of being seduced by bad company to impiety, to drunkenness, or to debauchery." Acknowledging that British and American sailors possessed "courage and generosity" to their shipmates, especially in wartime, he asked the crucial question: "What is your character in peace?"

The general public, he answered, accused sailors of being "ungrateful, turbulent, and riotous; and of getting drunk, and of quarreling, and fighting, and sometimes of causing the death of the natives."

> Now, as a man, and a man bred up in a Christian land, every sailor... should reflect and see how far these accusations are true in reference to himself; and if his conduct has heretofore given just occasion for these censures, let him resolve to alter his conduct. Let him think of his home, of his kindred, of his country, and of his Saviour, and no longer by his misconduct cause injurious reflections to be thrown on them. And let him think of his duty to himself; that he has a soul to be saved, as well as a body to be fed and clothed; and let him resolve to be true to her who is, or whom he intends (if Heaven will) to make his wife.

It was a description that must have stung. Hill pondered his own religious past and was not pleased with the memories.

On Several Occasions I had attended the Evening Service of that denomination of Christians called Methodists, & retired immediately afterwards with my companions to amuse ourselves by turning to Contemptuous Ridicule all that we could remember of the Service, and on one occasion I remember to have endeavored to convince my own Wife, that the System of Christianity was founded in falsehood.

But at certain Seasons of retirement, Conscience deman-ded to be heard, and my course of conduct, with the particular Occurrences of my past Life presented themselves in full View before my mind. Merciful God, was this thy kind admonishing Voice; how then couldst thou permit me still to enjoy thy Blessings, when I so often disregarded it!

He had, Hill reflected, renounced his wickedness on more than one occasion in the past, especially when he felt a "deep sense of the danger of [his] Situation." He had then "solemnly promised to turn to the ways of Righteousness, & seek the favour of the Lord God, & serve him." It was his practice to declare himself in writing, and put his thoughts on paper, even as he was doing at this moment. But the inspiration had always passed and he once again "relapsed into all [his] former wickedness."

In addition to his own lectures and writings, Morrison gave Hill *An Essay on the Divine Authority of the New Testament,* by David Bogue, who had been a mentor to Morrison in England. Morrison had been handing this book out freely to ships' captains since his first voyage to China twelve years earlier. As the *Packet* stretched eastward, Hill "employ'd most of my leisure in the Study of the Books received from Dr Morrison." He began with Bogue's *Essay,* and found it "so powerful & Convincing" that by the end of it, he wrote, "my former doubts had vanished, and I became so thoroughly convinced of the truth & Reality of the Divine Mission of Jesus Christ that I was astonished at my former Obstinacy & Ignorance."

For Hill, Bogue's book was filled with the "truth & reality of the Doctrines contain'd in the New Testament, & also of their divine Authority." Much of it is a tirade against what Bogue described as the hypocritical and dangerous "Popery" of the Catholic Church, and it must have influenced Hill's opinions of the Chileans whom he would shortly encounter again.

On September 6, the *Packet* arrived in Valparaiso harbor to find a squadron of Chilean Navy ships under their new British commander, Admiral Lord Thomas Cochrane (who would later serve as the model for Patrick O'Brien's Captain Jack Aubrey). The flagships were the *San Martin* and the *O'Higgins,* and there were three additional ships, four brigs, and a schooner in the fleet. The British frigate *Andromache* was also in the harbor, accompanied by another, smaller Royal Navy vessel, and there were some twenty merchant vessels, most of them American.

Hill quickly gathered the information that would bring him up-to-date on the revolutionary activity in South America. José de San Martín had gone to Argentina, leaving O'Higgins in charge in Chile. The expanded naval force had been marshaled to attack the ports of Peru. Revolutions were sweeping across the whole of the South American continent. San Martín was the force behind the revolutions in the southern colonies and his counterpart in the north was Simon de Bolivar. The two men would become known as the liberators of South America.

The free and open port of Valparaiso that Sam Hill had dreamed of for five years proved a disappointment in reality. Duties on legal imports were 34.5%. The duty on "prohibited" goods was 49%. Credit was limited to three months, and neither the high tariff nor the short grace period could be negotiated "on account of the urgent necessities of the Government." Hill found his ship and his cargo subject to a thorough and potentially destructive search.

He made arrangements for his cargo to be sent to Santiago and followed it there by the end of September. He still had high hopes that some of his goods, especially the Chinese silks, would find a ready market and a high price, but even that plan was dashed when another American ship carrying a similar cargo came in right behind him. And unfortunately, his clerk, Thomas Robinson had not been able to sell the remnants of their original cargo during Hill's absence.

Though it was not consistent with Thorndike's rather specific orders, Hill decided to take the remaining cash that Robinson had on hand and make another quick run to Canton and back. Robinson would once again remain in Chile running the store. Hill stayed in Chile until January 1, 1820, and then departed once again across the Pacific.

On March 11, Hill arrived in Hawaii, exactly fifteen years after his first visit there on the *Lydia*. He had been there many times and had both observed and contributed to enormous changes in the local culture, economy, and environment. On this and a subsequent visit before the *Packet* returned to Boston, he would note two events, the impact of which would resonate over the next two centuries. The first was the death of King Kamehameha I and the breakdown of the traditional system of *kapu* or taboo. The second was the arrival of the first American missionaries, whom Hill would meet on his next stopover.

The news of the King's death was brought instantly to the ship upon its arrival at Maui, and was written directly into Hill's log.

The former King of these Islands Tamahamahah died about 10 months Since and after some Slight Quarrels in which Teremyty (the former Kings Brother) and a few of his adherents were Killed, the Son of the late King, Rihu Rihu was proclaimed & supported unanimously as King of the Sandwich Isles.

Hill had known the old king for many years and had spent considerable time with the new king when he visited aboard the *Ophelia* four years earlier. While the former was acknowledged to have been a canny leader, Hill had not formed a favorable impression of the latter. Hill had predicted that when Liholiho (Rihu Rihu) succeeded his father there would be "many Irregularities Committed," but he had not anticipated the nature of the changes that had taken place.

The first Publick act of the Young King was the entire abolition of the Taboo, or that Religious Restriction which Supported the authority of the Priesthood & punished with Death every breach of its authority. By this act the Females are no longer prohibited from Eating what they Choose, or of going where they please, & are at free liberty to Eat & associate with the males at all times. The whole Number of their Eakosas or Wooden Deities were also abolished & no further respect or offerings made to their hidious forms, before held Sacred. Indeed they were at once pulled down & Cut to pieces & burned by Common Consent and never was a more favorable opportunity for Introducing a rational System of Religion amongst a People in Gross Ignorance, than is now offered at these Islands.

While Kamehameha lay dying, Hill was in Canton being born again, and his new religious outlook now tainted everything about the way he remembered the old King. Like many new converts Hill was, at this point in the experience, even more zealous than his teacher. Robert Morrison had gone to China to convert the heathen Chinese. He had become deeply interested in and sympathetic to their culture—not to the point where he became convinced that the Chinese did not require conversion to save their immortal souls—but he delved deeply into their language and lore. Morrison's primary motive was to use his new knowledge to develop conversion tools, but he was also informed and inspired by what he learned.

When Kamehameha was alive, Hill gave every indication of liking him, even admiring him as a leader in a challenging time, but that is not how he remembered the old King when he heard of his demise.

Thus about the middle of the Year 1819 Died Tamahahmahah; Sensible of his approaching Dissolution to the Last hour of his life, and extremely unwilling to leave this World, having supported a System of the most Unlimited Tyranny, ever known, over the Inhabitants of these Islands for more than Twenty Years, and with him Ceased the worship of Images or Idols, & that abominable System of Priestcraft & oppression the Taboo, which was the main Prop & Support of his Tyranny, & his leading Maxim was to Impoverish his People to the Last degree, that they might not become Rebellious or unsubmissive. His Death was regretted by none but the Cause of Rejoicing by thousands. At the time of his Death his son & heir, also his wives & all his near Kindred were by their ancient Customs obliged to embark in Canoes or vessels on the Water and remain until he had expired.

In Sam Hill's opinion, there was now hope for Liholiho only if he converted to Christianity. A visiting merchant had already baptized one of Kamehameha's principal advisors. The new King, who took the name Kamehameha II, might "be induced to follow his Example if proper means were used by some respectable & well Informed Person."

Kamehameha I had ruled during a time of extraordinary change. He was twenty years old when the two ships of the Cook expedition arrived in Hawaii in 1778. At that time, there were a number of chieftains in the island chain. By 1795, Kamehameha had conquered and united all the islands except Kauai. (Always referred to as "Atooi" by Hill and his contemporaries, Kauai had its own king, Kaumualii, or "Tomaree," who was also well known to Hill.)

In his consolidation of power, Kamehameha kept the control of Hawaii in the hands of the native people through a period when it was most threatened. He strictly controlled the exportation of sandalwood, its principal export, to Canton, deflected official British and commercial American interests in his autonomous authority, and even resisted an armed attempt by a Russian force to take control in 1816.

Kamehameha was a combination of inspirational leader and strongman. He kept his own people in line through the traditional system of taboos or *kapu,* an ancient code that defined and regulated social and religious behavior. It became harder and harder to maintain the kapu as explorers, and then traders, arrived in Hawaii and broke all the rules without seeming to suffer any of the promised retribution. The devastating loss of the Native population to diseases brought by foreign mariners further destabilized the traditional culture. By the time Liholiho came to the throne in 1819, the kapu was held together only by threats levied on the people by Kamehameha and his priests. It collapsed in the first days of the new rule and the timing was auspicious; the first ship of missionaries was already on its way.

Having lost much of the code that underpinned their traditional world view, the Hawaiian people were ripe for conversion. One of the greatest physical symbols of the old ways, the large wooden carvings of Kukailimoku, the patron deity of Kamehameha I, were destroyed along with the temples or *heiau* in which they stood, even before the missionaries arrived. (These *ku* figures were the "Eakosas or Wooden Deities" described by Hill. Three of them were removed from Hawaii prior to the destruction of the rest and survive today in museums in Honolulu; Salem, Massachusetts; and London.)

Hill's prediction several years earlier that Liholiho would be a weaker ruler than his father proved correct. During Kamehameha II's reign, the trade in sandalwood expanded, without any of the restrictions that his father had imposed, until most of the very valuable native trees had been cut and shipped to Canton. Missionaries began a full-scale dismant-ling of native Hawaiian culture, and battled with whalemen who arrived almost simultaneously, quickly outnumbering all other foreign visitors. Within a few decades there would be three hundred New England whaleships passing through Hawaiian waters annually. Young men swarmed ashore with rapacious desires for everything they had been denied on the ships. They craved coconuts and pineapples, roasted pork, liquor, and young women.

Bombarded by thousands of young men from visiting ships and by demands for trade and access, Liholiho courted English protection for his island world. Traveling on the English whaler *L'Aigle*, he took his favorite wife, Kamamalu to England to meet King George IV in November 1823. The following summer, the Hawaiian royal couple died of measles in London.

In late March 1820, Hill sailed for Canton. For almost the whole month of the passage to Asia, Hill was so ill that he did not leave his cabin except, he wrote, "on two occasions at a great hazard & with much pain." No one else on the ship was able to determine longitude, and Hill did not want to approach the coast without having taken any observations.

I now looked forward to the Period as being near at hand when my Extreme anxiety for the safety of my Ship, in

Navigating through the Ocean without being able to attend to the business, would Cease & however the Cares & fatigues of my business in Canton would require my immediate attention & great Exertions, yet it would not be attended with the same degree of anxiety as while Navigating the Ship at Sea. I had much reason to remember with the Strongest Sentiments of Gratitude, the Peculiar favor of the Almighty, on this Occasion, as during the whole of my Illness not a day of boisterous Weather was experienced, nor a Single Untoward Incident took place.

On May 2, the *Packet* anchored in the roadstead of Macao, and Hill took a boat into the town to check for mail. Thorndike had sent messages about the prices being fetched for Chinese goods in Boston and a list of sales, both long out of date by the time they came into Hill's hands. There were also letters from his children, which Hill says were "peculiarly gratifying" to receive. This small reference to his children is the only one he ever makes in the whole of his massive logbook of the five-year voyage.

When he left Chile, Hill says that it was his intention to go to China and there invest about two thirds of the cash he had on hand in "goods Suited to the American market," and ship them back to Boston on one of the ships at Whampoa. The rest of the money would be used to buy silks, which he would have specially made for the Chilean market.

Two American ships, the *Flying Fish* and the *Viper*, were loading silks for Chile when he arrived at Canton and as a result, the plans for the special-order silks were abandoned. Instead, he would buy sugar and whatever silks were available, along with yellow cotton nankings. "Had there been any prospect of making a Speedy remittance to my owners in the United States," Hill wrote, "I should have preferred & Certainly adopted the plan which I had originally in view," but there was no possibility of making such a shipment for at least six months. If he loaded and left immediately, he might be able to beat the American ships back to Valparaiso. He was able to make his purchases and leave Canton before the end of the month, but lost nine thousand dollars by not being able to wait longer for a better exchange rate on his Spanish dollars.

Four months later he was back in Chile. He wrote to Robinson at Santiago, who responded that "most of the former stock of Goods had been Sold," but that only a portion of the funds had been collected. Robinson thought that he would be able to wrap up business and be ready to depart "in a very short time if necessary," but it proved to be much more difficult to collect the money that was owed and sell the new products, and it wasn't until nine months later that Hill and Robinson were able to conclude this portion of the voyage. They finally sailed from Valparaiso for the last time on the Fourth of July, 1821, bound for Canton via the Hawaiian Islands.

***

Between November 1, 1815, when he anchored for the first time in Valparaiso Bay on the *Ophelia,* and July 1821, when he left there for the last time on the *Packet,* Sam Hill spent almost three full years on Chilean soil. During that period he became as knowledgeable as any American of the period of the intricacies of Chilean trade. In 1935, the Chilean historian Eugenio Pereira Salas wrote that Hill's persistent efforts to identify the cargoes that would work in the Chilean market were influential in inspiring the "first attempt of Independent Chileans at a free trade beyond the limits of the Spanish Empire. ... The return of the *Packet* to Valparaiso from Canton inspired Chilean merchants to begin their own fledgling attempts at a trade across the Pacific to Canton."

Hill's repeated trips to Valparaiso and the extended periods of time he spent in Santiago, made him a well-known personality in the insular, though increasingly cosmopolitan world of Chile. His success at trade was often moderated by circumstances beyond his control. The nature of a commerce so dependent on the vagaries of weather and wind, and the coverage of such vast tracks across the globe, meant that there was always a possibility that things well understood on departure would be at least subtly, and sometimes radically altered upon one's return. During Hill's time away from any port, changes occurred in consumer taste and product availability that could be irritating. In Hill's case the change was as often due to more dramatic economic upheaval, even political revolution.

Before he made his final departure from Chile, Hill took time to write extensively of the situation he would leave behind. He noted regulations on trade and the specific customs duties due on a wide variety of commodities. He reviewed the state of the Government, which he found "exceedingly corrupt & profligate of the Public money." (In contrast, he praised José San Martín as he tried to expand the boundaries of the independent nation.) Hill complained about the lack of a national currency and about the devastating duties levied on foreign trade while the local citizenry lived free of taxation. The expenses of the war, he claimed, were being paid by visiting merchants, and too much was spent on the showy aspects of it. Military parades and bands were everywhere in evidence, even at the theater and at funerals. In short, he concluded, "the Government at present is a Military Tyranny in the Strictest acceptation of the Term and the People long accustomed to Slavery... find consolation in the reflection that their present Self elected Masters are of their own Soil & not of foreign Growth."

Hill had mixed feelings about the Chilean people. They were addicted to gambling, which was "evidently productive of many disorders & Vices of Serious Magnitude." They had a distasteful exuberance for "Gaudy Pomp & Parade," and were too much in the clutches of priests. "The Consequence is they are made acquainted with the dogmas of the church, but in every branch of useful literature they are Grossly Ignorant especially the younger or rising Generation." This, despite the fact that the Catholic Church's influence was "rapidly declining to absurdities, daily becoming more Notorious," and destined for a collapse "into that State where no Religion is believed."

Much of Hill's tirade was obviously influenced by his recent conversion and his reading of the books given to him by Reverend Morrison. When he first arrived in Chile, he had been impressed by the kindness, beauty, and culture of the people, especially the women. Now he found them degraded by lack of education and by an "Ostentation and Vanity" that caused them "to Sacrifice every future

Consideration for the present possession of every Luxury & Extravagance, particularly in dress."

On the whole, the preachy Hill found that "their Native Pride & Indolence Causes them to look with Disdain on the drudgery of active life; while their Ignorance of the World & disinclination to travel abroad, renders them unfit & unequal to the task of mercantile Competition & blind to the gradual ascendancy of their Foreign Rivals."

> The General effect which may confidently be expected to Result from the operation of all the Foregoing Causes will be Simply this, that in the Course of a few Years many of the important offices of State will be either occupied by, or Influenced by Foreigners, English or Americans, & probably both, and all the wealthy & Influential Commercial Houses in Chile, will be composed of Foreigners, or Foreigners Connected with Chileans in which case the Foreign Copartner is always the Director, and in this way the Local Radical Change will be effected in the Habits, Manners, Morals, & Religion of the Inhabitants.

In his condemnation of the Chileans, Hill singled out an interesting exception: the lower classes with greater Native blood, and less influence from Spanish Catholicism, still had promise as honest workers and were worth cultivating.

He concluded his remarks on Chile by saying that the mineral resources seemed "Inexhaustible and it only Requires a due encouragement to Industry, & a well digested System of Finance to give Chile its due Consideration in the Scale of Nations, but at present their Extravagance & Ostentation has increased far beyond their Industry."

**

The *Packet* sailed from the coast of South America to the Hawaiian Islands, arriving on September 19, 1821 at Oahu, where it remained for about thee weeks. Still zealous in his Christianity, Hill was "happy to find the American Missionaries" had arrived, "sent out for Instructing the Natives of these Islands in the Principles of Christianity & to Establish Schools for Education amongst them."

Hiram Bingham and his party of Congregationalist missionaries had arrived the previous year "with several assistants male & females all of them being Married & having their families with them." Hill was pleased to see the work that they had already accomplished at Oahu and Kauai. "Two Schools had been formed & a Church had been Erected in which Divine Service was performed every Sabbath. And from the accommodating disposition of the Chiefs & King, I should think a fair Chance offered to hope & expect the best result from their undertaking."

Bingham invited Hill to visit the mission at Kauai, and he proceeded there with enthusiasm. "I beg leave to remark that I should not do Justice to my feelings were I to omit mentioning the Extreme Politeness & attention of Mr. Bingham & family to me," he wrote into his logbook. He also commented on the efforts, then underway for the first time, of creating a written orthography for the Hawaiian language. Hill described Bingham's "very Just & Judicious Remarks on the best & most expeditious mode of Reducing the Owhyhean Language to a Grammatical form," and his intelligent plan to consult with missionaries in Tahiti, who had been doing the same work for twenty years with a related Polynesian language. (Hill noted that between the two groups the "Oral Language, habits & manners & c. are so very Similar as to leave no doubt of their having descended from one Common Origin.")

Bingham was anxious to make a trip to Tahiti, and Hill was persuaded that his work "would be of Incalculable advantage both to the Teachers & Students at the Sandwich islands," but no vessel was available. Hill blamed merchant traders—"American Commercial men, on the Ground that their business & Interest would be Injured by Such Communication with English residents at Otaheite,"—for preventing Bingham's plans from coming to fruition. Had he not been so long away from home, he might have provided the *Packet* for the venture. The ship left Hawaii in the middle of October, carrying mail for the missionaries, and arrived at Canton a month later.

Once again Hill found himself managing his own trade and frustrated by a lack of instructions or assistance from Thorndike. The Boston merchant had sent him "New York & Boston Catalogues of sales, Schedules of Canton Goods, prices Current, ... lengthy remarks on prices of Goods, bad Markets, & c.," but "no positive directions respecting the kinds or qualities of Goods he would have me Invest for himself or the Gentlemen Freighters." Only one man with a stake in any of the freight sent instructions, and that was William Sturgis, who had been a managing partner in Hill's previous voyage on the *Ophelia.*

The final profits of the trip were inevitably going to disappoint Thorndike, and Hill may have been laying the groundwork to justify his actions to the ship's owner at this point in his log.

> I cannot but Remark how desirable it would be that owners & Freighters when writing to their Factors or Agents abroad, Should endeavour to give them all the Matter of Fact Information which they possess respecting prices, demand for particular goods & c & c., after which either have them to decide on the spot for the Investment of their funds, or else give positive directions to Invest Specific kinds of goods naming qualities or prices. This would relieve the Factor from much embarrassment.

Hill turned once again to John Cushing for advice. He made himself "acquainted with the State of the Canton Market & the Goods which had been Shipped to America with those ordered now in the market." He decided to devote a good share of his cash on hand to purchasing "fair quality Teas," as not much had been sent back to New England that season. "Such were the motions which governed my Conduct," he wrote, "I have only to hope that the assortment may be Satisfactory."

He spent his first few weeks in Canton lodged in the building leased by the Perkins Company. At the beginning of December he moved into the warehouse of Benjamin Wilcocks, who had provided him with assistance on his last voyage. Hill displayed his wares there for more than a month before he received bids that he thought were reasonable, selling the gold, silver, and copper that he had brought from Chile.

It was very difficult for Hill to work with the hong merchants, and Cushing offered only limited assistance. It took several weeks to make a workable connection and when Hill "at last Succeeded in forming a Contract with Namchong for the greater part of my Silks," he found that he would have to pay much higher prices than he expected. He negotiated with Puqua for sugar and Nanking cottons, but through Puqua's "unpardonable Negligence," and the "Embarrassments of the Hong Merchants," was delayed two additional months. He was not ready to leave Canton until February 1822 and this, to Hill, "though extremely mortifying was unavoidable."

The *Packet* had managed to take on enough cargo to necessitate shifting the water casks, spare rigging, anchors, spars, and lumber up onto the deck, and the ship was, in consequence, "very Crank," according to Hill. "But by a Close attention to the Sails in Squally weather, I had no doubt of making a safe passage," he wrote.

The route was south to Java, through the Sunda Straits, and into the Indian Ocean, headed around the Cape of Good Hope. In early April, high seas and gale-force winds pounded the *Packet,* and a serious leak was discovered in the hold. Hill sent men to the pumps as water began to rise at the rate of ten to fourteen inches per hour. "Very heavy Sea," Hill wrote, "most of the time running Mountains high." Down below, the men were pumping 150 to 200 strokes per hour trying to keep up. As the seas moderated the leak slowed, but sailors were required at the pumps for the rest of the voyage.

On April 11, 1822, Samuel Hill sailed past the Cape of Good Hope for the last time. The passage "was long & tedious," he wrote. The ship continued north and west in the Atlantic, passing to the west of the island of St. Helena on May 7.

On June 8, 1822, the Packet returned to Boston, having been gone one week shy of five years. Hill took "an ill turn" just before the ship reached home and "did not come to the possession of my faculties untill Some time after." He was escorted ashore and took "safe & Comfortable Lodgings at the Exchange Coffee House," near the waterfront in the North End. He made his last entry in his logbook as he sat there at a "little Booth."

Thus after an absence of 4 years 11 months & 24 days, during which I had experienced much Solitude & various

Vicissitudes I was again permitted to visit my Native Country & home. My life mercifully continued to me through frequent scores of Extreme Peril. Of my health I cannot Speak much, it having been much impaired during many severe Journeys on horseback to which I was from Necessity exposed in the Course of my business. With Sincere emotions of Gratitude & thanks to Almighty God for all his mercies to me I concluded the day in my Chamber, & had a refreshing night's rest and on Monday morning July 10th felt quite well though still feeble.

When he was recovered, Hill took his bundle of business papers to Israel Thorndike's office, delivered them to Thorndike's clerk, and returned to his lodging.

And what of his family? Hill probably thought that they were still in Framingham, but he does not seem to have made any attempt to get there in a hurry. Twice he had departed on long voyages leaving his wife and three children as lodgers in the home of another captain and wife. Elizabeth had apparently tired of the situation. At some point during Sam's absence on the *Packet* she had managed to move their little family back to Boston, where they rented their own apartment on Boylston Street, not far from where he was now lodged.

They would have been strangers to him. His sons were now seventeen and fourteen, his daughter eight. He knew Frederic better than the others because he had been on the *Ophelia* voyage, but he knew none of them well. In the last seven years he had spent less than four months at home.

Chapter IX

✺

Boston, *1822-1825:*
End of the Voyage

How Sam Hill, having been born again, dies.

In the first blush of Christian enthusiasm that followed his conversion, Samuel Hill made certain pledges to God and to himself. The most life-altering was a decision to leave the sea at the end of the *Packet* voyage, move with his family back to Machias, Maine, and spend the rest of his days as a farmer. As the nineteenth century progressed, this became the ideal of more and more sailors. It mirrored the larger national debate as the United States struggled to find its identity, a debate that had been played out in the experiment of the Embargo, and would continue through the Civil War. Was America—or should it be—global or insular, mercantile or agrarian? For individuals, it raised questions of sea or land, sailor or farmer, even savagery or civilization. The theme was often echoed in songs and stories that were shared on shipboard, where metaphors of the farm and field came into regular use as sailors stared into the unproductive furrows plowed by ships in their wakes. Where was home?

For the forty-two-year-old Sam Hill, as he desperately scribbled a version of his life in the summer of 1819, home had been the deck of a ship for more than twenty-six years. When he reflected on his life, those parts of it that had been lived well were in his childhood, in the home of his mother in Maine. "I adopted the following Resolutions," he wrote.

> Firstly to retire from the business of commerce when this voyage is ended, & go with my Family to the place of my Nativity & spend the remaining days or Years, (which it shall please the Divine Goodness to Continue me on Earth), in the Society of my Brothers & Sisters, on the Soil which was once my Father's; where it appears to me I may have opportunities of being useful to my Brothers.

The bubble may have burst long before the *Packet* dropped anchor in Boston harbor. Even had it not, the notion that he could return from sea after an absence of five years and announce to a family that barely knew him that he was going to drag them from their urban home into his distant farm fantasy, would undoubtedly have been greeted with skepticism and resistance.

Whether Samuel Hill's conversion experience was still with him when he got home is not clear. On the one hand, he sought out and joined a church; on the other, he seems to have manipulated the *Packet's* books enough to earn himself a healthy fortune, while simultaneously denying that Israel Thorndike's venture had been profitable. Thorndike sued him for $50,000.

In choosing to experiment in the Chilean trade in Thorndike's ship, and in the process to extend a two-year mandate into a five-year voyage, Samuel Hill erred. Had the voyage been a financial success, Thorndike might have been pacified, but the fact that Hill returned to him with a rather small purse was too much for the merchant. And it cannot have gone unnoticed by Thorndike that Hill—who was broke when he left Boston on the *Ophelia* seven years earlier— bought five pieces of property in Boston within a few years of his return on the *Packet.*

Israel Thorndike was no fool, nor was he inexperienced in the management of ships. As a teenager in the waning years of the Colonial Period, he was already the proprietor of a few fishing and coastal trading vessels He commanded three privateers in the Revolutionary War and owned principal shares in four others. In the years following the Revolution, Thorndike sent ships to the Caribbean in the slave trade, and tried his luck at trade in Europe, the Mediterranean, South America, and Asia. He was in the habit of writing very specific instructions to his captains.

Thorndike was a litigious man, constantly involved in lawsuits to recover money he claimed was owed him. At the time he sued Hill in 1822, Thorndike had been involved in at least one case every year for the previous dozen years. This case, however, was different from the others. Where renters owed debts to Thorndike as a property owner, for instance, the case was clear cut. The relationship between a ship's owner and a ship's captain was much more complex.

At the beginning of a voyage, the owner transferred all decision-making responsibility and authority to the captain for the duration of the voyage. If the cargo was poorly chosen, if markets had changed since the last information was received, if weather kept a ship from keeping to a schedule, even if clearly bad decisions were made along the way, unprofitable voyages were accepted by the mercantile community as part of the cost of doing business in such a complex and uncertain commercial world. Inept captains may not have received invitations to command subsequent voyages, but the owners did not generally sue them. To hold a captain responsible for the financial losses of a voyage in the courts of Massachusetts was not common and usually not successful. Thorndike lost his suit against Hill.

Thorndike appealed the case, this time concentrating not on the profitability of the voyage, but on the fact that Hill had disobeyed his direct instructions. Thorndike testified that he had directed Hill to take the *Packet* from Boston to Chile, from Chile to China, and there to "invest the proceeds in a return Cargo which he should Judge best adapted to the market in the United States," and return to Boston. Further, he had instructed that Captain Hill "should keep the sales of the goods shipped on freight distinct & separate from the Plaintiffs and from each other and should invest the proceeds in Merchandize according to the orders of the shippers."

That Hill had gone back and forth between Valparaiso and Canton not once, but four times had, he said, "deprived the Plaintiff of the use of his said Ship from that time... exposed her to great deterioration damage and loss, and wasted and lost a great part of the Cargo consigned to him." The other part of the case had to do with Hill's bookkeeping, which was clearly inadequate. Hill had never, according to Thorndike, rendered acceptable accounts of the voyage. What proportion of the profits belonged to Hill and what proportion belonged to Thorndike were the central questions. Hill could claim that *his* money had been made on his own account, within the "captain's privilege" that had been guaranteed him, but the accounts of the various investors and shippers had not been kept separate. Thorndike would finally win $5,000 in the appeal in 1826, but by that time Samuel Hill was dead.

Hill was fairly circumspect during the trial, holding his cards close to his chest and, for the most part, pleading ignorance. His seafaring career was clearly over, if not by choice then as a result of these circumstances. He wrote a detailed account of the suit, not for the court but for John P. Cushing in Canton. Nineteen pages of closely written text were required for Hill to explain to Cushing how he had been harassed by Thorndike and betrayed by his mates and clerk. He described how he had worked diligently through difficulties in Chile and behaved in a most aboveboard way while all around him were cheats and scoundrels.

"Perhaps an hour may occur when your mind is unemployed by your accustomed avocations that the following brief notice of the Suit Instituted against me by Col. Israel Thorndike may find a place in your attention," Hill began. It is a bizarre letter, filled with triple exclamation points, third person references to himself, reports of secret conversations that he could not have overheard, and sidebars, stage directions, and character analysis. The tone is sarcastic, manipulative and dramatic, with an edge of desperation, even paranoia. Hill is by turns astonished at the duplicity of those around him, deeply wounded by unprovoked and unwarranted character assassination, huffy at slights, the victim of elaborate plots and machinations, and an innocent in a cruel world.

However, buried within all this drama is a serious charge, which Hill wants to be the first to tell to Cushing, and to tell to him in a context that makes it seem meaningless: that Hill's first mate believed Hill might have forged Cushing's signature, or that of another agent for Perkins and Company, on invoices during the course of the *Packet's* voyage. Cushing had negotiated with Hill to carry freight for him to Chile, and Hill tells him that the lawsuit will probably ruin "nearly the whole of your adventure of Silks of the 2d adventure to Chile" (though he implies that the silks might have been damaged and consequently lost value anyway, as the passage across the Pacific "was four months & a boisterous one, being close hauled on a wind three fourths of the passage").

Hill may have used Cushing's name without his knowledge in order to convey cargo purchased at Canton, with money or goods belonging to Israel Thorndike, into a sham account. As the Perkins firm did not have an agent in Chile, Hill could have purchased goods there on a false Perkins' account and then claimed them as part of his own account when he returned to Canton.

Hill described to Cushing what happened when he returned home, how on the morning after his arrival in Boston he had proceeded to Thorndike's offices to find the merchant in close consultation with Thomas Robinson, Hill's clerk. The two stopped speaking immediately upon discovering Hill in their midst. As Robinson slunk away, Thorndike began accusing Hill of having failed to keep his accounts as instructed. Thorndike, wrote Hill, "understood I had carried a large amount of Freight & etc. of which he had no account." Hill explained that he had not yet brought the accounts up to date and that certain items "would require some explanations," about why they actually belonged to Hill rather than Thorndike. Hill then tried to pacify the merchant. "If the Freight so carried Should appear to belong to him," he wrote, "I should pay it, but if on the contrary it should appear to belong to me, I hoped he would cheerfully relinquish it."

The two spoke several times over the next few weeks, with Thorndike always demanding the accounts and Hill always putting him off, though for what purpose he does not make clear in his letter to Cushing. In every conversation, according to Hill, Thorndike "broke out into violent & passionate exclamations, found fault with the goods of the *Packet's* Cargo and said he was informed they were bo[ugh]t by outside merchants & were of bad qualities." Thorndike simultaneously questioned Hill's dependence on Robinson, especially the decision to leave him in Chile with cash and cargo during his absences in Canton. Most astonishing to Hill, Thorndike told him that he had been able to obtain "an exact account of all the *Packet's* business in South America & Canton from the officers & Others on Board."

Hill told Cushing that he always responded to these outbursts with "coolness & complacency," but he also began to perceive a plot against him by Thomas Robinson and the two mates, Crocker and Sumner. In his shipboard logbook, Hill always referred to the first mate as "Mr. Crocker," but in his letter to Cushing he consistently calls him "Doctor Crocker" or "the Doctor." It was clearly a derogatory slur, and it may have been meant to demean his position or performance on the *Packet,* as cooks on shipboard were regularly called "Doctor." The word was also a common slang term for a cheat—as when something is "doctored."

Thorndike had interviewed every man in the crew likely to know anything, including the carpenter, who reported that he "had been called to nail up Boxes of Specie & Bars of Bullion on Several occasions to a large amount." Hill believed that Crocker and Robinson were angling for a ship of their own on which to return to Chile, and that the two, having listened attentively to everything Thorndike said "conformed to his prejudices & suspicions in their answers."

> Doctor Crocker being fully convinced from the Col's arguments that he was an informed man, & being moreover a friend to strict retributive Justice, found that nothing stood in the way to his immediate promotion to the command of a Ship with an outfit for Chile, except a beggarly qualm of Conscience on swearing roundly to whatever the Col. should declare to be true, soon got over his doubts & perceived as clear as a Sun Beam, from the Lucid Statement of the Col. that Hill had

defrauded him, and of course it was his duty to do all in his power to enable the Col. to recover ample damages.

Hill complained that an incomplete workbook that he kept on shipboard had been altered by Thorndike's clerk in collaboration with Robinson and Crocker, and was being scrutinized as if it was the ship's accounts or "cargo" book. Words that altered the composition of the cargo—for example, "silk"—were added between lines, "in a hand very much resembling that of Col. Israel Thorndike & which but few can mistake." Despite his complaints at the inadequacy of the information Thorndike had about the voyage, Hill consistently failed to produce his own accounts.

In Hill's letter, the duplicitous nature of "Doctor Crocker" is dealt with in several pages of overblown text. The sneering "sunbeam" analogy is used more than once, and Hill refers to himself in the third person. "Doctor Crocker ... saw every charge which the Col. explained to him against Hill, to be facts as clear as a Sun Beam, & determined to prove himself a man of accurate & extensive Knowledge in the various branches of business in Chile & other parts of South America, he determined to go for the whole and at once become the acknowledged & distinguished favorite of a Great Man."

To Hill, it was obvious that Crocker and Robinson simply wanted a ship to return to Valparaiso. For Crocker it was to gain command of a vessel and for Robinson it was to move to the South American port where he had made himself comfortable for almost four years and where, according to Hill, "he wished to remain & to escape from his creditors in Boston, which object he finally accomplished by Shewing the Col. that a great profit might be made on a Shipment to Chile under proper management; and by keeping a grave face, looking wise & Shaking his head on all subjects of which he was Ignorant, and following suit on all subjects relative to the bad management of Hill in Chile."

Robinson tried to impress Thorndike with the names of Chilean merchants and government officials with whom he had close relationships. He claimed to know the locations of mines where great profits might be made. His report, interlaced with a good dose of information in Spanish, was, according to Hill, "perfectly unintelligible" to Thorndike and consequently "proof of Robinson's extensive knowledge of the men & business of that Rich Country."

Thorndike is portrayed in Hill's letter alternately as the dupe of Robinson and Crocker, and as their manipulator. The bottom line of their conversations was that Thorndike developed a "Strong prejudice against Hill which had fixed itself in his mind, & which he was now to have the means of gratifying, and moreover a new field of profitable business opened to him by the Sagacity of these Wizards."

The traitors got their wish. In the fall of 1822, Crocker took command of Thorndike's brig *Clarion,* bound for Chile with Sumner as first mate and Robinson as supercargo. Before he left, Crocker was deposed for the lawsuit.

> His evidence was delivered by reading it from a paper & he seemed to have got it pretty well fixed in his memory. He stated on the oath of his Maker, all the particulars of Goods Manifested & Goods not Manifested, of those which as he said paid Duties & those which did not, of Goods which he said were carried on Freight, & those on half profits, of Goods Smuggled, & the Charges incurred on them, of the amount of Specie carried on each Voyage, & of Bullion & c. and his perfect knowledge of the customs & modes of transacting business in Chile & c. & c. In Short he was deficient in nothing which would go to prove his perfect knowledge of the facts before Stated.

When the so-called "cargo book" was introduced, Crocker was asked about the insertions. "He did not," he testified, "write them himself, nor did he certainly know who wrote them, but on Reflections he was convinced they must have been written by Hill!!!" Crocker was then asked if he had ever seen on Captain Hill's desk "some Invoices which appeared to have the Signature of Perkins & Co. on them." Crocker said that "whether those Signatures were genuine or not he did not know; here the Col. rose & prompted him, and the Doctor then Stated that on Reflection he had reason to believe they were false Signatures written by Hill!!!" John Cushing, the agent of the Perkins' Company, was assured by Hill that Crocker had perjured himself and would be found out. Dozens of exclamation points were necessary to convey Hill's passionate outrage. The worst condemnation, however, was reserved for Thorndike.

> Could you my Dear Sir have believed that a man who holds a place amongst the Honorable of our Country, a man who Ranks amongst the Dignified & Wealthy Merchants of the United States, could so far forget himself as to Sacrifice every principle of Humanity as well as of Truth, to Support a Cause which he knows to be a bad one merely to gratify his Obstinacy or his Vanity, and to confront it himself so grossly before two such Miscreants as the Doctor & Robinson, whom he knows have no Character to lose, nor hopes of gaining one; Yet such is the truth & could you have seen the Interlineation in the Doctor's Hieroglyphical Cargo Book, you would have been as fully convinced as I am, that it was done by the Col. himself, and such was the decided opinion of the Gentleman who saw it & witnessed Crockers observations on the subject when it was first pointed out to him by me in my Room at the time when I borrowed this precious Memorandum from the Doctor in order to examine it.

As the *Clarion* made ready to sail from Boston harbor, Hill felt obliged to call on Thorndike "from a sense of that general duty which one civilized man owes to another in every Station & Situation in Life." He told him that the lies told by Crocker and Robinson, inflating the cargo of the *Packet,* put the *Clarion* enterprise in danger in Valparaiso. Surely the Chileans would seize any ship of Thorndike's "to answer for the deficit on the *Packet* exports," and "the Doctor & Robinson, being on the Spot & found to belong to the Owner of the *Packet,* would be also seized & Safely lodged in Prison for safe keeping, in common with the rest of his Property."

This was a nonsensical argument. How would the Chilean authorities know what arguments over cargoes were transpiring in Boston? Nonetheless, as Hill describes the scene, Thorndike instantly called for his coachman and ordered him to race for the harbor and prevent the *Clarion* from going to sea.

He next returned me a very great profusion of thanks, &
immediately adverted to his Suit against me & said he
felt it his duty to say he owed me an apology for having
commenced the suit so hastily & had he then have
known what he now knew, he should not have done it, &
he believed we two could settle all the points in dispute
between us better than by any other mode as the Law
was expensive & tedious.

There is, of course, no evidence that any of what Hill
says here is true. That Thorndike pursued him through this
lawsuit and an appeal, and kept at it after Hill was dead,
argues against his ever having wanted to settle, though Hill
told Cushing that Thorndike brought the subject up more
than once. The *Clarion* continued on its way.

Hill attempted to explain why Crocker and Robinson
were prejudiced against him. "I should also have stated,"
he wrote, that Crocker was asked during his deposition "if
he had any prejudice or cause of ill feeling against Hill. He
replied he had not, but that Hill was a man of anxious &
unhappy temper & that he had Several times reproved him
for negligence & for being asleep on Deck in the night
Watches, particularly on the homeward passage, which
reproofs were, he said, without cause & unjust." Hill
explains this:

It appears the Doctor was much irritated against me for
having rudely awakened him from frequent comfortable
Visions of the night when deep Sleep falleth on men,
during the homeward passage from Canton. Those
awakenings were sometimes followed by pretty Severe
Remonstrances, shewing the dangerous tendency of such
an example before the Ships Crew, and the Fatal
consequence which might result to the Ship, Cargo, &
Lives of all on board, and twice we were within an hairs
breadth of from his neglect.

Of Robinson, who had made two voyages with him, he says:

This wretch called on me a few days previous to his
departure, & after many apologies for the necessity he
had been under, of keeping on good terms with the Col.
told me he had stated many things in acquiescence with

the Col's prejudices against me, which he knew were not Strictly true, but as you know, said he, that the Col. would not have otherwise allowed me to go in the Clarion to Chile, so I hope you will excuse me as you know my Situation, & I thought you would be more offended If you discovered it after I was gone than if I told you of it here! I replied if you have done wrong & are sensible of it, you had better go to the Col. & explain yourself, as for my own part I do not wish to know any more of it; & he left me saying he did not like to Contradict himself to the Col. as it would make an Enemy of him, & begged I would not be offended!!!

There was no happy ending to this story for Samuel Hill. John Cushing must have found the letter suspicious and its author unstable and dishonest. Cushing sent the letter back to Boston where it was read by his uncle, Thomas Handasyd Perkins, and his cousin, T.H. Perkins, Jr., two men who already had a low opinion of Hill.

Sam Hill's seafaring days were over. He could no longer disguise his inability to manage the officers and crew who served under him, but he still tried to justify his misfortunes. According to Hill, the failures of the *Packet* voyage, like his misadventures on the *Polly,* the *Adventure,* the *Lydia,* the *Otter,* and the *Ophelia,* were all due to the faults and weaknesses of others. He was hapless against the plots of scheming supercargoes, manipulative mates, and conniving clerks.

His plan to move to the farm never materialized, but he did buy several pieces of property in Boston, with a value close to the $50,000 for which Thorndike sued him. During the two years following his return, he purchased a house for his family on Myrtle Street, the same street where they had lived from 1809 until his fortune collapsed in 1815, and four other houses nearby, from which he and his family drew rental income.

Hill's other large investment was a pew in the Park Street Church, which he purchased in January 1824 for the substantial sum of $600. He was, with difficulty, still trying to cling to some of the euphoria of his conversion experience but he feared it would not last. "In my moments of Retrospection," he wrote, "I frequently suffered the most poignant Sensations of Shame & Sorrow... my Conscience told me I was wrong & condemned me... for this my wickedness, when perhaps in Six hours afterwards I have repeated the same crime in order to produce the Jest, the Laugh, & the applause of the unthinking."

But on some occasions of extraordinary deliverance from extreme dangers, from Scenes, at the bare recollection of which my Soul Shudders with Horror, I was so fully convinced of the immediate aid of Divine Power, that I trembled at the Idea of my unworthiness; and when I knelt in Prayer before the Almighty, I was ashamed & confounded at the remembrance of my wickedness, & could not Pray, for I knew in mine heart that I should repeat the same wicked practices again, and I was afraid to mock the Almighty lest he should destroy me.

The Park Street Church, which he chose to make his parish, shared his evangelical zeal. It also supported missionary work in Asia, and Hill's association of his own conversion with the work of the Reverend Robert Morrison, made this church a logical choice. Beyond the overt gestures of purchasing a pew and making heartfelt declarations, however, Hill found it hard to live the life of a Christian.

At some point between the time he returned home in June 1822, and the time of his death in September 1825, Sam Hill moved out of the family house on Myrtle Street and back to a room on Prince Street in the North End. He and Elizabeth had very little experience in living together, and it was too late to develop the habit now.

***

As his relationship with his wife was breaking down, the country was consolidating. In December 1823, President James Monroe delivered a message to Congress that has come to be known as the "Monroe Doctrine," declaring that the American continents were "henceforth not to be considered as subjects for future colonization by any European powers." The message was particularly addressed to the Russians on the Northwest Coast, but it was also a statement in support of the newly independent South American nations. Samuel Hill had been intimately involved with the events that led to the development of American policy in both regions. Few Americans could have known more about those distant places than he.

In his own lifetime, Hill never achieved the reputation or fame that he had tried to create through his activities and writing. John Jewitt became a well-known figure, having expanded his *Journal Kept at Nootka Sound* into a larger and more detailed account, *A Narrative of the Adventures and Sufferings of John R. Jewitt,* which was published in 1815. In it, Samuel Hill was acknowledged as Jewitt's rescuer with only brief mention.

Hill might have gained fame from his appearance in the Lewis and Clark journals, which were published in 1814. But having been described by the explorers as the captain famous for having "a woman in his Canoe who [he] was fond of," he could not very well identify himself as the "Captain Haley" of the narrative.

Separated from his family, Hill spent his last year living among the sailors, boarding houses, bars, and bordellos of the Boston waterfront, as he had more than thirty years before when he first arrived on the ship *Jane* from Machias. He died in obscurity on September 1, 1825. The cause of death given on his death certificate is "paralytic," which may refer to alcoholism or to some form of the mental illness that manifested itself throughout his life. References to his death in the Boston newspapers gave only his name and age. Even the *Columbian Centinel,* to which he had contributed articles, simply said: "DIED: In this city, on Thursday, Capt. Samuel Hill, aged 49." He was buried in a tomb in the Granary Burying Ground, adjacent to the Park Street Church.

On the day after Christmas, 1825, a full inventory of Hill's estate was entered into the record of the Suffolk County Probate Court. The probate ghouls, like the ghost of Christmases yet to come, must have been in his house on Myrtle Street in the days leading up to the holiday. They examined his clothes: his coats of broad cloth and bombazine, his black hat, white hat, vests, and shirts. They even inventoried his underwear, distinguishing between "drawers new" and "drawers old." They counted out his twelve pocket handkerchiefs, worth a total of $6.00. Room by room, the Myrtle Street house was examined—front chambers up and down, back chamber, bed chamber, garret, kitchen—and a list was made of tables, side board, parlor carpets, looking glasses, plates, glasses, silverware, tea sets, lamps, hallstands, featherbeds, counterpanes, bed curtains, wash stands, wearing apparel, and books. With his "Pew No. 61 in the Broad Aisle of Park Street Meeting House," his personal property was worth $1987.82.

His real estate, the house on Myrtle Street and the four other houses on Bowdoin Street and Somerset Place, were worth an additional $45,000. Israel Thorndike persistently tried to claim $5,000 from Elizabeth over the next several years, and she steadily refused to give it to him. Some of the rental property was sold immediately to provide twenty-year-old Frederic with money to marry and set himself up as the publisher of a short-lived magazine called the *Lyceum,* described as "A Literary and Critical Review."

Elizabeth survived her husband by more than twenty years. He had apparently purchased space for her to accompany him into tomb number nineteen in the Granary Burying Ground but she, having ceased to lie with him while they both lived, did not choose to alter the situation when they were both dead. Three tombs down from John Hancock, the mortal remains of Samuel Hill moldered away for a century and more, until his bones were swept away with the rest of the tomb to make way for an expansion of the Park Street Church.

Frederic, who became a poet and playwright, published his first book of verse, "The Harvest Festival and other Poems," the year his father died. He never alluded to his sea voyage on the *Ophelia* or to his father's career in his poems or plays. He concentrated on writing about knights, shepherdesses, and country dances, in texts laced with Roman illusions and Latin quotations. His plays included "The Shoemaker of Toulouse," "The Chevalier de Faublas," "Ten Quakeresses," and "Cupid on Crutches." His most famous play was a six-part melodrama called "The Six Degrees of Crime: or, Wine, Women, Gambling, Theft, Murder and the Scaffold." The starring role of Julio Dormilly was played in the premiere performance by Frederic Hill himself.

It would later become a favorite role of John Wilkes Booth, the murderer of Abraham Lincoln.

Frederic's son, Frederic Stanhope Hill, Jr., did follow a sea career, and served as both a merchant mariner and in the U.S. Navy. He wrote a number of books on naval history and a narrative of his own seafaring career, called *Twenty Years at Sea, or Leaves from My Old Log Books.* In the first chapter he acknowledged that "it was just possible that my old grandfather, who was a famous sea captain in his day, had transmitted to me a strain of his sailor blood, rather than my poet father; so instead of fitting for college or going into a counting-room, my parents at last consented that I should go to sea."

That was his only mention of his grandfather, Captain Samuel Hill. He did not claim for him the honors of having been the first American to live in Japan, the rescuer of Jewitt, the courier of Lewis and Clark's letter, an eyewitness to events of the Chilean Revolution, or the acquaintance of two Hawaiian kings. He had, as F. Stanhope Hill claimed, been famous "in his day." He had also been infamous. The mariner grandson could not admit that his grandfather had never been able to keep a chief mate loyal to him through even one voyage as captain or that he had cheated on his wife and embezzled from his employers. He didn't want to acknowledge that his grandfather had abducted and abused a Hawaiian teenager and instigated battles on the Northwest Coast that left dozens dead. At the end of his life, the closest Samuel Hill came to the fame he craved was the nearness of his tomb to that of John Hancock. His infamy inevitably obscured his fame.

Afterward:
What in Sam Hill?

In the introduction to his book, *Ned Myers,* James Fenimore Cooper says, "It is an old remark, that the life of any man, could the incidents be faithfully told, would possess interest and instruction for the general reader." For more than five years, I have tried to determine whether Captain Samuel Hill was representative of the mariners of his time, or an exception. In the end, I still can't say.

I first encountered Hill in the *Lydia* journals of Isaac Hurd and William Walker and was, consequently, suspicious of him from the start. This was not true of other historians who, in the early decades of the twentieth century, began their studies of Hill with his own logbooks from the *Ophelia* and the *Packet* voyages and believed that Hill's descriptions of his adventures could be taken at face value.

Many times in the writing of this book I doubted my own reading of Hill's character. But again and again I caught him lying, exaggerating, obfuscating, justifying, and, in his beautiful and convincing prose, editing, softening, and even reordering events in his life to make himself perennially either the victim or the hero (or both!).

I copied large portions of Hill's writing, including his "autobiography," correspondence, articles he had published in Boston newspapers, and excerpts from his logs, along with descriptions of him by Walker, Hurd, and others, and sent this material to my friend and colleague, Captain William Hallstein, M.D. I thought that, as both a practicing psychiatrist and a master mariner, Bill might have something interesting to say about Sam Hill. He did.

"Real sociopaths are very few and far between," Bill said, "but Sam Hill probably was one." The term, he said, is generally used too casually and, as a result, the real impact of the sociopathic personality is not fully understood by the general public. "Their style and way of operating makes all those other people you thought were sociopaths seem like amateurs."

My objective in asking for Bill's assistance was not just to find some way to label Samuel Hill's behavior, but to understand to what extent it might have been based on mental illness rather than the exigencies of the shipboard experience. Certainly the seafaring community was one that accepted eccentricity, even violent strangeness. When James Bennett was asked under oath if Hill was a good captain, he answered, "When he was well." In a separate court case, another mate, Mr. Crocker, described Hill as "a man of anxious & unhappy temper." Both men, who were mistreated by Hill on shipboard and accused by him later of behavior that was at least unprofessional if not criminal, were so influenced by their experiences at sea that they considered Hill's behavior within the realm of normal and acceptable.

I asked Dr. Hallstein how Sam Hill could have functioned as a sea captain for so many years, and he responded that "being a captain is a job a sociopath can get away with, because they can attempt total control in a small universe."

Sociopaths, despite their bad performance, are good talkers. Hill displayed bad judgment but he was not stupid. He was skilled at weaving a story and the stories, importantly, couldn't be entirely false or people would catch on. But the stories have flaws: they are basically all about *him.* An important distortion and elaboration on reality is part of the sociopath's mode of operation. As the story unfolds you don't learn about anyone else, no other characters are developed.

Hill didn't feel shackled by morals or conscience; he sold his schemes with little foundation in fact or reality as most people know it, but was able to make people trust him with money and ships. Sociopaths are crazy in ways that don't stop them at first. They are not cognitively impaired and can be highly intelligent.

Bill Hallstein found Hill to be a "hyper-vigilant observer," though the details he chronicled were as often meaningless as meaningful. He was "not bound by fact or conscience or any moral obligation." He didn't know what was true. He was not capable of hearing that there could be another point of view. He did not acknowledge the contributions of his crew and fellow captains. This made him the sole rescuer of Jewitt and Thompson and the only person able to see what was wrong on the *Polly.*

When recounting his past, Hill was able to manipulate not only facts, but time. He reordered events, but clung to the reality of individual moments, to isolated details that could be exaggerated. This allowed him to ground his version of his life in a self-proclaimed truth.

In his autobiography, Sam Hill purports to confess his sins, but he never mentions any in particular. He does not recognize himself as a thief, rapist, and murderer, though he was all of those things. It does not seem to have bothered him that he was robbing his employer even as he declared his new, good intentions. And although he dramatically proclaimed his guilt in a text that was ostensibly between him and God, he could not help but look over his shoulder to see who else might read it in his wake.

As he told it, Sam Hill was as much victim as sinner and he always had an explanation or context or even a justification for his sins. He blamed others for much of what happened to him. His collapse in Canton at the end of the *Lydia's* voyage had nothing to do with his own behavior and everything to do with a conspiracy among other captains. The poor Hawaiian girl abducted during the voyage is nowhere mentioned in Hill's account. He took no responsibility for the death of his men on the *Otter;* it was the mate's fault. And the dead Indians had simply been dealt retributive justice for *their* sins. Mates were to blame for financial failures on both the *Ophelia* and *Packet.* When Hill was not portraying himself as a victim, he assumed the role of hero. Whenever he could make that claim, he did it with gusto. As he represented it, he had saved two ships when no one else had the wherewithal to do it. He had rescued captives of Indians and pirates.

What were the circumstances that allowed Captain Samuel Hill to develop a violent shipboard kingdom in an age when the fledgling United States was still celebrating its great democratic experiment? In large part, it was the nature of the shipboard experience on a long voyage. That he was often violent does not necessarily separate him from his fellow mariners.

The men who manned American ships in the age of Samuel Hill, set in action a national legacy that was not decided in the halls of Congress by elected officials, but *de facto* on the quarter decks by captains like Samuel Hill. Sailors lived for months and years in situations far from home, separated from their families, isolated from society, crowded into small spaces, and forced into endlessly repetitive schedules. They were poorly fed, often brutalized, and had no contact with women. When they suddenly found themselves on shore, they were not at home. Around them were people babbling in languages they did not understand, but beckoning with gestures that they liked to believe they *did*. It was easy to dehumanize people who refused to understand plain speaking in one's own language and fellow sailors provided ready examples that one did not need to behave in foreign ports in the manner that was expected back home.

And a return home was not always a return to normalcy. Some sailors found it very hard to conform to social expectations. Others felt rejected by society. Ships were populated by young men from every religion, race, and ethnic group in America. It was a heterogeneous human stew that lived in the forecastle of a ship, far removed from the civilizing influence of laws, women, and organized religion.

An accepted standard of behavior developed on ships that often lacked humanity, humility, honesty, sensitivity, and even reason. This was the standard that Samuel Hill used in his interactions with his men, the native people he encountered around the globe, his employers, and even his wife and children.

Samuel Hill was one of the earliest Americans to encounter Northwest Coast Indians, Hawaiians, and Chileans, and he treated them with arrogance, easy violence, and a rapacious appetite for profit and sensual gratification. His actions, and those of his comrades on shipboard, set in motion events and established patterns of relationships with which we still live two centuries later.

Acknowledgments:

Many of the ideas I explore in this book were developed over a dozen years of teaching Maritime Studies at the Sea Education Association in Woods Hole, Massachusetts. I am grateful to my students and colleagues there for always providing me with a ready sounding board. John Kingsbury brought this book to press and for that has my greatest thanks. Captain Alan Hickey was especially helpful in sharing his experiences in the waters around Cape Horn and along the coast of Chile, and Captain Steve Tarrant brought the *Robert C. Seamans* into long-abandoned village sites on the coast of Alaska and British Columbia so that I could see where Sam Hill sailed on the *Lydia* and the *Otter.* For help with nagging details and for listening to developing ideas, my thanks go to John Jensen, Paul Joyce, Matthew McKenzie, Liz Maloney, Jim Millinger, Dwayne Williams and Erik Zettler.

I first encountered Sam Hill while writing my dissertation at Brown University. My advisors there, Patrick Malone and Shepard Krech III, continue to influence me long after graduation. The weekly lunch for Fellows of the John Carter Brown Library provided me with many opportunities to gain from the experience of scholars more knowledgeable than myself, especially Norman Fiering, Susan Danforth, Pepe Amor, and Douglas Cope. Their casual conversation about the independence movements in South America was more helpful than they know.

In grappling with the Dutch East India Company's endeavors in Japan, I had help from friends and advisors in Japan and the Netherlands, and at the Peabody Essex Museum in Salem. The early visits of the *Franklin, Eliza,* and other American vessels to Nagasaki under the auspices of the VOC was a topic of conversation twenty years ago with Peter Fetchko at the PEM and with Els van Eyck van Heslinga, then at the Nederlands Scheepvaart Museum. Cynthia Viallé and Leonard Blussé corresponded with me about details of their extraordinary project, *The Deshima Dagregisters.* My thanks go especially to my friend Joost

Schokkenbroek of the Nederlands Scheepvaart Museum, who promptly responded to my questions with good humor and all available information, and who aided me in translations from the Dutch. Likewise, Hiroko Makino always seemed ready to drop everything to help me with research on Deshima, translate Japanese texts, and serve as my initial liaison to sources in Nagasaki. In Japan, Mitsuo Egashira and Miyuki Takada at the Dejima Restoration Office sent source material and information. Hayato Sakurai helped me to secure permission to publish images from Japanese collections. Maria-José Sanchez Blanco, my student from Harvard, provided a similar service with Spanish museums. My niece Kate Huber was my able assistant in The Netherlands.

Rhys Richards, who served for a number of years as New Zealand's Ambassador to the Solomon Islands, responded with detailed answers to my questions about Sam Hill's route through those waters. George Miles at the Beinecke Library at Yale first introduced me to the journals of Isaac Hurd and William Walker, which largely inspired this whole enterprise. Lyle Dick, the British Columbia historian for Parks Canada shared his research and ideas as we worked on complementary projects. Paul Lauenstein was a helpful friend long before I knew that he had the *Otter* journal of his ancestor Thomas Robinson. Brian Bockelman translated Eugenio Pereira Salas' articles from Spanish and steered me toward background materials on the Chilean Revolution. Elizabeth C. Bouvier of the Massachusetts Supreme Judicial Court Archives found and provided me with copies of Hill's two lawsuits. Harold F. Worthley, Librarian-Historian at the Congregational Library and Archives in Boston helped me to document the pew Hill purchased at the Park Street Church. Mark Hanna checked the records of HMS *Indefatigable* at the Public Record Office in London. Ed Lefkowics helped me to identify which voyage collection was used by David Porter. Gina Canepa provided a Chilean's perspective on Hill's adventures in her country. Kelly Thomas of the Historic Burying Grounds Initiative of the Boston Park Department located Hill's burial site in the Granary Burying Ground. Castle McLaughlin and I debated the Nootka Sound hats in the Lewis and Clark collection while she prepared an exhibit and catalog on the subject at the Peabody Museum of Archaeology and Ethnology at Harvard. Numerous other friends and colleagues entered enthusiastically into this project, including Daniel Fenimore at the Peabody Essex Museum; Robin Wright at the Burke Museum of Natural History and Culture at the University of Washingon; Michael Dyer, Laura Pereira, and Hayato Sakurai at the Kendall Institute of the New Bedford Whaling Museum; and Deborah Harrison, who read through early versions of the text and made helpful and intelligent comments. My sister, Peggy Malloy, read through the final manuscript and knows how much I love and appreciate her without my having to make declarations of favoring her over my other siblings.

My thanks to a very patient family for listening, especially my mom, Dolores Malloy (who really wanted this to be a Romance Novel); my aunts Theresa Malloy and Gladys Paxton, who share my love of history; and my mother-in-law, Pearl Frank. Dr. William Hallstein, Kit Ward, and especially Captain Peg Brandon, get my warmest thanks for being friends as well as advisors on this book. They offered support when it was needed most. And finally, last and most, I thank my husband, Stuart Frank, for never asking "What the Sam Hill?!" during all the years that Captain Samuel Hill lived in our house and wouldn't leave.

Sources:

An extraordinary wealth of materials about Samuel Hill and his many ventures survives, including two manuscript journals from the *Lydia* voyage, three from the *Otter,* and one each from the *Franklin,* the *Ophelia,* and the *Packet.* There are also logbooks and journals from several of the ships Hill encountered. The Chinook Indians described "Captain Haley" to Lewis and Clark, and he appears in the explorers' journals. There are also court records from Hill's two lawsuits. Surviving documents authored by Samuel Hill include two newspaper articles, his epic letters to the owners of the *Ophelia* and to John Cushing, an unpublished manuscript that includes his detailed logbooks kept aboard the *Ophelia* and the *Packet,* and an "Autobiography" written aboard the *Packet* after his evangelical experience. Detailed sources for each chapter are described below.

Note:

Idiosyncratic spellings have been maintained for quoted passages from shipboard texts, but punctuation has been added occasionally where needed for clarity.

Prologue (*Boston* of Boston):

John Jewitt published two different versions of his experiences: *Journal Kept at Nootka Sound* (1807), which includes only the terse entries from his diary, and an expanded account, *Narrative of the Adventures and Sufferings of John R. Jewitt; Only Survivor of the Crew of the Ship Boston, During a Captivity of Nearly 3 Years Among the Savages of Nootka Sound, with an Account of the Manners, Mode of Living, and Religious Opinions of the Natives* (1815). These two books provided details for the description of the capture of the *Boston,* and the life of Jewitt and John Thompson in the household of Maquinna. There have been many subsequent editions of Jewitt's *Narrative,* some of which are edited or abridged. Hilary Stewart's 1987 University of Washington edition has especially good illustrations and commentary.

Captain James Cook named "Nootka Sound" and called the people who lived there "Nootka Indians," and though anthropologists and historians followed his lead for two hundred years, it was never a name that the people living there used to describe themselves. In the late twentieth century, the indigenous people of the west coast of Vancouver Island chose the name "Nu-cha-nulth" to identify themselves as a group, but when Jewitt was a resident there, the people identified themselves by their villages, and that is what I have chosen to do in the chapters describing Samuel Hill's movements in the waters of Vancouver Island. As a political entity, the modern descendents of Canada's original occupants call themselves "First Nations." After consulting with friends in British Columbia and Alaska, I have decided to use the term "Indians" because it conforms to the historical sources. I hope readers will understand that I mean to imply no judgments or stereotypes in my use of the word.

Chapter One *(Lydia):*

Two shipboard accounts of the *Lydia's* remarkable voyage survived, both now at the Beinecke Library at Yale University. Isaac Hurd kept a journal from the time the ship departed Boston in August 1804, until he transferred to the *Atahualpa* on the Northwest Coast in July 1805. The second account was kept by William Walker who was promoted from the forecastle to become Captain Hill's clerk when Hurd left the ship. Walker's journal was kept in a ledger that came onto the *Lydia* with John Jewitt and John Thompson after their rescue at Nootka Sound. It has Thompson's name written on the title page, though the illiterate Thompson never managed to acquire the skills that would let him take advantage of it. Walker identifies himself as the volume's keeper in the text. Walker regularly quoted Hill's abusive language in the pages of his journal, and that material provided the quotations for Chapter I.

Samuel Hill's account of the rescue of the *Boston* survivors comes from two sources, his "Autobiography" at the New York Public Library, and an article he wrote in a Boston Newspaper, the *Columbian Centinel,* which appeared on May 20, 1807. His suit against Theodore Lyman is documented in "Hill v. Lyman, Suffolk County Court of Common Pleas," for January 1809, at the Massachusetts Supreme Judicial Court Archives.

The murder of the captain of the *Atahualpa* was described in the shipboard journal of Ebenezer Clark of the *Vancouver,* who had transferred temporarily to the *Atahualpa* to help prepare cargo. Clark's journal is also in the Beinecke Library at Yale. After he transferred to the *Atahualpa,* Isaac Hurd collected additional details from the survivors, especially Joel Richardson.

Information about Lewis and Clark comes primarily from their journals, and from annotations and editorial comments in two editions of their journals: Nicholas Biddle's *History of the Expedition under the command of Captains Lewis and Clark..,* published in 1814; and an edition published in 1990 by the University of Nebraska Press, edited by Gary E. Moulton. Correspondence from the expedition was published in *Letters of the Lewis and Clark*

Expedition, with Related Documents, 1783-1854 (Urbana: University of Illinois Press, 1962), edited by Donald Jackson.

The Nootka Sound hats collected by Lewis and Clark (which were probably delivered to the Columbia River aboard the *Lydia),* are in the collection of the Peabody Museum of Archaeology and Ethnology at Harvard University. They are described and illustrated in my book *Souvenirs of the Fur Trade: Northwest Coast Indian Art and Artifacts Collected by American Mariners* (Cambridge: Peabody Museum, Harvard University, 2000).

Chapter Two *(Jane, John Jay, Lydia, Polly):*

Samuel Hill outlined the chronology of his voyages in his manuscript "Autobiography," now in the collection of the New York Public Library (NYPL). That information has been augmented with shipping records found in Boston newspapers and the *Boston Ship Registers* to identify further details of vessels not included by Hill. Notes by Hill's grandson, the maritime historian Frederic Stanhope Hill, accompanied the gift of his papers to the NYPL.

F. Stanhope Hill may have planned to write about his grandfather at some point. He gave a lecture in June 1897 at the New England Historic Genealogical Society in Boston entitled "An Old Time Shipmaster," which "related to the life of Capt. Samuel Hill" (NEHGS *Proceedings*, 1897, vol. 51, p. 499). Sadly, no text of the lecture has been found, though F. Stanhope Hill's incomplete notes at the NYPL, titled "An Old Logbook" appear to be the start of a biography of some sort. They are written on the back of stationary from the "Commonwealth of Massachusetts, Massachusetts Nautical Training School, State House, Boston... F. Stanhope Hill, Secretary." In an accompanying letter he says, "My grandmother (Hill) gave me before she died the journal of my grandfather, Captain Samuel Hill," and describes the incident in which Sam Hill was flogged by his father.

In his "Autobiography," Hill described books he had read and I have tried to quote from translations and editions that were available in his lifetime. The translation of Voltaire quoted here, for instance, is probably the same one encountered by Hill, published in Catskill, N.Y. in 1796 as

The Philosophical Dictionary, For the Pocket: Translated from the French Edition.

The quotation from John Masefield comes from a letter he wrote to Elizabeth Robins, in the Berg Collection at the New York Public Library. I found it in *John Masefield* by June Dwyer, where it appears on page 11. The journals of Philip Van Buskirk are in the collection of the University of Washington Library, and have been extensively described in B.R. Burg's book, *An American Seafarer in the Age of Sail: The Erotic Diaries of Philip C. Van Buskirk, 1851-1870.* Burg's introduction provided me with ideas for considering homoerotic behavior on shipboard, as did two articles by Arthur N. Gilbert, "The *Africaine* Courts-Martial" and "Buggery and the British Navy." It was in the second of those articles that I found the quote from David Hannay's *Naval Courts Martial* (Cambridge, England, 1914), about that "class of case of which I shall not be expected to speak" (p. 94, footnote no. 57).

Susanna Haswell Rowson's *Charlotte Temple: A Tale of Truth,* (first published in England in 1791, and in America in 1794), is still in print, in a Penguin Classics edition. My husband Stuart Frank's unpublished book, *Ballads and Songs of the Whalehunters,* mines the song texts of American whalemen and provides an interesting window into the perceptions sailors shared about women. Chantey texts appear in Stan Hugill's *Shanties of the Seven Seas.* I discuss these at some length in my article, "The Sailor's Fantasy: Images of Women in the Songs of American Whalemen," in *The Log of Mystic Seaport* (Summer, 1996).

Chapter Three *(Franklin):*

The visit of the ship *Franklin* to Nagasaki is described all too briefly by Samuel Hill in his "Autobiography," and Captain James Devereux's logbook of the voyage is also frustratingly terse about the crew's actions in Japan. Fortunately, Leopold Willem Ras of the Dutch East India Company (VOC), kept a daily journal all through the visit of the Americans to Nagasaki in 1799. Ras's journal has been translated from the Dutch and published along with other journals kept by VOC employees as *The Deshima Dagregisters,* edited by Cynthia Viallé and Leonard Blussé. (Ras's journal is in *Volume X, 1790-1800,* published in 1997.)

The Japanese artist, Kawahara Keiga, painted wonderful scenes of daily life at Deshima, which give vibrant visual details of the island shortly after the visit of the *Franklin.* Kawahara's paintings are in the collection of the Nagasaki Municipal Museum, which also has Hendrik Doeff's letter to the local government regarding the future of his son Michitomi Jokichi (which was translated for me by Hiroko Makino). Pictures of Deshima from the late eighteenth and early nineteenth centuries have been published in *Deshima: Its Pictorial Heritage: A Collection of Historical Maps, Sketch Maps, Drawings and Paintings Illustrative of the Changing Spectacle of the Islet off Nagasaki in Japan, 1634-1904* (Nagasaki: Nagasaki City Council on Improved Preservation at the Registered Historical Site of Deshima, 1987).

Captain James Devereux's logbook and other shipping papers, including his charter from the VOC, instructions for entering the port of Nagasaki, and his account of souvenirs purchased at Deshima, are all in the collection of the Peabody Essex Museum in Salem, Massachusetts. That museum also has many of the artifacts brought back by Devereux, and paintings of the *Franklin* by Dutch and Japanese artists.

Hendrik Doeff wrote a memoir of his time in Japan, which was published in the Netherlands in 1833 as *Herinneringen uit Japan.* It has not been published in English, but my friend Joost Schokkenbroek, of the Nederlands Scheepvaart Museum, read through the book with me and provided a running translation.

Note on the spelling of "Deshima": The orthography of Japanese names in English is not entirely consistent, and the spelling "Dejima" is currently preferred by the Dejima Restoration Office at the Nagasaki City Board of Education. As I have relied so heavily on Dutch and American sources, however, I have chosen to use the spelling found more commonly in those materials.

Chapter Four *(Helen, Adventure, Mary, Indus)*:

Notions about the sexuality of Polynesian women were widely discussed in the seafaring literature of the nineteenth century. The manuscript of Ebenezer Dorr's journal, which represents the private observations of many American mariners, is in the collection of the John Carter Brown Library at Brown University. David Porter's account of his cruise in the Pacific during the War of 1812 was originally published in 1815. A second edition quickly followed, in which Porter responded to critics who had damned him for the licentious behavior of his crew at the Marquesas Islands. In his response, Porter quoted the passages from James Cook and others that I use in this chapter. There are numerous editions of Cook's writings, but Porter seems to have obtained all of his quotations from a single compilation of voyages, G. W. Anderson's *A Collection of Voyages Round the World,* published in London in 1790 and widely available in the United States in Porter's time.

Marshall Sahlins' interpretation of the sexual behavior of Polynesians in *Islands of History* has been widely misstated in the years since it was first published. The notion that "white" men were perceived as gods, and therefore desirable sperm donors for the progeny of Hawaiian women, is a simplistic version of Sahlins' theory that I have heard described by otherwise thoughtful and knowledgeable historical interpreters in Hawaii. The sudden and unexpected appearance of alien people on their islands certainly caused confusion among Hawaiians about who the strangers were and where they originated. But a supernatural origin was an explanation that could not be sustained over time, and in later descriptions of sexual encounters with Hawaiian, Tahitian, and Marquesan women, the encounter had clearly become as much a commercial transaction as anything else, often with the young women the exploited victims of male relatives and foreign sailors.

Greg Dening's description of Marquesan society and sexual practices appears in his book *Islands and Beaches: Discourse on a Silent Land, Marquesas 1774-1880* (Honolulu: University of Hawaii Press, 1980).

Chapter Five *(Otter):*

Robert Kemp's evocative, often passionate journal of his life aboard the *Otter* is in the collection of the Peabody Essex Museum. It starts with the beginning of the voyage and ends the day before he was murdered. Samuel Fergurson's incomplete journal is at the Beinecke Library at Yale. It begins in March 1809 and ends abruptly two years later, while the *Otter* was still on the Northwest Coast. Thomas Robinson's journal, which documents the voyage from Boston to Hawaii, is still in the collection of his descendants in Massachusetts.

Hill wrote a statement about the attack by the Chilkat Tlingit (the incident in which Robert Kemp was killed), which appeared in the *Columbian Centinel*, July 8, 1812. His altercation with the Russians was described in a report sent from Alaska to St. Petersburg by Ivan Kuskov in 1810. It was published, in Russian, in *Materials for the History of the Russian Colonies on the Shore of the Eastern Ocean* (part 3, p. 7). I was not able to locate either the original document or see a copy of this book, but Kuskov's report was translated and quoted by C.L. Andrews in a letter dated October 5, 1830, to Edmond S. Meany, editor of the *Washington Historical Quarterly*. Andrews' letter was written in response to an article by Frederick W. Howay, "The Attempt to Capture the Brig *Otter*," which had appeared earlier that year.

"Possibly the following notes relating to [Samuel Hill] may be of value," Andrews wrote, before providing the following translation from Kuskov.

> In May of this year [1810] a party was sent in the straits. For protection of it, and for trade with the Kolosh were sent two large sailing ships; 'Juno', under Mr. Benjamin, and the 'American Winship'. The head commander of the expedition was Mr. Kuskof. The party, arriving at the Dundas Island, lying near the Charlotte Islands, began to gather sea otter, being continually threatened by the Kolosh [Haida].
>
> In this time there was found there an American ship for trade, and from it one Hill clearly showed

displeasure and threatened Mr. Kuskof, that, if occasion arose, that they would unite with the Kolosh, and would use all means to hinder our hunting.

In the same matter, at one time a multitude of boats with armed people surrounded our ships, and Hill on his ship tacked about at a little distance, being in readiness with to cooperate [with the Haida]. ... Eluding the unfriendliness, Mr. Kuskof decided to leave, after losing already on other occasions eight Aleut men.

A footnote to this passage (which according to Andrews appears in "part 4, page 55"), says that "When Mr. Kuskof in 1810, on the ship 'Juno' under the command of Mr. Benjamin, was found protecting a party of Aleuts at Dundas Island, the Kolosh, after much violence, fell again upon the party. The foreigner Hill, maneuvering at a little distance, gave to know that if Kuskof were to fight the Kolosh, that his strength would all be thrown on the side of the Kolosh. Kuskof was compelled to go away, losing meantime in killed by the Kolosh, eight Aleuts."

Records in Russia and the Soviet Union were moved from one collection to another during the twentieth century and a number have been lost or destroyed. Yelena Andryushenkova, a research assistant at the American Consulate in St. Petersburg, kindly searched Russian archives for the original documents related to Samuel Hill's encounter with Ivan Kuskov, but was unable to locate them for me. A copy of Andrews' letter to Meany is in the Howay collection at the University of British Columbia Library in Vancouver. The journals of the *New Hazard* and the *Hamilton,* vessels encountered by Hill soon after the attack at Chilkat, are both at the Peabody Essex Museum Library in Salem, Massachusetts.

Chapter VI *(Ulysses)*:

Information about the numbers of naval vessels and privateers in the War of 1812 came from F. Stanhope Hill's book, *The Romance of the American Navy as Embodied in the Stories of Certain of our Public and Private Armed Ships from 1775 to 1909.* Ralph Eastman's *Some Famous Privateers of New England* provided context on the perspective of Bostonians on the War. The capture of the *Ulysses* is documented in *American Vessels Captured by the British during the Revolution and War of 1812: The Records of the Vice-Admiralty Court at Halifax, Nova Scotia* (Salem, MA: Essex Institute, 1911), and in *The Naval War of 1812: A Documentary History,* Vol. II, (Naval Historical Center, 1992), William S. Dudley, Editor.

Descriptions of life aboard the prison ships and in the prison camp at Melville Island in Halifax, were found in Benjamin Franklin Palmer's *The diary of Benjamin F. Palmer, privateersman, while a prisoner on board English war ships at sea, in the prison at Melville Island and at Dartmoor...* (New Haven: The Tuttle, Morehouse & Taylor Press, 1914), and in James Fenimore Cooper's *Ned Myers; or, A Life Before the Mast* (Philadelphia: Lea and Blanchard, 1843). Ira Dye's article, "American Maritime Prisoners of War, 1812-15," in *Ships, Seafaring and Society: Essays in American Maritime History,* edited by Timothy J. Runyan, helped me to understand the management of prisoners-of-war.

Chapter VII & VIII *(Ophelia* and *Packet)*:

Unlike the other voyages described in this book, Hill's last two voyages are presented principally from descriptions that he wrote himself. His massive and detailed logbooks of the *Ophelia* and *Packet* voyages are, with his "Autobiography," in the collection of the New York Public Library. Significant portions of both were published in the 1930s by two scholars. In 1935, they were translated into Spanish by Eugenio Pereira Salas and presented as *Revista Chilena de historia y geografia.* In 1937 and 1939, James W. Snyder, Jr., published the logbooks in the *New England Quarterly* and *Americana, the Quarterly Historical Magazine.* Salas' commentary was especially helpful, as he consulted Chilean records of the "Capitania General," which would otherwise have been unavailable to me. Brian Bockelman of Brown University translated Salas' notes from Spanish for me.

- 294 -

A description of the capture of the *Pearl* was found in Samuel Burr Johnston's Letters *Written during a Residence of Three Years in Chili, Containing an Account of the Most Remarkable Events in the Revolutionary Struggles of that Province...* (Erie, Pa., R.I. Custis, 1816). David Porter's journal of the *Essex* voyage was first excerpted in Washington Irving's *Analectic Magazine* in October 1814, and subsequently published in its entirety, first in 1815, and then with additional commentary in 1822. William Sturgis corresponded with Porter and referred to it in his instructions to Captain Hill; both the letter and instructions are in the Bryant and Sturgis papers at the Baker Library at the Harvard Business School.

Captain Caleb Reynolds' instructions from the owner of the ship *Sultan*, are in the collection of the Peabody Essex Museum, and were quoted in Stuart Frank's "The Origins of Engraved Pictorial Scrimshaw," in *The Magazine Antiques* in October 1992. Places described by Hill with names that are now archaic were identified in Lippincott's 1858 *Complete Pronouncing Gazetteer, or Geographical Dictionary, of the World.*

Chapter IX (Boston):

The record of Israel Thorndike's lawsuit against Samuel Hill is "Thorndike v. Hill, Suffolk County Supreme Judicial Court Record Book, Vol. 1827: March-November" at the Massachusetts Supreme Judicial Court Archives in Boston. Hill's long letter to John P. Cushing is in the Perkins Papers at the Massachusetts Historical Society. Thorndike was prominent enough in Boston and Beverly, Massachusetts, to be described in a number of works. The most useful was J.D. Forbes' *Israel Thorndike, Federalist Financier* (New York: Exposition Press for the Beverly Historical Society, 1953). John Cushing's biography is given in L. Vernon Briggs' *History and Genealogy of the Cabot Family* (Boston: Goodspeed & Co., 1927).

Both Thorndike and Cushing were among the wealthiest men of their time. Briggs says that Cushing "amassed a fortune of $7,000,000, probably the largest in New England for his generation." Thorndike is listed as the fiftieth wealthiest American of all time in *The Wealthy 100: From*

Benjamin Franklin to Bill Gates—A Ranking of the Richest Americans, Past and Present, by Michael Klepper and Robert Gunther (Carol Publishing Group, 1996). Thomas H. Perkins is also on the list at number 78.

The Boston residences of Elizabeth and Samuel Hill were traced through the Boston City Directories (published as *The Massachusetts Register and United States Calendar)* for 1803, 1806, 1807, 1809, 1810, 1813, 1820, 1823, and 1825-1829 at the Boston Public Library. A copy of Hill's death certificate was found at the New England Historic Genealogical Society in "Deaths Registered in the City of Boston (Listed Alphabetically) from 1801 to 1848 Inclusive." His probate record is "administration, case no. 27718" in the Suffolk County Probate Records for 1825, which are at the Commonwealth of Massachusetts Archives in Boston.

Bibliography:

Anderson, G.W. *A Collection of Voyages Round the World* (London: Alex Hogg, 1790).

Andrews, C.L. Letter to Edmond S. Meany, October 5, 1930 [copy], Howay collection, University of British Columbia Library, Vancouver, B.C.

Biddle, Nicholas. *History of the Expedition under the command of Captains Lewis and Clark, to the sources of the Missouri; thence across the Rocky Mountains and down the River Columbia to the Pacific Ocean; Performed during the years 1804-5-6; by order of the Government of the United States* (Philadelphia: Bradford and Inskeep, 1814).

Bogue, David. *An Essay on the Divine Authority of the New Testament* (London: Printed by C. Whittingham for T. Williams, 1804).

Briggs, L. Vernon. *History and Genealogy of the Cabot Family* (Boston: Goodspeed & Co., 1927).

Bryant & Sturgis. Letter Book, Baker Library, Harvard Business School, Cambridge, MA.

Burg, B.R. *An American Seafarer in the Age of Sail: The Erotic Diaries of Philip C. Van Buskirk, 1851-1870* (New Haven: Yale University Press, 1994).

Clinton, Ebenezer. Journal of *Vancouver* and *Atahualpa* (1804-1806), Beinecke Library, Yale University.

Collier, Simon and William F. Sater. *A History of Chile, 1808-1994* (Cambridge University Press: 1996).

Dana, Richard Henry, Jr. *Two Years Before the Mast* (New York: Harper & Brothers, 1840; reprinted by Penguin Classics, 1986).

Dening, Greg. *Islands and Beaches: Discourse on a Silent Land, Marquesas 1774-1880* (Honolulu: University of Hawaii Press, 1980).

Doeff, Hendrik. *Herinneringen uit Japan* (Haarlem: 1833).

Drisko, George W. *Narrative of the Town of Machias: The Old and the New, The Early and the Late* (Machias: Press of the Republican, 1904).

Dudley, William S., Editor. *The Naval War of 1812: A Documentary History,* Vol. II (Washington, D.C.: Naval Historical Center, 1992).

Dwyer, June. *John Masefield* (New York: Ungar, 1987).

Dye, Ira. "American Maritime Prisoners of War, 1812-15," *Ships, Seafaring and Society: Essays in American Maritime History,* edited by Timothy J. Runyan. (Detroit: Wayne State University Press, 1987), 293-320.

East India Marine Society. "Catalogue of the Articles in the Museum," *The East India Marine Society of Salem* (Salem, 1821; revised 1831).

Eastman, Ralph M. *Some Famous Privateers of New England* (Boston: State Street Trust Company, 1928).

Essex Institute. *American Vessels Captured by the British during the Revolution and War of 1812: The Records of the Vice-Admiralty Court at Halifax, Nova Scotia* (Salem, MA: Essex Institute, 1911).

Fetchko, Peter. "Salem Trading Voyages to Japan During the Early Nineteenth Century," *The American Neptune,* XLVI, no. 1 (Winter, 1986), 50-54.

_____. "Winds of Change: American Ships at Nagasaki," *Worlds Revealed: The Dawn of Japanese and American Exchange* (Tokyo and Salem: Edo Tokyo Museum/Peabody Essex Museum, 1999).

Forbes, J.D. *Israel Thorndike, Federalist Financier* (New York: Exposition Press for the Beverly Historical Society, 1953).

Frank, Stuart M. *Ballads and Songs of the Whale-hunters, 1825-1895: From Manuscripts in the Kendall Whaling Museum,* Brown University Dissertation in American Civilization, 1985.

_____. "The Origins of Engraved Pictorial Scrimshaw," *The Magazine Antiques,* Vol. CXLII, No. 4 (October 1992), 509-521.

Furgerson, Samuel. Journal of the *Otter* (1809-11), Beinecke Library, Yale University.

Gilbert, Arthur N. "The *Africaine* Courts-Martial: A Study of Buggery in the Royal Navy," *Journal of Homosexuality* 1 (1974), 111-22.

_____. "Buggery and the British Navy, 1700-1861," *Journal of Social History* 10 (1976), 72-98.

Haswell, Robert. Log of the *Columbia* (1787-88), Massachusetts Historical Society, Boston.

Hildreth, Richard. *Japan As It Was and Is* (Boston: Phillips, Sampson and Co., 1855).

Hill, Frederic S. *The Harvest Festival, with Other Poems* (Boston: True and Greene, 1826).

_____. *The Memorial: A Christmas & New Year's Offering* (Boston: True and Greene, 1827).

_____. *The Shoemaker of Toulouse, or, the Avenger of Humble Life* (Boston: W.V. Spencer, [1856?]).

_____. *The Six Degrees of Crime: or, Wine, Women, Gambling, Theft, Murder and the Scaffold* (New York: S. French [1876?]).

Hill, F. Stanhope. *The Lucky Little Enterprise and her Successors in the United States Navy* (Boston: 1900).

_____. *The Romance of the American Navy as Embodied in the Stories of Certain of our Public and Private Armed Ships from 1775 to 1909* (New York: G.P. Putnam's Sons, 1910).

_____. *Twenty-six Historic Ships: the Story of Certain Famous Vessels...* (New York and London: G. P. Putnam's, 1903).

_____. *Twenty Years at Sea, or Leaves from My Old Log-Books* (Boston and New York: Houghton, Mifflin, and Co., Riverside Press, 1893).

Hill, Samuel. Autobiography, June 14, 1819, New York Public Library.

_____. Letter to Thomas Handasyd Perkins, James Perkins, and William Sturgis, February 28, 1817, Perkins Family Papers, Massachusetts Historical Society.

_____. Letter to John P. Cushing at Canton, March 8, 1823, Perkins Family Papers, Massachusetts Historical Society.

_____. Logbook of the *Ophelia* (1815-1817) and Logbook of the *Packet* (1817-1822), New York Public Library.

_____. "Loss of the *Boston*," *Columbian Centinel*, May 20, 1807, 1.

_____. Probate record of Samuel Hill, Administration Case no. 27718, in Suffolk County Massachusetts Probate Records for 1825, at Commonwealth Archives, Boston.

_____. "Savage Attack on the Brig OTTER," *Columbian Centinel*, July 8, 1812, 1.

Hill v. Lyman, Suffolk County Court of Common Pleas, January 1809. Massachusetts Supreme Judicial Court Archives, Boston.

Howay, Frederick W. *The Atahualpa: Which Vessel was Attacked by Natives on the Northwest Coast of America in June of 1805* (Fairfield, WA: Ye Galleon Press, 1978).

_____. "The Attempt to Capture the Brig *Otter*," *Washington Historical Quarterly*, v. 21 (1930), 179-189.

_____. "An Early Account of the Loss of the *Boston* in 1803," *Washington Historical Quarterly*, vol. 17 (1926), 280-287.

_____. "Indian Attacks Upon Maritime Traders of the Northwest Coast, 1785-1805," *Canadian Historical Review*, 6 (April 1925), 287-309.

_____. "A List of Trading Vessels in the Maritime Fur Trade," published in five parts in the *Transactions of the Royal Society of Canada*, (Third Series, Volumes XXIV, XXV, XXVI, XXVII, and XXVIII; Ottawa: 1930-34). Republished with editions by Richard A. Pierce, (Kingston, Ontario: Limestone Press, 1973).

_____. "A Short Account of Robert Haswell,'" *Massachusetts Historical Society Proceedings* (May 1936), 592-600.

_____. "The Trading Voyages of the *Atahualpa*," *Washington Historical Quarterly* (January 1928), 3-18.

_____, ed. *Voyages of the* Columbia *to the Northwest Coast 1787-1790 and 1790-1793* (Boston: The Massachusetts Historical Society, 1941).

_____, ed. *Voyage of the* New Hazard *to the Northwest Coast, Hawaii and China, 1810-1813, by Stephen Reynolds, a member of the crew* (Salem: Peabody Museum, 1938; reprinted by Ye Galleon Press, Fairfield, WA., 1970).

Hugill, Stan. *Sailor town* (London: Routledge & Kegan Paul, 1969).

_____. *Shanties from the Seven Seas* (London: Routledge & Kegan Paul, 1969).

Hurd, Dena D. *A History and Genealogy of the Family of Hurd in the United States, 1640-1910* (Boston: 1910).

Hurd, Isaac. Journal of the *Lydia* and *Atahualpa* (1804-1805), Beinecke Library, Yale University.

Index of Obituaries in Massachusetts Centinel and Columbian Centinel, 1784-1840 (Boston: G.K. Hall & Co, 1961).

Jackson, Donald, ed. *Letters of the Lewis and Clark Expedition, with Related Documents, 1783-1854* (Urbana: University of Illinois Press, 1962).

Jewitt, John. *A Journal Kept at Nootka Sound* (Boston: 1807).

_____. *A Narrative of the Adventures and Sufferings of John R. Jewitt; Only Survivor of the Crew of the Ship Boston, During a Captivity of Nearly 3 Years Among the Savages of Nootka Sound, with an Account of the Manners, Mode of Living, and Religious Opinions of the Natives* (Middletown, CT: 1815).

Johnston, Samuel Burr. *Letters Written during a Residence of Three Years in Chili, Containing an Account of the Most Remarkable Events in the Revolutionary Struggles of that Province...* (Erie, PA: R.I. Custis, 1816).

Kemp, Robert. Journal of the *Otter* (1809-11), Beinecke Library, Yale University.

Klepper, Michael, with Robert Gunther. *The Wealthy 100: From Benjamin Franklin to Bill Gates—A Ranking of the Richest Americans, Past and Present* (New York: Carol Publishing Group, 1996.)

A Complete Pronouncing Gazetteer, or Geographical Dictionary, of the World... (Philadelphia: J.B. Lippincott & Co., 1858).

Long, David F. *Nothing Too Daring: A Biography of Commodore David Porter, 1780-1843* (Annapolis: U.S. Naval Institute Press, 1970).

Malloy, Mary. *"Boston Men" on the Northwest Coast: The American Maritime Fur Trade, 1788-1844* (Fairbanks: Limestone Press, University of Alaska, 1998).

_____, ed. *A Most Remarkable Enterprise: Lectures on the Northwest Coast Trade and Northwest Coast Indian Life by William Sturgis* (Hyannis, MA: Parnassus Imprints, 2000).

_____. "The Sailor's Fantasy: Images of Women in the Songs of American Whalemen," *The Log of Mystic Seaport,* Vol. 49, No. 2 (Autumn, 1997), 34-43.

_____. *Souvenirs of the Fur Trade: Northwest Coast Indian Art and Artifacts Collected by American Mariners* (Cambridge: Peabody Museum, Harvard University, 2000).

The Massachusetts Register and United States Calendar (Boston City Directory) for 1803, 1806, 1807, 1809, 1810, 1813, 1820, 1823, and 1825-1829, Boston Public Library.

Meany, Edmond S., Jr. "The Later Life of John R. Jewitt," *British Columbia Historical Quarterly,* Vol. 4, No. 3 (1940), 1-18.

Memorial of the Centennial Anniversary of the Settlement of Machias (Machias, Maine: Printed by C.O. Furbush: 1863).

Morison, Samuel Eliot. *The Maritime History of Massachusetts, 1783-1860* (Cambridge, Massachusetts: The Riverside Press, 1923).

Morrison, Robert. *A parting memorial consisting of miscellaneous discourses, written and preached in China, at Singapore, on board ship at sea in the Indian Ocean, at the Cape of Good Hope, and in England: with remarks on missions, &c. &c.* (London : W. Simpkin and R. Marshall, 1826).

Morrison, Robert, Mrs. *Memoirs of the Life and Labours of Robert Morrison... Compiled by his Widow* (London: Longman, Orme, Brown, Green, and Longmans, 1839).

Moulton, Gary E., editor. *The Journals of the Lewis & Clark Expedition,* Vol. II: November 2, 1805—March 22, 1806 (Lincoln and London: University of Nebraska Press: 1990).

Neumann, William L. "United States Aid to the Chilean Wars of Independence," *The Hispanic American Historical Review,* Vol. 27, No. 2 (May, 1947), 204-219.

Ogden, Adele, *The California Sea Otter Trade 1784-1848* (Berkeley: University of California Publications in History, Vol. 26, 1941).

Palmer, Benjamin Franklin (1793-1824). *The diary of Benjamin F. Palmer, privateersman, while a prisoner on board English war ships at sea, in the prison at Melville Island and at Dartmoor...* (New Haven: The Tuttle, Morehouse & Taylor Press, 1914).

Porter, David. *Journal of a cruise made to the Pacific Ocean, by Captain David Porter, in the United States frigate Essex, in the years 1812, 1813, and 1814 Edition 2d ed. To which is now added ... an introduction, in which the charges contained in the quarterly review, of the 1st ed. of this Journal are examined ...* (New York: Wiley & Halsted, 1822; reprinted with introduction by R.D. Madison and with notes by Madison and Karen Hamon; Annapolis: U.S. Naval Institute Press, 1986).

Reynolds, Stephen. Journal of the *New Hazard* (1810-13), Peabody Essex Museum, Salem.

Richards, Rhys, and Mary Malloy. "United States Trade with China in the First Two Decades, 1784-1804," in *United States Trade with China, 1784-1814* (Special supplement to *The American Neptune,* Salem: 1994), 10-44.

Robinson, Thomas. Journal of the *Otter* (1809-10), Collection of Paul Lauenstein, Sharon, Massachusetts.

Rowson, Susanna Haswell. *Charlotte Temple: A Tale of Truth,* (London, 1791; New York, 1794).

Rotundo, E. Anthony. "Romantic friendship: Male intimacy and middle-class youth in the Northern United States, 1800-1900," *Journal of Social History* 23 (1) (1990).

Salas, Eugenio Pereira. "Un comerciante norteamericano en nuestras costas: Samuel Hill y sus viajes (1815-1822.)," *Revista Chilena de historia y geografia,* Tomo 76, No. 84, p.

390-400; and Tomo 77, No. 85, p. 74-97 (Santiago, Chile, 1935).

Snyder, James W. Jr. "The Voyage of the *Ophelia*," *New England Quarterly*, Vol. 10, No. 2 (June 1937), 355-380.

_____. "Voyage of the Ship *Packet* to South America and China, 1817," *Americana, the Quarterly Historical Magazine*, Vol. XXXIII, No. 3 (July 1939).

Sterne, Laurence. *The Works of Laurence Sterne: Complete in Eight Volumes* (London: 1790).

Steward, Scott C. and John Bradley Arthaud. *A Thorndike Family History...* (Privately printed: 2000).

Stewart, Hilary. *The Adventures and Sufferings of John R. Jewitt* (Vancouver: Douglas & McIntyre, 1987).

Thorndike v. Hill. Suffolk County Supreme Judicial Court Record Book, March-November 1827, Massachusetts Supreme Judicial Court Archives, Boston.

Vancouver, George. *A Voyage of Discovery to the North Pacific Ocean, and Round the World; in which the Coast of the North-west America has been carefully examined and accurately surveyed... 1790, 1791, 1792, 1793, 1794, and 1795* (London: G.G. and J. Robinson, and J. Edwards, 1798).

van Gulik, Willem. *The Dutch in Nagasaki—19th-century Japanese Prints* (Uitgeverij Stichting Terra Incognita: n.d.).

van Opstall, Margot E., Frits Vos, Willem van Gulik, Jan de Vries. *Vier Eeuwen Nederland-Japan: Kunst, Wetenshap, Tall, Handel* (Lochem: 1983).

Viallé Cynthia and Leonard Blussé, *The Deshima Dagregisters: Volume X, 1790-1800* (Leiden: Institute for the History of European Expansion, 1997).

Voltaire (Francois Marie Arouet). *The Philosophical Dictionary, For the Pocket: Translated from the French Edition* (Catskill, N.Y.: 1796).

Work Projects Administration. *Ship Registers and Enrollments of Machias, Maine, 1780-1930* (Washington, D.C.: prepared by The National Archives Project, Division of Community Service Projects, 1942).

Works Progress Administration, Survey of Federal Archives, *Ship Registers & Enrollments of Boston and Charlestown, Vol. 2, 1796-1800,* The National Archives Project (Boston, 1942).

Works Progress Administration, Survey of Federal Archives, *Alphabetical List of Ship Registers, District of Boston, Massachusetts, 1802-1810,* The National Archives Project (Boston, 1939).

Works Progress Administration, Survey of Federal Archives, *Alphabetical List of Ship Registers, District of Boston, Massachusetts, 1811-1820,* The National Archives Project (Boston, 1939).

Works Progress Administration, Survey of Federal Archives, *Alphabetical List of Ship Registers, District of Boston, Massachusetts, 1821-1830,* The National Archives Project (Boston, 1939).

Picture Credits

Cover, Ship *Franklin* of Salem, Massachusetts, in Batavia, ca. 1790. Peabody Essex Museum, M11,925

Figure 1: Plate by Gustave Doré illustrating *The Rime of the Ancient Mariner* by Samuel Taylor Coleridge, Amilcare Pizzi, Milano 1966.

Figure 2: Hat collected by Lewis and Clark, Peabody Museum of Archaeology and Ethnology, Harvard University, 99-12-10/53080.

Figure 3: Entry from William Clark's journal, American Philosophical Society, Philadelphia, Codex j48.

Figure 4: Entry from Meriwether Lewis's journal, American Philosophical Society, Philadelphia, Codex I 144.

Figure 5: Portrait of Maquinna by Tomas de Suria, 1791, Museo de America, Madrid, CE00367.

Figure 6: Detail, "Map of part of the continent of North America: Whereon is laid down the Missouri, Jeffersons, Lewis's, Clarks, and the Columbia Rivers, from the Mississippi to the Pacific Ocean, as corrected by the celestial observations of Messr. Lewis & Clark during their tour of discovery in 1805. Copied by Nicholas King," Boston Athenaeum, $[Triangle]8.G5 1.

Figure 7: American vessels *Franklin* and *Eliza* in Nagasaki Harbor, ca. 1799, by Shiba Kokan, Peabody Essex Museum, M13,393.

Figure 8: Deshima in the late eighteenth century, by a Japanese artist, Courtesy of Nagasaki University Library, Economic Branch, Library Muto Collection.

Figure 9: Portrait of Hendrik Doeff with a Javanese servant, by Shiba Kokan, National Museum of Ethnology, Leiden, The Netherlands, 2821-1.

Figure 10: Dutch Men with Japanese women and a Javanese servant observing a ship at Deshima, by Kawahara Keiga, Courtesy of Nagasaki Museum of History and Culture.

Figure 11: The kitchen at Deshima in the early nineteenth century, by Kawahara Keiga, Courtesy of Nagasaki Museum of History and Culture.

Figure 12: Dutch merchants sharing a meal at Deshima, by Kawahara Keiga, Courtesy of Nagasaki Museum of History and Culture.

Figure 13: A game of billiards at Deshima, by Kawahara Keiga, Courtesy of Nagasaki Museum of History and Culture.

Figure 14: Haida argillite carving of an American mariner, ca. 1840's, Peabody Museum of Archaeology and Ethnology, Harvard University, 94-57-10/R207.

Figure 15: Reverend Robert Morrison with Chinese students, from *Memoirs of the Life and Labours of Robert Morrison... Compiled by his Widow* (London: Longman, Orme, Brown, Green, and Longmans, 1839).

Index

Dorthy, John, 13

Douglas, James, 167

Dutch East India Company (VOC), 98, 100-105, 108, 114-115, 282, 288-289

Eagle, 234

Eayrs, George Washington, 138

earthquakes, 113, 219, 242, 245

East India Marine Society, 118, 297

Ebbets, John, 24, 34, 40, 53, 62, 216

Ebenezer Dorr, 129, 290

Edes, Sam, 198-202, 206-210, 231

Eliza, 5, 96, 99, 101, 107, 109, 112, 114-115, 204, 305

Embargo, 136-140, 144, 263

Endeavor, 133

Essex, 184, 195, 196, 197, 203, 293, 301,

Estakhunah, 149

Eu-stoch-ee-exqua, 18

Francis Xavier, St., 98, 103

Forrester, 216

Forster, George, 131

Fort Clatsop, 70

Fort Ross, 156

Framingham, 183, 262

Frank, Stuart M., 284, 288, 293, 297

Franklin, 2, 4, 5, 29, 94, 96-97, 102-103, 107, 112, 114-121, 123, 219, 282, 284, 288-289, 305

Friendly Cove, 14, 17, 66

Furgerson, Samuel, 143-144, 147, 150, 152, 154-159, 161, 169, 297

Fyffe, John, 206, 209

Galapagos Islands, 186-188, 212, 225

Geenemans, Leendert, 115

General Pickering, 174

George IV, King of England, 254

Gilchrist, James, 115

Governor Strong, 71

Grace, 98

Gray, Robert, 19, 88-89

Gray's Harbor, 31, 33

Griffith, Edward, 175

Haida Gwaii. *See* Queen Charlotte Islands.

Haida Indians, 5, 33, 35, 39, 58, 142, 149-151, 155-156, 306

Haley, Capt. (a.k.a. Samuel Hill), 48, 68, 72, 275, 284

Halifax, 8, 175-177, 179-180, 183, 204, 293, 297

Hallstein, William, 278-279, 284

Hamburg, 90-91, 93, 127

Hamilton, 24, 36, 57, 59, 148, 152, 155, 157-158, 164, 292

Hancock, John, 276-277

Hannah, 90

Hannah, James, 19

hardtack, 27

Hardy, Tilly, 145, 169

Harraden, Andrew, 121, 123, 174

Harraden, Jonathan, 174

Haskins, Ralph, 28

Haswell, Robert, 78-79, 88-90, 93, 127, 298-299

Havana, 121, 123

Hawaii (Sandwich Islands), 8, 29, 43, 61-62, 128, 138, 147-149, 162, 168, 189, 212, 214-216, 218, 229, 232, 251, 253-254, 259, 290-291

Hawaiian crewmen under Hill's command, 29, 37, 62, 157-158, 169